A GUIDE TO MALPRACTICE LIABILITY FOR LEGAL AND LAW-RELATED PROFESSIONS

A GUIDE TO MALPRACTICE LIABILITY FOR LEGAL AND LAW-RELATED PROFESSIONS

Warren Freedman

Q

QUORUM BOOKS
Westport, Connecticut • London

Library of Congress Cataloging-in-Publication Data

Freedman, Warren.
A guide to malpractice liability for legal and law-related professions / Warren Freedman.
p. cm.
Includes index.
ISBN 0–89930–909–7
1. Lawyers—Malpractice—United States. 2. Malpractice—United States. I. Title.
KF313.F74 1995
346.7303—dc20
[347.30633] 94–38536

British Library Cataloguing in Publication Data is available.

Library of Congress Catalog Card Number: 94–38536
ISBN: 0–89930–909–7

First published in 1995

Quorum Books, 88 Post Road West, Westport, CT 06881
An imprint of Greenwood Publishing Group, Inc.

Printed in the United States of America

The paper used in this book complies with the Permanent Paper Standard issued by the National Information Standards Organization (Z39.48–1984).

10 9 8 7 6 5 4 3 2 1

Contents

A GUIDE TO MALPRACTICE LIABILITY FOR LEGAL AND LAW-RELATED PROFESSIONS

Chapter 1

Introduction

PART A: MALPRACTICE AND PROFESSIONALS

The law of professional malpractice extends across a wide range of specialized activities, as illustrated by the chapters hereinafter, although in the public mind, malpractice is most frequently associated with lawyers and with physicians. All professions, however, are involved with malpractice actions, and the battleground of fashioning a unified standard of care persists for all professions. In times of accelerating social and economic as well as political changes, the role of malpractice law becomes all the more important. The search for the normative function of malpractice law continues, for the function of tort law is clearly to reflect social norms. The moral thrust of tort law is evidenced in Section 870 of the Restatement (Second) of Torts, which delineates the "innominate tort" as imposing liability on one who "intentionally causes injury to another . . . if his conduct is generally culpable and not justifiable under the circumstances"; such conduct calls forth a remedy even though it "does not come within a traditional category of tort liability."

At the outset, it should be observed that actions for malpractice may fall into the broader category of negligence actions. An action for negligence requires that the defendant be found to owe the plaintiff a legal duty to conform to a particular standard or course of conduct and that the defendant has in fact failed to conform to that standard or course of conduct. In most professions, Codes of Ethics or Statements of Professional Conduct raise that standard or course of conduct *above* the standard for negligence.[1] In short, negligence is conduct that "falls below the standard established by law for the protection of others against unreasonable risk of harm."[2] Malpractice is perhaps more sophisticated and subtle. The New York court in *Miller v. Albany Medical Center Hospital*[3] pointed out the distinction between negligence and malpractice as turning on "whether the acts or omissions complained of involve a matter of medical science or art requiring special skills not ordinarily possessed by lay persons, or whether the conduct complained of can instead be assessed on the basis of common everyday experience of the triers of fact." Eight years later, however, in 1991, another New York appellate court in *Safier & Vogelman v. Kalvin*[4] ruled that the counterclaim in the medical malpractice case sounded in common-law negligence, not medical malpractice:

> In the case at bar all parties conceded (the doctor by his conduct and the patient in his pleadings) that the performance of polypectomy would be contrary to accepted medical standards where a patient has recently ingested aspirin. There is no prima facie need for expert testimony on this conceded fact. The standard of good and accepted medical practice is not an issue in the case. The issue that may be decided by the jury without the need of expert testimony (if defendant's version of the facts is accepted) is whether the doctor was negligent in failing to advise his patient, prior to the day scheduled for the colonoscopy, not to take aspirin, or whether the doctor was negligent in not asking his patient if he had taken aspirin prior to commencing the colonoscopy procedure, rather than asking the question after he first observed the polyp through the scope. We note that the counterclaim does not involve improper diagnosis or assessment of defendant's condition or the degree of required supervision (see, *Halas v. Parkway Hospital*, 158 A.D.2d 516). Since the counterclaim asserted that Dr. Safier's postponement of the polypectomy was correct there was no need for expert medical testimony as to its propriety. The fundamental issues to be determined at trial are whether Dr. Safier or his staff advised defendant to abstain from aspirin, and also, whether Dr. Safier was negligent in not asking his patient if he did take aspirin prior to commencing the colonoscopy procedure. Since these issues may readily be assessed based upon common everyday experience of the trier of facts, without the need of expert testimony, the action sounded in ordinary negligence (see, *Halas v. Parkway Hospital*, supra; *Huntley v. State of New York*, 62, N.Y.2d 134). Similarly, since the counterclaim sounded in negligence the recitation of a stated amount of damages was not barred by CPLR 3017(c).

Also,

> an act of omission or commission may be negligent conduct and if committed by a physician is designated as a medical malpractice action. The standard of conduct is made up by medical doctors practicing in a given community. Whether Dr. Safier, by failing to instruct his patient to abstain from ingesting aspirin, under the circumstances, departed from good and accepted medical practice is a question of fact requiring expert medical testimony. The defendant, as a lay person, testifying that Dr. Safier did not tell him to abstain from taking aspirin does not suffice to prove a case since there must be expert medical testimony as to whether Dr. Safier departed from

good and accepted medical practice (see, *Scott v. Uljanov*, 74 N.Y.2d 673 where the court held that "conduct may be deemed malpractice, rather than negligence, when it 'constitutes medical treatment or bears a substantial relationship to the rendition of medical treatment by a licensed physician.' *Bleiler v.* Bodnar, 65 N.Y.2d 65, 72.")

Indeed, when defendants are professionals, the standard of conduct required is that they exercise the "skill and knowledge normally possessed by members of that profession in good standing."[5] When professionals are sued, proof that they conformed to the customary practices of the profession will generally relieve them of liability.[6] It necessarily follows that testimony by experts is central to malpractice suits against professionals. And evidence of what constitutes generally accepted professional conduct encompasses Codes of Ethics, professional policy statements, organizational rules, internal evaluations, and the like.[7]

It is well to note, as did the New Jersey Supreme Court in 1980, that professionals, whether employees or independent entrepreneurs, "owe a special duty to abide not only by federal and State law but also by the recognized codes of ethics of their professions."[8] In this case, the court acknowledged that this special duty may require a professional employee to decline to follow his employer's directions. Yet the professional employee's general invocation of professional obligations will not permit the overturning of employer discretion. The professional must point to a specific standard or ethical duty, not to a broad statement of principle, to support a claim premised upon public policy, for example.[9] Indeed, the professional employee must adhere to the Code of Ethics of his or her profession[10] as well as federal licensing laws for his or her profession; and the employer must not be allowed to subvert the protection of the public provided by the governmental program of licensing professions.[11]

Nevertheless, whether licensed or not, the professional gives no guaranty of good results; the professional is liable for malpractice only if he, she, or it acted without the requisite minimum skill and competence, not merely because the operation, lawsuit, or the like, was not successful. The professional is not liable for "mere error of judgment"—or, in the case of a lawyer, for a "mistake in a point of law which has not been settled by the court of last resort . . . and on which reasonable doubt may be entertained by well-informed lawyers."[12] The correct standard of behavior for the professional has always been the level of skill of the minimally qualified member in good standing, not the average member—the point being that those who have less than median or average skill may still be competent and qualified.[13]

But professional standards themselves can be held to have been negligently promulgated, and therefore the professional can be held liable for following such standards, as seen in *Helling v. Carey*,[14] dealing with the standard practice among ophthalmologists. Here the plaintiff, under 40 years of age, was a patient of two ophthalmologists, the first of whom treated her for problems associated with the wearing of contact lenses but who did not perform a simple glaucoma test since it is rare to find glaucoma in a person under 40 years of age. The second ophthalmologist discovered that plaintiff had glaucoma, and plaintiff thereupon sued the first ophthalmologist for his failure to give the glaucoma test. According to the Washington court: "The precaution of giving this pressure test . . . to patients under the age of 40 is so imperative that, irrespective of its disregard by the standards of the ophthalmology profession, it is the duty of the courts to say what is required to protect the patients."[15] Thus, the court substituted its own judgment for that of the professional ophthalmologist and applied the objective judicial test in place of the medical test. In 1940, Judge Learned Hand in *The T. J. Hooper Case*[16] uttered the oft-quoted statement that "[i]n most cases reasonable prudence is in fact common prudence; but strictly it is never its measure; a whole calling may have unduly lagged in the adoption of new and available devices. It never may set its own tests, however persuasive may be its usages. Courts must in the end say what is required; there are precautions so imperative that even their universal disregard will not excuse their omission."

The court can indeed establish an objective standard, as the North Carolina appellate court in *Heath v. Swift Wings Inc.*[17] stressed the importance of an objective standard for the professional person. Here a professional pilot in piloting a small plane was allegedly responsible for the death of his passenger. The trial court applied the standard of an ordinary prudent pilot "having the same training and experience"; but the appellate court prevailed and favored the objective standard of "minimum standard generally applicable to all pilots."

This professional standard may well vary with the geographical area, although the Michigan Supreme Court in *Naccarato v. Grob*[18] did not agree; here two pediatricians in the Detroit area were sued in 1970 for malpractice in failing to diagnose phenylketonuria, or PKU, a rare childhood disease that begins at birth and results in progressive mental deterioration. The court opined:

> It is therefore unnecessary to consider in this opinion whether a standard of parochial negligence can obviate the requirement of reasonable care by a local practitioner. At issue here is the standard of care owed to a patient by a community of specialists. Whatever the considerations were that allowed the area practice to set the standard for the country general practitioners—they are not relevant to a metropolitan specialist—calling a specialist parochial or bucolic is hardly appropriate. The reliance of the public upon the skills of a specialist and the wealth and sources of his knowledge are not limited to the geographic area in which he practices. Rather his knowledge is a specialty. He specializes so that he may keep abreast. Any other standard for a specialist would negate the fundamental expectations and purpose of a specialty. The standard of care for a specialist should be that of a reasonable specialist practicing medicine in the light of present day scientific knowledge. Therefore,

geographical conditions or circumstances control neither the standard of a specialist's care nor the competence of an expert's testimony. [Citations omitted]

What constitutes "professional services" is also an important issue. In *Multinomah County v. Oregon Auto Insurance Co.*,[19] the Oregon court observed that the liability policy had excluded injury due to the rendering of or a failure to render any professional service. The court defined professional services as services arising out of a vocation, calling, occupation or employment involving specialized knowledge, labor or skill, and "the labor or skill involved is predominantly mental or intellectual rather than physical or manual." Accordingly, the act or omission must be looked to and not the title or character of the party who performs or fails to perform the act.[20]

Time is frequently a prime factor in professional malpractice, as illustrated in *Stellema v. Vantage Press Inc.*[21] Here a fraud action was brought in 1978 by 2,200 victimized authors who had paid the defendant "vanity" publisher to have their manuscripts published, only to discover that their manuscripts were not published. It was not until 1990 that the case went to trial and resulted in a jury finding that the defendant was liable in fraud for holding itself out as a legitimate book publisher. At the time of trial, only 830 authors had remained in the lawsuit to share the damages totaling $3.5 million.[22]

What is the rule when an injured party is prevented from discovering the malpractice by the intentional misrepresentation of the defendant professional?[23] The New York court in *McIvor v. DiBenedetto*[24] authorized the invocation of collateral estoppel unless "the plaintiff possesses 'timely knowledge' sufficient to place him or her under a duty to make inquiry and ascertain all the relevant facts prior to the expiration of the applicable statute of limitations." Accordingly, the physician's motion for partial summary judgment dismissing the malpractice action insofar as it was asserted against the physician was barred by the New York two-year statute of limitations.[25] The existence of a default judgment or a confession of judgment will collaterally estop a malpractice action arising from the same transaction.[26] In *Kossover v. Trattler*[27] the defendant physician in defending a malpractice action had previously sued the plaintiff-patient to recover for professional services rendered; when the plaintiff failed to answer the complaint, a default judgment was entered. Subsequently, plaintiff commenced the action for medical malpractice covering the same period of time, and prior to trial the physician moved to amend his answer to include the affirmative defenses of collateral estoppel and *res judicata*, contending that the default judgment precluded the malpractice claim. But the trial court denied the motions, pointing out that collateral estoppel should not apply since plaintiff's "absence" in the prior action prevented the court from considering the malpractice issue. On appeal, it was pointed out that the lack of identical issues between the prior and subsequent actions negated the invocation of the preclusion device. However, the concurring opinion of the

New York appellate court commented that "implicit in the finding (in the first action) that the fee was earned . . . was a finding that the treatment was beneficial and therefore not the proper subject for future litigation on the malpractice action by the plaintiff."[28]

The defenses for professionals who are sued for malpractice run the gamut of contract and tort defenses. For example, in *Goetzman v. Wichern*[29] the plaintiff alleged that the defending physician was negligent in his diagnosis and treatment of her breast cancer over a period of four years. She alleged that his negligence caused her to have a mastectomy and to undergo radiation therapy and chemotherapy, both procedures causing substantial injuries and damages. The physician's defense was that the patient herself was negligent in failing to follow his advice and cooperate with his diagnostic and treatment recommendations. The Iowa jury rendered a verdict for the defendant physician based upon her "contributory negligence." But the Iowa Supreme Court reversed:

> "Whatever may have been the historical justification for [contributory negligence], today it is almost universally regarded as unjust and inequitable to vest an entire accidental loss on one of the parties whose negligent conduct combined with the negligence of the other party to produce the loss. [Citation omitted.] . . . Only the pure form of comparative negligence proportions a reduction of recovery to a person's fault in all cases and prevents a party at fault from escaping liability in any case. As demonstrated in the reasoning of the courts that have adopted the pure form, it is the fairest, most logical, and simplest to administer of all available systems. It is the system endorsed by most of the commentators. . . . It is also the form recommended by the National Commissioners on Uniform State Laws in the Uniform Comparative Fault Act (1977). . . .": "We hold that in all cases in which contributory negligence has previously been a complete defense, it is supplanted by the doctrine of comparative negligence. In such cases contributory negligence will not bar recovery but shall reduce it in the proportion that the contributory negligence bears to the total negligence that proximity caused the damages."

Incidentally, the plaintiff's choice of venue in bringing the malpractice action generally prevails, as illustrated in the New York case of *Champion v. City of New York*:[30] "Defendant Nassau County has made no showing of any substantial prejudice except the inconvenience of the county and its doctors. This inconvenience in and of itself is insufficient to restrict granting consolidation in accordance with prevailing principles. The consent of the defendants in the first action to consolidation in Nassau County is not determinative. Their mere willingness to proceed in Nassau County should not frustrate plaintiff's choice of venue."

Of more than passing interest to professionals generally are computer systems that are professional tools available to professionals. Note that computer technology costs more than $88 billion annually, or 3 percent of the gross national product.[31] Increasingly, professionals are using computers while rendering professional services.[32] Computerization has drastically changed the methodology of most professions including law, engineering, architecture, *inter alia*. The imposition of liability for nonuse of a computer system would require proof that such nonuse was the cause of the injury suffered. The conclusions of one writer are noteworthy:

> The expanding personal use of computer systems by professionals has resulted in the use of machines for tasks that traditionally required practitioners' personal attention. The machines will begin to figure more prominently in malpractice litigation as computers slowly make the transition from experimental innovations to required tools. The threat of malpractice liability will force professionals to use available computer systems, and to be competent in doing so. The ready availability of information will probably result in an expansion of the duty of professions to warn their clients of potential dangers. The current "custom" of not consulting such systems is unlikely to prevail as defense once the utility of the systems is established, while the mere availability of useful systems could lead to an inference of negligence when they are not used. When computer systems are recognized as "authorities" for even limited questions, plaintiffs who can establish causality should prevail in malpractice actions premised on violations of practitioners' "duty to consult." National access to such systems will result in the demise of the "locality rule" in cases involving the transfer of information.[33]

In today's economy, it is common to find professionals involved with nontraditional services. For example, a lawyer may well offer to clients investment counseling or other business sales and services. The prevalence of such nontraditional services invites the query whether valid claims can be pressed against the lawyer for breach of fiduciary duty as opposed to legal malpractice.[34] Also, do such nontraditional services fall within the protection of the professional liability insurance policy?[35] Recently, in *Heine v. Colton, Hartnick, Yamin & Sheresky and Newman*,[36] a former partner of the law firm was dismissed for allegedly "engaging in a large pattern of financial transactions appearing to be lacking in substance." The dismissed partner then sued the law firm (and two other law firms) for several millions of dollars, and the federal district court in New York concluded that the law firm owed a fiduciary duty to the plaintiff based on certain allegations in the complaint that did not give rise to the attorney-client relationship.[37] In *Sheinkopf v. Stone*[38] the issue was "whether an entrepreneurial attorney, who unwisely conducts personal business from his law office, thereby implicates his partners, leaving them (and their law firm) liable for investments gone sour." The First U.S. Court of Appeals affirmed summary judgment in favor of the defendants: "The record will not support a finding that an attorney-client relationship came into being, and there does not seem to be any other legal basis for a claim against the remaining partners of the firm."[39]

Indeed, the law of privilege has long been the most controversial area of federal evidence law.[40]

NOTES

1. *See* PROSSER AND KEETON, THE LAW OF TORTS (5th ed. 1984), at 164–165; and *note* Section 328A of RESTATEMENT (SECOND) OF TORTS.

2. *See* Section 282 of RESTATEMENT (SECOND) OF TORTS. Malpractice today arises out of situations where the error can be subtle and no more apparent in retrospect than when the advice was given. Increasingly, lawyers are being sued almost as insurers of the financial success of their clients' business transactions, where the client—who has taken some business risk and lost—can demonstrate that the loss could have been avoided if the lawyer had provided different advice.

3. 95 A.D.2d 977 (N.Y. App. Div., 3d Dept., 1983).

4. _____ N.Y.S.2d _____ (Unreported, App. Div., 2d and 11th Depts., 1991).

5. *See* Section 299A of RESTATEMENT (SECOND) OF TORTS.

6. *See* Note, 27 DUQUESNE L. REV. 237 (1989), at 240.

7. *See* Lind and Ullberg, *Are Professional Codes of Ethics Acquiring the Force of Law?* 11 ALI-ABA COURSE MATERIALS J. 63 (1987).

8. *See* Pierce v. Ortho Pharmaceutical Corp., 417 A.2d 505 (N.J. 1980).

9. *Cf.* Suchodolski v. Michigan Consolidated Gas Co., 316 N.W.2d 710 (Mich. 1982), holding that the Code of Ethics of internal auditors was not consonant with public policy. In Martin v. Malcolm Pirnie, Inc., 949 F.2d 611 (2d Cir., Dkt. 91–6138, Nov. 20, 1991), the Second U.S. Court of Appeals defined "professional" under the Fair Labor Standards Act (FLSA) as an employee working not less than eight-hour days! An employer who inadvertently treats otherwise eligible professional employees as hourly wage earners has a "window of correction" to preserve their FLSA "salaried status" by reimbursing them and promising future compliance.

10. Ethics and conduct are significant issues in the professions, and CODES OF PROFESSIONAL RESPONSIBILITY, published by The Bureau of National Affairs in Washington, D.C . (R. Gorlin ed. 1990), is the starting point for an analysis of ethics and professional conduct.

11. *See generally* Note, *A Remedy for the Discharge of Professional Employees Who Refuse to Perform Unethical or Illegal Acts: A Proposal in Aid of Professional Ethics*, 28 VAND. L. REV. 805 (1974).

12. *See* Hodges v. Carter, 80 S.E.2d 144 (N.C. 1954).

13. *See* Section 299A of RESTATEMENT (SECOND) OF TORTS; and *note* The T. J. Hooper Case, 60 F.2d 737 (2d Cir. 1932).

14. 519 P.2d 981 (Wash. 1974).

15. *See* Curlender v. Bio-Science Laboratories, 165 Cal. Rptr. 477 (1980), where the court ruled that a cause of action was stated by allegations that the defendant negligently performed a test upon plaintiff's mother that, if performed competently, would have revealed the high probability that the plaintiff would be born with Tay-Sachs disease. As a result of the disease, the plaintiff is mentally and physically disabled and has a life expectancy of four years. The complaint also alleged that if plaintiff's mother had been fully informed, she would have had an abortion. In upholding the complaint the California court stated at 488–489:

> We have no difficulty in ascertaining and finding the existence of a duty owed by *medical laboratories* engaged in genetic testing to parents and their as yet unborn children to use ordinary care in administration of available tests for the purpose of providing information concerning potential genetic defects in the unborn. The public policy consid-

erations with respect to the individuals involved and to society as a whole dictate recognition of such a duty, and it is of significance that in no decision that has come to our attention which has dealt with the "wrongful-life" concept has it been suggested that public policy considerations negate the existence of such a duty. Nor have other jurisdictions had any difficulty in finding a breach of duty under appropriate circumstances or in finding the existence of the requisite proximate casual link between the breach and the claimed injury; we find no bar to a holding that the defendants owed a duty to the child plaintiff before us and breached that duty. The real crux of the problem is whether the breach of duty was the proximate cause of an *injury cognizable at law*. The injury, of course, is not the particular defect with which a plaintiff is afflicted—considered in the abstract—but it is the birth of plaintiff with such defect. The circumstance that the birth and injury have come hand in hand has caused other courts to deal with the problem by barring recovery. The reality of the "wrongful-life" concept is that such a plaintiff both *exists* and *suffers*, due to the negligence of others. It is neither necessary nor just to retreat into meditation on the mysteries of life. We need not be concerned with the fact that had defendants not been negligent, the plaintiff might not have come into existence at all. The certainty of genetic impairment is no longer a mystery. In addition, a reverent appreciation of life compels recognition that plaintiff, however impaired she may be, has come into existence as a living person with certain rights. One of the fears expressed in the decisional law is that, once it is determined that such infants have rights cognizable at law, nothing would prevent such a plaintiff from bringing suit against its own parents for allowing plaintiff to be born. In our view, the fear is groundless. The "wrongful-life" cause of action with which we are concerned is based upon negligently caused failure by someone under a duty to do so to inform the prospective parents of facts needed by them to make a conscious choice *not* to become parents. If a case arose where, despite due care by the medical profession in transmitting the necessary warnings, parents made a conscious choice to proceed with a pregnancy, with full knowledge that a seriously impaired infant would be born, that conscious choice would provide an intervening act of proximate cause to preclude liability insofar as defendants other than the parents were concerned. Under such circumstances, we see no sound public policy which should protect those parents from being answerable for the pain, suffering and misery which they have wrought upon their offspring. . . . The extent of recovery, however, is subject to certain limitations due to the nature of the tort involved. While ordinarily a defendant is liable for all consequences flowing from the injury [citation omitted], it is appropriate in the case before us to tailor the elements of recovery, taking into account particular circumstances involved.

16. 60 F.2d 737 (2d Cir. 1940).
17. 252 S.E.2d 256 (N.C. App. 1979).
18. 180 N.W.2d 788 (Mich. 1970).
19. 470 P.2d 147 (Ore. 1970).
20. A provision in a consulting engineering firm's general liability policy excluded, *inter alia*, "engineering services," and the Texas appellate court in Aetna Fire Underwriters Insurance Corp. v. Southwestern Engineering Co., 626 S.W.2d 99 (Tex. App. 1981) found the phrase to be ambiguous. The phrase would be construed as not including the act of locating underground pipelines, so that coverage would be afforded for damage suits brought against the insured engineering firm after it struck an underground pipeline in the course of digging a trench to lay cable.
21. *See* 411 N.Y.S.2d 191 (App. Div., 1st Dept., 1978); 47 N.Y.2d 882 (1979); 470 N.Y.S.2d 507 (1983), *rev'd*, 492 N.Y.S.2d 390 (1985); *inter alia*.
22. *See* Chapters 2 through 6 hereinafter.

23. *See* WARREN FREEDMAN, THE BUSINESS TORT OF FRAUD AND MISREPRESENTATION (1989 *et seq.*), at ch. 1 thereof.

24. 503 N.Y.S.2d 836 (App. Div., 2d Dept., June 24, 1986).

25. *See* WARREN FREEDMAN, RES JUDICATA AND COLLATERAL ESTOPPEL: TOOLS FOR PLAINTIFFS AND DEFENDANTS (1988), at 65 *et seq.*

26. *See* 56 ST. JOHN'S L. REV. 171 (1981).

27. 442 N.Y.S.2d 554 (1981), *aff'g* 428 N.Y.S.2d 402 (1980).

28. *Cf.* Section 58 of RESTATEMENT (SECOND) OF JUDGMENTS, which in Comment b, Illustration 3, poses the same set of facts, to wit: A, a physician, brings an action against B for medical services rendered to B. B fails to plead, and judgment by default is given against B. B is not precluded from subsequently maintaining an action against A for malpractice!

29. 327 N.W.2d 742 (Iowa 1982).

30. _____ N.Y.S.2d _____ (Unreported, Kings County Apr. 6, 1992).

31. *See generally* Willick, *Professional Malpractice and the Unauthorized Practice of Professions: Some Legal and Ethical Aspects of the Use of Computers as Decision-Aids*, 12 RUTGERS COMP. & TECH. L.J. 1 (1986).

32. *See* A.B.A.J. (Feb. 1985), at 136.

33. *See* Matthew, *Architects, Engineers, Computer Products and the Law: A Matter of Anticipation*, 3 COMPUTER L.J. 337 (1982), at 340–341.

34. *See generally* Arnoff and Klampert, *The Risks in Providing Non-Traditional Services*, N.Y.L.J. (Apr. 28, 1992), at 3, 6, and 7.

35. *See* Part B hereinafter. *Note* the language in the typical insurance policy:

> [T]o pay on behalf of the insured all sums which the insured shall become legally obligated to pay as damages because of any claim or claims first made against the insured and reported to the company during the policy period or extended reporting period, arising out of any act, error or omission of the insured *in rendering or failing to render professional services for others in the insured's capacity as a* [professional], *fiduciary* or Notary Public, and caused by the insured or any other person for whose acts, errors or omissions the insured is legally responsible, except as excluded or limited by the terms, conditions and exclusions of this policy.

Note one of the relevant exclusions, to wit:

> [This policy does not apply] to any claim made by or against or in connection with any business enterprise (including the ownership, maintenance or care of any property in connection therewith), not named in the Declarations, which is owned by any insured or in which any insured is a partner, or employee (except where he is an employee solely by virtue of having been retained to perform legal services) or which is directly or indirectly controlled, operated, or managed by any insured in a non-fiduciary capacity.

36. _____ F. Supp. _____ (Unreported, S.D.N.Y. 1992).

37. *Infra* note 34 at 6.

38. 927 F.2d 1259 (1st Cir. 1991).

39. *Infra* note 34 at 6.

40. *See* Note, *Making Sense of Rules of Privilege Under the Structural (IL) Logic of the Federal Rules of Evidence*, 105 HARV. L. REV. 1339 (1992).

PART B: PROFESSIONAL MALPRACTICE INSURANCE

Professional malpractice or professional liability insurance is unique in many respects, the most obvious aspect being the rule that allows the insured professional to have veto power over insurance settlements.[1] This unusual feature is justifiable on the grounds that the professional's very reputation is at stake, that is, his or her ability to earn a living, in every settlement situation. However, professional liability insurance generally excludes claims that result from dishonest, fraudulent, or criminal acts or omissions by the insured professional or by anyone for whose acts or omissions the insured professional is legally responsible.[2] Some professional liability policies exclude claims for punitive damages, but in many cases, the insurer has been required to pay punitive damages.[3]

Deductibles are quite common in professional liability insurance policies and may encompass within the deduction "claims expenses" such as attorneys' fees, court costs, investigation expenses, and adjusters' fees, *inter alia.*[4] Coverage is generally written with limits for each claim of malpractice as well as an aggregate limit applicable to annual policy periods.[5]

Professional liability insurance is principally based on "claims-made" coverage[6] because the damages are generally multiple and are not known for perhaps years after the error or omission on the part of the insured professional. According to *Fremont Indemnity Co. v. Gierhart*:[7] "Coverage is effective 'if the negligent or omitted act is discovered and brought to the attention of the insurer within the policy term. . . . The essence, then, of a claims-made policy is notice to the carrier within the policy period.' " On the other hand, "occurrence" coverage has the inherent and difficult problem of assigning a date for the occurrence of the error or omission or negligence on the part of the professional, and that date triggers the claim, if within the policy period.[8]

Unfortunately, the term *professional services* is not defined in the typical professional liability insurance policy. However, courts have not been inclined to declare the term ambiguous, as seen in *Albert J. Schiff Associates Inc. v. Flack*,[9] where the New York court ruled that a suit by the insurance agent against another insurance agent over the use of a marketing plan conceived by one agent did not involve professional services. But in *Continental Casualty Co. v. Burton*,[10] where the lawyer accepted funds from a client for the purpose of investing the funds in a fiduciary capacity, the court found no problem with coverage under the professional malpractice policy when the lawyer absconded with the funds.[11]

Summary judgment is precluded where there is a question of material fact regarding the intentions of the parties to the professional liability policy, as seen in *Dunham v. American Home Insurance Co.*[12] Here plaintiff-insured professional contended that one policy covered "occurrences" that took place during a five-year period and that the second policy covered "claims made" during a one-year period in that five-year period; a third policy allegedly was a "modified claims-made" policy covering prior acts or omissions for current customers of the plaintiff! The prevalence of a question of fact was indeed obvious!

In the Arizona case of *Fremont Indemnity Co. v. New England Reinsurance Co.*,[13] the court found that the policy unambiguously provided coverage for acts that were committed by the professional prior to the inception of the policy only if covered by "other insurance"; nevertheless, here there was no coverage for the acts of malpractice committed prior to the inception of the policy that were covered by an earlier professional liability insurance policy.

"Errors and omissions" insurance[14] policies form the equivalent to malpractice insurance for occupations other than those in professional fields. Errors and omissions coverage was applicable to a physician, however, in *Pacific Indemnity Co. v. Linn*,[15] where the insured physician had written a diet book and was sued for injuries and the death of readers! Generally, errors and omissions insurance excludes "any dishonesty, intentional fraud, criminal or malicious act."[16] Insurance agents and brokers[17] often carry "errors and omissions" coverage; but where the agent is the subject of a claim for unfair competition and usurpation of trade secrets, as in *Albert J. Schiff Associates Inc. v. Flack*,[18] no coverage existed in the absence of a negligent act in the performance of the agent's professional capacity.

Sexual conduct between doctor and patient is not a "medical incident" covered by the malpractice insurance of the doctor, as illustrated in *Snyder v. Major and National Union Fire Insurance Co.*[19] The federal district court declared that the defendant insurer was not liable for any damages awarded a patient for her alleged rape by the insured plastic surgeon. However, malpractice insurance coverage would be available for sexual conduct when "the physician is a psychiatrist and the sexual incident arises out of a therapeutic relationship." In short, sexual misconduct is not an insurable medical incident under the facts of this case!

In many states, there are mandatory malpractice insurance statutes empowering the state to enjoin the physician, for example, from practicing medicine until he or she has obtained medical malpractice insurance as required by state statute.[20] The Kansas statute, as seen in *State ex rel Schneider v. Liggett*,[21] excluded nurses and dentists from the proscription for malpractice insurance. Subsequently, the Kansas Health Care Provider Insurance Act was enacted to protect the physician's due process rights by giving him or her the opportunity to attend and represent his or her interests at settlement hearings.[22] In order to render the malpractice insurer liable under the policy, it is generally essential that the physician's liability policy be in effect at the time that the patient sustained the injury due to malpractice.[23]

Malpractice insurance rates have been on the increase in recent years, making it exorbitant for the professional to obtain the necessary insurance coverage. ALAS, or Attorneys Liability Assurance Society, for example, raised its rates in April 1992 by 20 percent, an increase that followed a 7 percent rate increase earlier in 1992.[24] Other insurers have done likewise in the medical field.

NOTES

1. *See* WARREN FREEDMAN, FREEDMAN'S RICHARDS ON INSURANCE (1990) at Section 1.55A therein.
2. *Note* that most lawyers' professional liability insurance policies contain an express exclusion for "any claim arising out of any dishonest, fraudulent or malicious act, error or omission of any insured." *See* Brake v. Enzien, 562 N.Y.S.2d 1010 (1990).
3. *See* Mazza v. Medical Mutual Insurance Co., 319 S.E.2d 217 (N.C. 1990).
4. *See* Miller, *Understanding Professional Liability Insurance*, TRIAL MAGAZINE (May 1990), at 48 *et seq.* A detailed analysis of the many policy coverage issues can be found in *The Lawyers Desk Guide to Legal Malpractice*, which is published by and available from the Standing Committee on Lawyers' Professional Liability, American Bar Association, Chicago, Ill. A new study published by the Standing Committee compares policy coverages on a company-by-company basis.
5. *See* Empire Casualty Co. v. St. Paul Fire & Marine Insurance Co., 764 P.2d 1191 (Colo. 1990).
6. *Infra* note 1 at Section 11.7(c) thereof.
7. 560 So.2d 1223 (Fla. App. 1990).
8. *See* Gulf Insurance Co. v. Dolan, 433 So.2d 512 (Fla. 1983). *See generally* Arnoff and Klampert, *The Applicable Statute of Limitations*, N.Y.L.J. (July 31, 1991), at 3 and 5, pointing out that a determination of the applicable statute of limitations is "essential to understanding this cause of action" for attorney malpractice liability.
9. 417 N.E.2d 84 (N.Y. 1990).
10. 795 F.2d 1187 (4th Cir. 1990).
11. Miller, *infra* note 4. Termination of employment did not constitute the rendering of professional services so that a suit by an employee against an employer for wrongful termination was not covered by the employer's professional liability policy in Inglewood Radiology Medical Group, Inc. v. Hospital Shared Services, Inc., 266 Cal. Rptr. (1990).
12. 17 C.L.T. 29 (Conn. Super., Dkt. 334031, June 26, 1991).
13. *Infra* note 1 at Section 6.7 thereof.
14. *See id.* at Section 1.38.
15. 766 F.2d 754 (3d Cir. 1985).
16. *See* St. Paul Insurance Co. v. Bonded Realty Inc., 578 S.W.2d 191 (Tex. App. 1979).
17. *See* chapter hereinafter.
18. 435 N.Y.S.2d 972 (1980).
19. ______ F. Supp. ______ (Unreported, S.D.N.Y., Dkt. 85 CIV 9812, 1992).
20. *See* Couch on Insurance 2d at Section 44.369. As of November 1993, only the state of Oregon took that deliberate step. In Oregon, insurers are required to

write insurance for every applicant in the legal profession. The insurance business appears to be thriving in that one out of every ten Oregon lawyers is involved in lawyer professional liability claims! In Virginia, an integrated bar, all members are required to disclose whether they have malpractice insurance as a condition of being licensed to practice law in Virginia. The state of Rhode Island requires malpractice insurance for court-appointed lawyers. *See* A.B.A.J. (Nov. 1993), at 44 and 45.

21. 576 P.2d 221 (Kans. 1978).
22. *See* Harrison v. Long, 734 P.2d 1155 (Kans. 1987).
23. *See* Waterman v. Fidelity & Guaranty Co., 209 Ill. App. 284 (1917).
24. *See* Note, N.L.J. (Apr. 12, 1992), at 3 and 24.

Chapter 2

Attorneys

While attorneys are considered by many provocateurs to be guilty of provoking malpractice actions involving both attorneys and nonattorneys, the fact of the matter is that attorneys have in recent years found themselves weighed down by myriads of lawsuits for their own legal malpractice.[1] Lawyers, being officers of the courts, have additional professional responsibilities delineated in countless Codes of Ethics and Statements of Professional Conduct and Practice. Legal malpractice may be said to take diverse forms, not only with respect to plaintiffs who are clients of the attorney but also with respect to plaintiffs who are not clients of the attorney, or with respect to plaintiffs who may have hired the lawyer indirectly and hopefully established the attorney-client relationship.[2]

This diversity of plaintiffs who bring legal malpractice actions generally commences with the rendering by the attorney defendant of a "legal opinion" that is customarily delivered to a party or parties to the transaction. Although the initiation of that legal opinion comes from the recognized client, the substance of the legal opinion is generally negotiated by the client and even by third parties in the transaction. This third-party legal opinion has been the subject of a 1990 report by the Section of Business Law of the American Bar Association (ABA),[3] based upon the following premises:

1. The transaction documents, as the record of a completed negotiation, take into account the parties' realized goals and accurately reflect their bargains.
2. The Report does not imply that there must always be a third-party legal opinion or that it would be imprudent for the parties, taking into account cost and other

considerations, either to dispense with a third-party legal opinion or to alter its scope from the typical opinion contemplated by the Report.

3. A third-party legal opinion is an expression of professional judgment on the legal issues specifically addressed. By rendering a professional opinion, the opinion giver does not become an insurer or guarantor of the transaction or of the future performance of the client.
4. The Report does not replace careful, knowledgeable, transaction-specific legal work as the basis for a third-party legal opinion.
5. The Report does not purport to deal with traditional legal opinion issues in a comprehensive way. For example, it does not address the "due incorporation" opinion.
6. The materials that follow are offered as a sound basis upon which to request, prepare and deliver a third-party legal opinion and as a resource for the understanding of its scope and limits.
7. The Report, including the Accord, is an endeavor to establish a common ground meeting the needs of the opinion giver and the opinion recipient. While believed to provide a framework that is both sound and fair, it has no official sanction and its use is a matter of voluntary action.
8. The Report is intended for prospective use only, and neither the full Report nor the Accord itself is to be used as a frame of reference for evaluating opinions rendered in the past or critiquing earlier third-party legal opinion practices. Relatedly, the positions taken in the Accord are not intended to have, and should not be interpreted as bearing in the future upon third-party legal opinions that do not adopt the Accord.
9. State bar groups may develop, in due course, supplements to the Accord that will take into account relevant laws, regulations or case law of a unique character found in their respective jurisdictions.[4]

The New York Court of Appeals in November 1992 decided *Prudential Insurance Co. v. Gilmartin, Poster & Shafto*,[5] making it abundantly clear that a lawyer may have liability arising from giving a legal opinion to a person other than a client, that is, a third party.[6] The defendant law firm acted as counsel to U.S. Lines in connection with a restructuring of debt that U.S. Lines negotiated with its lenders. As part of the closing of the restructuring transaction, the firm gave a remedies opinion to Prudential and other lenders qualified by a practical realization limitation. It also gave a separate opinion as to the perfection of various ship mortgages. The debt was secured by U.S. Lines ship mortgages; these documents had been prepared by counsel to the lenders. Unfortunately, there was a mistake in one of the mortgages, to wit: the omission of three zeros in the description of the amount of the debt. (The mortgage showed $92,000 in debt rather than $92,000,000!) The court affirmed summary judgment in favor of the law firm on the basis of the fact that the legal opinion was not incorrect; it gave no advice as to the amount of the debt beyond referring back to the mortgage. The court concluded that the opinion letter related only to the smaller amount of the debt stated in the mortgage and therefore the opinion letter could not have caused the loss to Prudential!

"Opinion standards" of counsel for third parties in these transactions have been promulgated by the several states, as illustrated by the Report on Standards for Opinions of Florida Counsel of the Special Committee on Opinion Standards of the Florida Bar Business Law Section (hereinafter set forth in Appendix "A"). A "legal opinion" is therein defined as "a formal writing expressing the lawyer's informed understanding of the legal principles applicable to a specific transaction or a particular aspect of that transaction."[7] Chief Judge Cardozo more than 60 years ago in *Ultramares Corp. v. Touche, Ross & Co.*[8] was deeply concerned about the liability of lawyers for their legal opinions:

> Liability for negligence if adjudged in this case will extend to many callings other than an auditor's. Lawyers who certify their opinion as to the validity of municipal or corporate bonds with knowledge that the opinion will be brought to the notice of the public, will become liable to the investors, if they have overlooked a statute or a decision, to the same extent as if the controversy were one between client and adviser.

Lawyers have also been held liable for their actions and inactions in a variety of situations. For example, in *Growth Center City, Ltd. v. Sildorf Boardman Duignan & Eisenberg,*[9] the law firm attorney misused confidential information to compete with the client's business venture. Liability was predicated upon breach of fiduciary relationship and not upon professional legal grounds. In *Boles v. Simonton,*[10] the cause of action was for the negligent drafting of an installment contract to buy a service station; the contract called for acceleration, allowing payment of the full balance due on the contract in event of default. There was no saving clause in the contract that would have permitted the makeup of late payments. The Montana Supreme Court, in affirming the unfortunate dismissal of the complaint, held that the cause of action accrued when the parties read and signed the contract, not when plaintiff discovered or should have discovered the attorneys' negligence.[11] But in *Murphy v. Smith*[12] the highest Massachusetts court tolled the statute of limitations in a legal malpractice case based on malpractice in the certification of good title to real property. The court tolled the statute of limitations from the beginning of the representation under the "continuing representation doctrine" until the termination of the attorney's representation. Note that the attorney here continues to represent the client![13] Indeed, legal malpractice damages claims frequently raise statute of limitations questions.[14] One writer[15] opined:

> The malpractice claim matures or accrues when the lawyer's negligence has caused injury to the client. One recurrent problem that has split U.S. jurisdictions is whether

the possibility of remediation should toll the statute of limitations. No uniform national rule currently exists to resolve the issue of claim accrual. Some jurisdictions adopt an "exhaustion of appeal" or "remediation" rule. Under this approach, the statute of limitations is tolled until the underlying action, on which the malpractice claim is based, is concluded and the amount of injury has been fixed. Other jurisdictions decline to impose an exhaustion requirement. In these jurisdictions, the malpractice claim is not tolled by the possibility that later events will undermine or nullify the effects of the lawyer's errors.

In proof of legal malpractice, the plaintiff must prove by a preponderance of the evidence that there was in existence the lawyer-client relationship, that the lawyer was negligent or at fault in handling the client's affairs, and that such negligence or at-fault conduct was the proximate cause of the client's injury, damage, or loss.[16] In the lawyer-client relationship, legal malpractice is readily ascertainable, as illustrated by *Dier v. Hamilton*;[17] here the attorney for the plaintiff not only gave improper legal advice with respect to property encumbered by a recorded judgment against the former owner of the property but himself had an undisclosed interest in the encumbered property! A lawyer may indeed be found guilty of the tort of "spoliation of evidence,"[18] as where an attorney prejudicially alters a medical record or a tape recording so as to affect a legal claim that the opposing party would otherwise have been able to assert.[19] Where an attorney disposes of motor vehicle parts that he or she had agreed to preserve and that might reveal the cause of the accident, the new tort of spoliation of evidence has been committed. In *Tetuan v. A. H. Robins Co.*,[20] the plaintiff-wife suffered severe physical injuries from the use of the defendant's IUD contraceptive device. Attorneys for the defendant product manufacturer allegedly suppressed evidence of the company's known propensity to imperil users of the device. The Kansas Supreme Court, in affirming an award of $1.7 million in compensatory damages and $7.5 million in punitive damages, castigated the defendant not only for concealing unfavorable results of its safety studies on the product but also in "consigning hundreds of documents to the draft furnace rather than inform women that the Dalkon Shield carried inside their bodies was a bacterial time-bomb which could cause septic abortions, PID, and even death."[21] Spoliation or destruction of evidence by an attorney should bring the weight of judicial censure as well.

But where third parties are involved, the question of the lawyer's liability is not clear, although the U.S. Supreme Court many years ago, in *National Savings Bank v. Ward*,[22] observed that a lawyer who supplies a certificate of title to a client is *not* answerable to a third person whom the lawyer did not intend to serve: "Neither fraud nor collusion is alleged or proved; and it is conceded that the certificates were made by the defendant lawyer at the request of the applicant for a loan, without any knowledge on the part of the defendant lawyer what use was to be made of the same or to whom they were to be presented."[23] Lawyers, while generally not liable to nonclients for negligence, many be liable to nonclients in fraud situations where the lawyer has an underlying financial interest.[24] But such fraud claims against the lawyer may be defeated where the attorney was not shown to have actual intent to defraud or where the attorney never made any representation to the plaintiff.[25]

In the state of New Jersey, according to *Grunwald v. Bronkesh*,[26] decided by the New Jersey Supreme Court, the "discovery rule" applies in lawyer malpractice actions,

> "triggering the New Jersey six-year limitations period when the client suffers injury or loss and knows, or should know, it is attributable to any attorney's malpractice. The court observed that it had previously applied the discovery rule in medical malpractice actions because plaintiff may reasonably be unable to identify the necessary facts forming the basis of the malpractice claim. The court reasons that applying the discovery rule would preserve the attorney's fiduciary duty of full disclosure by removing the incentive to conceal material facts until after the statute of limitations had run. Noting that both injury and fault are required to satisfy the discovery rule, the court rejected the position that plaintiffs' damages are speculative until an adverse judgment is affirmed on appeal. That damages may later be reduced or extinguished does not change the time the underlying injury or loss occurs. Moreover, delaying the accrual of a cause of action until the appellate process has been completed would defeat the purpose of statute of limitations periods, i.e., fairness to the defendant—because plaintiffs could litigate stale claims. Here the attorney had erroneously advised plaintiff that a prospective buyer had entered into an enforceable contract to purchase plaintiff's property. When the buyer refused, plaintiff sued for specific performance. The lower New Jersey chancery court refused to enforce the contract and held that plaintiff had unreasonably relied on the legal advice. Plaintiff then sued the attorney more than 6 years later, and the trial court granted summary judgment for defendant, concluding that the claim was barred by the 6-year statute of limitations since plaintiff knew or should have known that he had suffered damages as a result of the attorney's malpractice when the lower court had rendered its decision." The New Jersey appellate court reversed, holding that the damages were speculative until the appellate process was complete. But the New Jersey Supreme Court *reversed* and reinstated the trial court's decision rendering summary judgment in favor of the defendant!
>
> It is the general, accepted rule that the mere breach of duty does not cause a claim to accrue in the hands of the person to whom the duty is owed. In the context of a professional malpractice claim, the rule is the same: The mere breach of a professional duty, causing only nominal damages, speculative harm or the threat of future harm—not yet realized—does not suffice to create a cause of action for negligence. . . . Until the client suffers appreciable harm as a consequence of his attorney's negligence, the client cannot establish a cause of action for malpractice.
>
> Until the client suffers some actual injury, the malpractice claim is inchoate. Once actual injury is suffered, the malpractice claim accrues. Actual injury can include loss of a legal right, injury to a legal interest or damage that is reasonably certain to occur in the future. [footnotes omitted]

See *Laid v. Blackner*[27] and *Alhino v. Starr*,[28] two California decisions sustaining the above conclusions.

The Illinois Supreme Court in *Collins v. Reynard*[29] ruled that a plaintiff seeking to recover damages for purely economic loss may not recover under a tort theory of legal malpractice. Plaintiff had retained the defendant law firm to negotiate an installment sale contract for her business. It turned out that the buyer had pledged the assets of the business to a bank, which, due to the law firm's alleged malpractice in drafting the contract, was able to obtain a perfected security interest superior to that of plaintiff. In essence, plaintiff argued that the law firm had failed to draft the contract so as to reflect her intention to retain a first and prior security interest in the business and its related assets. The bank later repossessed the assets and sold them, with the result that plaintiff was unable to sell the business to an alternate buyer. In her malpractice suit, plaintiff sought damages in the amount due under the installment sale contract. The court opined that the mere existence of the attorney-client relationship does not suggest that there are duties present beyond those contracted for between the parties; to recover in a malpractice action, the plaintiff must establish harm beyond that of disappointed economic expectations. In *Hankin v. Hamernick*[30] the attorney moved to dismiss plaintiff's action for payment of stenographic services on the ground that he was absolved of liability because he had disclosed to the plaintiff that he was the agent for his client. But the New York court held that in the absence of a disclaimer the attorney was liable for any costs incurred on behalf of the client. Indeed, an attorney who exhibits gross or wanton negligence may be liable to clients for punitive damages. In Texas, an attorney's professional services fall under the Texas Deceptive Trade Practices Act as a consumer complaint![31]

When does a preliminary interview with a prospective client create a lawyer-client relationship that gives rise to the duty to avoid conflicts of interest? The federal district court in Illinois held that a law firm should be disqualified from representing the defendant when the plaintiff had a preliminary interview with the firm as part of a "beauty contest" to pick substitute counsel.[32] Note that here the plaintiff and the law firm never entered into a representation agreement, never filed an appearance on behalf of the plaintiff, and never received a fee from the plaintiff.[33] In short, the court found an implied attorney-client relationship. However, to avoid disqualification in such situations, "the lawyers should adopt reasonable procedures appropriate for the size and type of firm and practice to determine . . . the parties and issues involved and to determine whether there are actual or potential conflicts of interest."[34] However, to avoid disqualification in such situations, "the lawyers should adopt reasonable procedures appropriate for the size and type of firm and practice to determine . . . the parties and issues involved and to determine whether there are actual or potential conflicts of interest."[35] The lawyer should also warn the client at the outset not to volunteer excess information but to divulge only what is necessary to determine whether a conflict or potential conflict of interest does exist.[36] Furthermore, the lawyer should advise the potential client that any information divulged in the preliminary interview will not be confidential; a written statement to that effect should suffice.

In the *Matter of the Estate of Weinstock*,[37] the New York Court of Appeals had found the father-son team of attorneys guilty of such impropriety and overreaching as to preclude them from serving as named executors of the decedent's will. The two attorneys were also found guilty of constructive fraud in advising decedent with respect to appointment of executors. The New York Court of Appeals nevertheless felt impelled to state its conclusion that

> [w]e do not wish to be understood as implying that when a testator selects the attorney who draws his will as his executor any presumption or inference of impropriety arising from the circumstance that such attorney is otherwise a stranger. That fact alone does not give rise to any obligation on the part of the attorney to come forward with an explanation. It may well be that the testator sought to assure that his estate would be administered by an outsider free from the competing interference of obsequious members of his family. In any event, it is only where, as here, the evidence warrants an affirmative finding of impropriety and overreaching, predicated on more than the fact of appointment, that courts would be warranted in interfering with the testator's manifested intention and excluding the attorney as executor.

Awarding of attorney's fees[38] has also been the subject of legal malpractice. In an action for reimbursement of legal fees allegedly due under an insurance policy,[39] the federal district court in *Mutual Life Insurance Co. of New York v. Liberty Mutual Insurance Co.*[40] disqualified plaintiff's counsel from acting as pretrial counsel since she had previously represented plaintiff in an action commenced against another party in which defendant had approved plaintiff's selection of counsel and paid its legal fees for four years until a dispute arose between defendant and plaintiff over the amount of legal fees being incurred. The court held that the disqualification was warranted under DR 5–101(B), which provides that a lawyer shall not act, or accept employment that contemplates the lawyer's acting, as an advocate before any tribunal if the lawyer knows or it is obvious that the lawyer ought to be called as a witness on behalf of the client. The court concluded:

> It may seem trite to remind lawyers that they are officers of the Court and that, as such, they are required to exercise independent professional judgment at all stages of a litigation, e.g., to evaluate with a dispassionate eye the validity and non-validity of the positions their client wishes them to take and to render professional advice to their client as to the best method of achieving the proper result at a minimum legal expense to their client. These judgments can only be made by independent counsel, not by counsel seeking to justify the very expenses she incurred for her client.

In *Chambers v. NASCO, Ltd.*[41] the Louisiana federal district court used the inherent power of the court to award more than $1 million in attorney fees to the winning party in a breach of contract suit. The attorneys for the party, after the contract for the sale of a television station was apparently breached, discovered that the agreement had not been recorded and devised a plan to take advantage of a Louisiana doctrine to avoid specific performance if NASCO sued by transferring the property to the sister of plaintiff in a trust and recording the transfer on the morning of the day that NASCO informed them it would breach the contract. The attorneys planned to argue that the transfer had priority under Louisiana law because it was recorded before the purchase agreement was recorded. Two years later the court ruled in favor of NASCO in the "massive and unnecessary lawsuit."[42]

An attorney may be compelled to refund fees in excess of reasonable value of work done, according to *Cass & Sons Inc. v. Stag's Fuel Oil Co.*:[43]

> Under applicable law, I not only have the authority to determine the reasonableness of fees charged, but to order a refund of fees already paid. (*Fugazy v. Fugazy*, 149 A.D.2d 664; *Jacobson v. Sassower*, 113 Misc.2d 279, *aff'd* 107 A.D.2d 603, *aff'd* 66 N.Y.2d 991). In my opinion, a reasonable fee for the services rendered including out of pocket expenses amounts to five thousand dollars. It is unnecessary for me in making this evaluation to precisely spell out how I weighed the various factors in making this finding. (*Shrauger v. Shrauger*, 146 A.D.2d 955). Accordingly, the attorneys are directed to deliver to the present attorneys for the defendant all sums received by them as fees over and above five thousand dollars. In addition, they are to deliver to the present attorney for the defendant all papers they are retaining as a lien for their services.

The liability of the lawyer for securities fraud is predicated, *inter alia*, upon Section 12 of the Securities Act of 1933, which provides, in part, that a person who "offers or sells a security" in violation of the registration requirement of the act, or by means of fraudulent statements or omissions, "shall be liable to the person purchasing such security from him." The U.S. Supreme Court in *Pinter v. Dahl*,[44] however, restricted that potential liability for attorneys rendering legal services to clients engaged in the sale of securities by defining who is an offeror or seller under Section 12:

> The range of persons potentially liable under Section 12(1) is not limited to persons who pass title. . . . A natural reading of the statutory language would include in the statutory seller status at least some persons who urged the buyer to purchase. For example, a securities vendor's agent who solicited the purchase would commonly be said, and would be thought by the buyer, to be among those "from" whom the buyer "purchaseed," even though the agent himself did not pass title.

In short, liability extends to anyone

> who successfully solicits the purchase motivated at least in part by a desire to serve his own financial interests or those of the securities owner. . . . But: "[s]ection 12's failure to impose express liability for mere participation in unlawful sales transactions suggests that Congress did not intend that the section impose liability on participants collateral to the offer or sale. When Congress wished to create such liability, it had little trouble doing so. . . . By injecting these concepts into [s]ection 12(1) litigation, the substantial factor test introduces an element of uncertainty into an area that demands certainty and predictability . . . and affords no guidelines for distinguishing between the defendant whose conduct rises to a level of significance sufficient to trigger seller status, and the defendant whose conduct is not sufficiently integral to the sale.

Thus, the highest court concluded that the mere performance of legal services in connection with a securities transaction does not expose attorneys to Section 12 liability: "The buyer does not, in any meaningful sense, purchase the security" from the attorney." See such cases as *Marshall v. Quinn-L Equities Inc.*[45] and *Abell v. Potomac Insurance Co.*[46] In *Mercer v. Jaffe, Snider, Raitt and Heuer, P.C.*,[47] the court opined that "quite obviously buyers commonly do not say that they purchased securities from lawyers or law firms that helped to prepare promotional material or offering statements."

In *Kaplan v. E. F. Hutton Group Inc.*,[48] the court ruled that a law firm representing class members could not communicate with other class members from another lawsuit unless contacted first by those class members. Unauthorized communications with class members is a subject of constant concern in class actions, as noted in *Christensen v. Kiewit-Murdoc Investment Corp.*[49]

How do lawyers protect their fees? Under ABA Model Rule 1.8(j), a lawyer is prohibited from gaining a proprietary interest in a cause of action or litigation unless it is acquired by a legally established lien to secure fees or a contingency fee arrangement.[50]

There are indeed a multitude of defenses that lawyers utilize in defending against legal malpractice claims. The Illinois Supreme Court in *Collins v. Reynard*[51] ruled that a client's recourse for economic loss allegedly caused by the attorney (typically the chief injury stemming from legal malpractice) can rest only on contract law: "The mere fact that there is an attorney-client relationship does not, by itself, suggest that there are duties present above and beyond that which is contracted for. . . . Contract law provides a superior basis . . . for resolution of issues concerning the failed expectations of clients and professionals. . . . Contract damages . . . do not expose professionals to unlimited and unforeseen damages for economic loss."[52] The court here stated that malpractice actions might still be based on tort theories if they involve allegations of fraud or "where extracontractual fiduciary or ethical duties are at issue." A Wisconsin attorney was not liable for failure to diligently pursue a claim that resulted in a lower recovery than plaintiff client would have received if the defendant attorney had settled earlier.[53]

The Racketeering Influenced and Corrupt Organizations Act, or RICO,[54] has been applied to professionals including lawyers, although the U.S. Supreme Court in *Reves v. Ernst & Young*[55] in 1993 restricted RICO in terms of liability for accountants by imposing an additional requirement that a defendant's unlawful conduct must involve the "operation and management" of the affairs of the enterprise. Clearly, this requirement by the highest court would tend to exclude lawyers who readily deny participating in the operation or management of their client or clients. Yet the language of Section 1962(c) of RICO provides that it is unlawful "for any person employed by or associated with any enterprise . . . to conduct or participate, directly or indirectly, in the conduct of such enterprise's affairs through a pattern of racketeering activity." An accountant was found to have participated in the conduct of its client's/enterprise's affairs through its audit work.[56] In contrast thereto is *University of Maryland at Baltimore v. Peat, Marwick & Main Co.*,[57] holding that RICO cannot be used against an accounting firm that issued erroneous and misleading financial statements for a client that later became insolvent. The accounting firm simply did not sufficiently participate in the client's activities to make RICO applicable. According to the court:

> The accounting firm in *Reves* made a critical, erroneous decision that affected the solvency of the [client] and did not tell the [client's] board of directors about it. Yet, even this decision-making did not rise to the level of directing an enterprise.
>
> These services, like the audits, were merely financial services provided for the insurance company, just as lawyers or computer technicians have provided valuable services. Simply because one provides goods or services that ultimately benefit the enterprise does not mean that one becomes liable under RICO.
>
> It cannot be said that by merely performing what are generic financial and related services to an insurance company, even if they are later found to be deficient, an accounting firm has opened itself to liability under RICO.

An attorney is precluded or collaterally estopped from asserting a defense because of a disbarment proceeding that found him guilty of converting plaintiff's funds, as seen in *Burton v. Kaplan*.[58] The present action by the plaintiff for damages presented the same issues as in the prior action including malpractice, breach of fiduciary duty, fraud, and attorney misconduct. The fact that an attorney was experiencing disciplinary problems with the attorney registration and disciplinary commissions during his representation of the defendant did not support the defendant's claim that the attorney rendered ineffective assistance of ineffective assistance of counsel.[59] Note that an injury in an attorney negligence action occurred when the trial court in the underlying case entered an adverse order.[60] In *Vargas v. Zapp*, the New York court held that the action against the attorney was not time-barred because plaintiff's claim arose from the alleged contractual relationship between the parties, and therefore the plaintiff in New York was entitled to a six-year statute of limitations.[61] Note that the plaintiff had argued that he was entitled to

> a tolling of the running of the statute under the doctrine of continuous representation. This doctrine recognizes that the person seeking professional assistance has a right to repose confidence in the professional's ability and good faith and realistically cannot be expected to question and assess the techniques employed in the manner in which the services are rendered while he is still being represented by that professional (*Greene v. Greene*, 56 N.Y.2d 80, 94). Thus, in claims of medical or legal malpractice, the time limitation may, in some circumstances, not run until after the professional relationship has terminated. The application of the doctrine is limited to cases where the attorneys' involvement after the alleged malpractice is related to the same matter and is not merely a continuance of the general professional relationship (see, *Luk Lamellon U Kupplungbau GmbH v. Lerner*, supra; *Little Princess Truck Rentals v. Pergament*, 145 A.D.2d 179).[62]

In New York the six-year statute of limitations is clearly applicable to lawyer malpractice actions, as seen in *Sager v. DeRiggi*,[63] holding that the six-year statute of limitations "governs an action to recover damages to property or pecuniary interests where the obligations alleged to have been violated by defendant, whether verbalized as in tort for professional malpractice or as in contract for nonperformance of particular provisions of the contract, arose out of the contractual relationship of the parties." A law firm that failed to file papers of incorporation for a corporate client was not liable to an accounting firm that had failed to file tax returns for the corporation in *Prescott Investors Inc. v. Blum*.[64]

It should be noted that communications from an attorney to an expert witness relating to subjects about which the expert witness will testify are discoverable, even if they would otherwise be covered by the attorney "work product doctrine," according to *Intermedics Inc. v. Ventritex, Inc.*[65] The question was raised during discovery by parties to a patent infringement suit. According to the court, Rule 26(b)(3) of the Federal Rules of Civil Procedure generally protects attorney work product from discovery, while Rule 26(b)(4) allows discovery of facts known and opinions held by experts. Noting an "unresolved tension" between these provisions, it applied a balancing test. The work product doctrine aims to allow counsel to "think dispassionately, reliably, and creatively both about the law and the evidence" in a case, the court said. It conceded that these are important interests but said they wouldn't be seriously harmed by allowing discovery of communications with expert witnesses. Permitting such discovery wouldn't stop lawyers from thinking dispassionately and creatively about a case or recording their thoughts, it said. Counsel would merely have to choose between having an uninhibited exchange with a nontestifying expert and paying the extra cost for this or having exchanges with the testifying expert, knowing that such communications may have to be disclosed. On the other hand, the court said, Rule 26(b)(4) is intended to allow for probing cross-examination on complicated issues to help the trier of fact judge the persuasive power and reliability of expert testimony. Such cross-examination often wouldn't be possible if counsel couldn't "explore thoroughly in pretrial discovery the mental route that the expert had travelled on the way to his or her conclusions," it said. Moreover, it added, the trier of fact may find it valuable to know that communications from counsel to an expert witness may have included counsel's editorial comments and thus influenced the expert's reasoning and opinion on an issue. Therefore, the court held that written and oral communications from a lawyer to an expert witness on matters about which the expert will testify are discoverable, even if they would otherwise be deemed work product, "absent an extraordinary showing of unfairness that goes well beyond the interests generally protected by the work product doctrine."

Note that the ABA Model Code of Professional Responsibility does not undertake to define standards for civil liability of lawyers for professional conduct. The ABA Model Rules of Professional Conduct takes the same postion:

> Violation of a Rule should not give rise to a cause of action nor should it create any presumption that a legal duty has been breached. The Rules are designed to provide guidance to lawyers and to provide a structure for regulating conduct through disciplinary agencies. They are not designed to be a basis for civil liability. . . . Accordingly, nothing in the Rules should be deemed to augment any substantive legal duty of lawyers or the extra-disciplinary consequences of violating such a duty.

Nevertheless, a jury can be told about the ethics rules, as determined by the California Court of Appeals in *Mirabito v. Liccardo*.[66] The court opined that while there is no independent cause of action for the breach of a disciplinary rule, the rules are a proper standard of conduct to use "to help prove whether Leonard had breached his fiduciary duties." The contrary view is seen in *Lazy Seven Coal Sales, Inc. v. Stone and Hinds*,[67] holding that such rules are not intended to determine civil liability.

Courts have unique roles in disciplining lawyers for actions or inactions that amount to malpractice. In *Waldman v. Levin*[68] the appellate court affirmed a jury verdict against two attorneys who, with the consent of their client in open court and on the record, had settled the client's medical malpractice case. The settlement figure was well below the expectations of the client; and despite the fact that two other judges had approved the settlement amount, the client hired a new attorney to set aside the settlement, alleging negligence by the original two attorneys in accepting a "low-ball" offer of settlement.[69] The appellate court here found that the jury properly determined negligence on the part of the original two attorneys who had failed to contact a certain medical expert in a particular field when they had in fact contacted a number of other medical experts in related fields and had found but one expert that supported the client's position. Furthermore, the two original attorneys should have called on an expert economist. Thus, the original attorneys' negligence was the proximate cause of the client's loss. This case represents the view that accepted modes of attorney conduct can be rendered negligent by judicial fiat! And in a Maryland case, *Morgan v. Cohen*,[70] the trial court threw out a claim by a client against her two former attorneys alleging that they should not have permitted her to sign a settlement reflecting a favorable resolution of the personal injury suit despite the absence of any disfigurement or permanent injuries. Her new attorney argued that she had a viable suit against a third party that was lost by the settlement! The Maryland appellate court reversed in an unreported opinion![71]

May sanctions be imposed in federal court on a party who signs a pleading or other paper that contains erroneous information and that is later deemed to be meritless if the party acted in good faith? The U.S. Supreme Court in *Business Guides v. Chromatic Communications Enterprises*[72] responded in the affirmative: "Where a represented party appends its signature to a document that a reasonable inquiry into the facts would have revealed to be without merit, we see no reason why a district court should be powerless to sanction the party in addition to, or instead of, the attorney." Under Rule 11 the client is held to the same standard of conduct as his or her attorney! Sanctions against attorneys have been varied, as shown in *Fields v. Iowa District Court*.[73] The attorney who conducted research for a medical negligence action was sanctioned by the court. The attorney here had inappropriately relied on his client's version of the facts and had therefore failed to conduct an adequate investigation that would be expected of a reasonable attorney. On the other hand, the second U.S. Court of Appeals in *Healey v. Chelsea*[74] ruled that the sanctioning of a lawyer for bringing a frivolous lawsuit was inappropriate because the suit ultimately failed largely due to the client's shortcomings as a trial witness. Rule 11 sanctions can only be imposed after the submission of frivolous papers: "In determining whether or not a claim was totally unfounded, courts must strive to avoid the wisdom of hindsight in determining whether a pleading was valid when signed and any and all doubts must be resolved in favor of the signer."[75]

In New York City, Part 130 of the Rules of the Chief Administrator gives the New York court the discretion to impose sanctions on any party or attorney in any civil action or proceeding for costs and expenses reasonably incurred as a result of frivolous conduct, defined as follows:

> (1) [I]t is completely without merit in law or fact and cannot be supported by a reasonable argument for an extension, modification or reversal of existing law; or (2) it is undertaken primarily to delay or prolong the resolution of the litigation, or to harass or maliciously injure another. . . . In determining whether the conduct under-

taken was frivolous, the court shall consider, among other issues, (1) the circumstances under which the conduct took place, including the time available for investigating the legal or factual basis of the conduct; and (2) whether or not the conduct was continued when its legal or factual basis was apparent or should have been apparent to counsel.[76]

In *Forstman v. Arluck*[77] two doctors sought an order for costs and sanctions against plaintiff's counsel. When it became apparent that the specific allegations of malpractice against the doctors were wholly without merit, the court imposed sanctions on plaintiff's counsel for continuing the litigation against the doctors.[78] The New York Court of Appeals in *Matter of Anonymous*[79] analyzed the imposition of disciplinary sanctions for unethical conduct of attorneys and gave broad discretion to local disciplinary authorities and courts to sanction lawyers who criticize a judge, for example.[80]

Lawyers, like other professional businesspeople, have in recent years resorted to advertising for the marketing of their services, and these advertising practices have plagued both federal and state courts since the 1977 decision of the U.S. Supreme Court in *Bates v. State Bar of Arizona*,[81] permitting lawyers to advertise their legal services.[82] The 1988 U.S. Supreme Court decision in *Shapero v. Kentucky Bar Association*[83] held that direct-mail solicitation by attorneys was constitutionally protected free speech. And in 1990 the highest court in *Peel v. Attorney Registration and Disciplinary Commission of Illinois*[84] ruled that a state cannot bar a truthful communication of a nonstate-sponsored certification of specialization by lawyers.[85] In New York in May 1991 the Association of the Bar of the City of New York proposed that advertising of private certification as a lawyer specialist be permitted.[86]

State bar associations have figured in substantial litigation with their lawyer-members. For example, in *Keller v. State Bar of California*[87] the U.S. Supreme Court ruled unanimously that state bar associations may not use compulsory dues to support members' wishes to support such political activities as "nuclear freeze," polygraph testing, air pollution regulation, sex discrimination, prison construction, crime victim's bill of rights, gun control, *inter-alia*![88] State bar associations have also been concerned with lawyer advertising, as evident by the statement of the New York State Bar Association on December 4, 1990, that New York lawyers may use client testimonials in their advertising![89] The Florida Supreme Court in 1990 imposed new restrictions on lawyers who advertise in Florida: Advertised fees must be honored for at least 90 days unless the ad specifies a shorter time. Fees advertised in the Yellow Pages must be honored for a year. Lawyers may not make "self-laudatory" statements in ads or statements that describe the quality of the lawyer's services. Lawyers may not use trade names in their advertising if they do not actually practice under them. This prevents firms from inventing contrived names only to gain higher placement in alphabetical listings. All ads must be submitted to the bar's new Standing Committee on Advertising, which will review them and offer advisory opinions on whether they comply with the rules. Lawyers may be required to forfeit any fees collected as a result of advertising that violates the rules.[90]

According to Bodine,[91] "advertising can reduce the cost of legal services," citing a 1984 survey by the Cleveland, Ohio, office of the Federal Trade Commission (FTC) to the effect that in states with fewest restrictions on lawyer advertising, consumers tended to pay 5 to 13 percent less for legal services:

> The important point is that advertising effectively helps clients in the difficult task of finding a lawyer. The ABA "Aspirational Goals for Lawyer Advertising" states, "People sometimes do not receive needed legal services, either because they are unaware of available services, don't understand how they can benefit from those services or don't understand how to obtain them. Therefore, it is also the legal profession's responsibility to inform the public about the availability of legal services and how to obtain and use them. Advertising is one of many methods by which lawyers can inform the public about legal services. Most people have more information about price and quality when they need a washing machine than when they need someone as important as a lawyer. Advertising can fill this gap. After seeing an ad, a person can at least learn what the lawyer looks like, the office address and fees, and what kind of cases the firm handles. If restrictions were removed, ads would allow lawyers to distinguish themselves by listing their specialty certifications, past accomplishments and client testimonials. The issue is whether "the public is better kept in ignorance than trusted with correct but incomplete information. We suspect the argument [against advertising] rests on an underestimation of the public," the Supreme Court said in 1977 in the *Bates* case. The public is trusted with making tough choices using conflicting information when electing a president or buying a house. The people are also smart enough to sort through lawyer ads.[92]

Legal malpractice, according to an ABA Standing Committee study of professional liability claims against attorneys,[93] has somewhat been focused in recent years upon claims arising from family law matters. In *Cornett v. Johnson*,[94] for example, an unhappy client filed a malpractice claim against an attorney who represented him in proceedings to obtain a divorce. Dissatisfied with the division of property by the court, the disgruntled husband alleged an improper distribution of marital assets resulting from the attorney's failure to call certain witnesses and introduce certain evidence during the divorce hearing. The disgruntled client even had an affidavit of the judge who had presided in the divorce hearing; that judge testified that had the additional evidence been submitted, he would have ruled more favorably toward the husband in dividing up the marital estate. But in the legal malpractice action the trial court disregarded the affidavit as "speculative" and granted summary judgment in favor of the attorney since the client failed to present other evidence including evidence of damages sustained. In *Haynes v. Kuder*[95] the unhappy female client sued her divorce attorney for unspecified acts of malpractice, and her attorney moved to compel arbitration pursuant to a provision in their retainer agreement. The client alleged that her attorney never explained to her the meaning or significance of the arbitration clause. But the trial court granted the attorney's motion to compel arbitration, and the appellate court affirmed.

It is obvious that a large number of complaints against lawyers could be eliminated by requiring written contracts setting forth the fee schedule as well as simplified versions of other important and necessary clauses.[96] That was the recommendation of the National Organization of Bar Counsel in a September 1990 report, which also recommended mandatory arbitration for attorney-client fee disputes in the absence of a written agreement. Failure to give the client notice of how the fee is set is unethical.[97]

Attorney-client sexual relations is a popular and inviting topic, as illustrated in *Suppressed v. Suppressed*,[98] where the Illinois Supreme Court reviewed factual presentation that on three separate occasions the defendant male attorney requested, and the female client submitted to, intimate conduct while the defendant was representing her in a divorce case. She alleged that she complied with his advances because she was fearful that "her refusal to do so would jeopardize the defendant's willingness to adequately represent her and her children's interest." After this sexual harassment, she dismissed the attorney and retained new counsel. Three years later she filed a formal complaint with the Illinois Attorney Registration and Disciplinary Commission, which promptly closed the proceeding. Then five years later came the present suit, which was dismissed by the trial on the ground of the two-year statute of limitations governing personal injury actions in Illinois. She appealed on the ground that the applicable statute was a five-year one for contract actions, but the Illinois appellate court again rejected her appeal. Above all, the attorney's alleged sexual relationship with a client, although unethical, did not amount to legal malpractice: "[We do not believe that] the higher standard of care required of a fiduciary should extend to an attorney's personal relationships with his clients, unless there is tangible evidence that the attorney actually made his professional services contingent upon the sexual involvement or that his legal representation of the client was, in fact, adversely affected. . . . Although defendant's behavior may have been unethical, we do not think that it equates with legal malpractice."[99]

Sexual relations between attorney and client is seen in *Edwards v. Edwards*,[100] especially after the court imposed monetary sanctions and costs in the amount of $10,000 for the attorney's frivolous conduct:

> We hold that where the conduct claimed to be frivolous consists of the refusal of a party or an attorney to perform a particular act, e.g., voluntary withdrawal as counsel, the party who sought to compel performance must establish that under the facts

and circumstances of the particular case such performance was clearly and unequivocally mandated by existing law. In this case, that standard was not met. The propriety of the order under review must be weighed against the background of this not atypical emotionally-charged matrimonial dispute. . . . The only New York case to have come to our attention which has addressed the issue of an attorney's sexual involvement with clients is *Matter of Bowen* (150 AD2d 905, *app. den.* 74 NY2d 610), an attorney disciplinary proceeding in which respondent was alleged to have entered into a sexual relationship with three clients and to have attempted to pursue personal relationships with four other women who sought professional advice regarding matrimonial problems. The court, in sustaining the charges, held that respondent "repeatedly attempted to use the attorney-client relationship and the trust engendered thereby in furtherance of sexual relationships, taking particular advantage of clients whose matrimonial difficulties placed them in a highly vulnerable emotional state." (*Id.* at 908). In none of these cases was it the sexual relationship *per se* which constituted a breach of professional responsibility but rather the attorney's attempt to exploit the professional relationship to gain unsolicited sexual favors. Here, of course, even assuming the truth of the allegations, there is not the slightest hint that Golub, who knew the wife since 1981, took advantage of her or the attorney-client relationship. She has made no such complaints.[101]

Law firms have particularly been defendants in gender discrimination cases, as illustrated by *Ezold v. Wolk, Block, Schorr, and Solis-Cohen.*[102] Here the federal district court in Pennsylvania found that the defendant law firm had engaged in unlawful "disparate treatment" of a female associate when it did not extend a partnership offer to her. Note that in employment discrimination cases[103] plaintiffs can attempt to prove discrimination on the ground of disparate treatment, which is based on discriminatory intent, or disparate impact, which means that a facially neutral employment practice has a statistically adverse effect on a protected class.[104] Here plaintiff Nancy was hired by the Philadelphia law firm in 1983 as a litigation associate. Throughout her five years with the law firm her performance was regularly evaluated: She received low marks for her analytical ability but positive evaluations for her courtroom skills. In 1989 the executive committee of the law firm voted not to make her a partner, and she thereupon resigned and sued the law firm under Title VII of the Civil Rights Act of 1964. The trial court opined that she had successfully presented a *prima facie* case of discrimination; the trial court did not find that her low marks for "analytical ability" were "worthy of credence." But the Third U.S. Court of Appeals, in reversing and remanding for entry of judgment in favor of the law firm, pointed out that favorable performance evaluations in categories other than the proffered one were not relevant to a finding of pretext. The lower court had impermissibly substituted its own judgment for that of the law firm, according to the federal appellate court.[105]

Where a lawyer practices in more than one state, he or she is subject to the disciplines of each state; if the disciplines are in conflict with each other, the problem is addressed in ABA Formal Opinion 91–360, dated July 11, 1991, which elected a principled compromise approach to determine which state's public policy should control. See A.B.A.J. (Feb. 1992) at 93, identifying the case of *Bernick v. Frost*,[106] where the New Jersey court construed an attorney-client contingency fee agreement between a New Jersey lawyer and a New Jersey client under the New Jersey limitation on contingency fees even though the tort action was filed in New York!

The growth of complex transactions and the mobility of modern life have led to a huge increase in interstate litigation. Barring national uniformity in rules of professional conduct—unlikely to occur in the near future—multilicensed lawyers must be aware of the varied and sometime conflicting obligations they assume.

An interesting unanswered question in the 1990s is whether or not the everyday standard of care lawyers owe their clients as professionals is virtually impossible to maintain without computer literacy.[107] Today it is estimated that almost 90 percent of all written information is computerized and accessible through online databases; even court decisions, revised statutes, and other "tools of the trade" are distributed on computer media.

Still another relatively unanswered question is whether the Federal Deposit Insurance Corporation (FDIC) has the right to pursue a legal malpractice claim against a law firm for its representation of a defunct savings and loan association. The Ninth U.S. Court of Appeals in *O'Melveny & Myers v. FDIC*[108] decided that the FDIC had the right "to rescue the economy and the victims of failing thrifts" and the law firms "can claim no stronger ethical position than did the wrongdoers within the corporate entity." In contrast thereto are decisions of the Fifth U.S. Court of Appeals[109] that state laws take precedence and limit the ability of the FDIC to sue professionals.

Solicitation of clients is another instance of legal malpractice, as illustrated by *Ohralik v. Ohio State Bar Assn.*,[110] decided by the U.S. Supreme Court in 1978. The lawyer here in person solicited two victims of an automobile accident after hearing about the accident and contacting the parents of one of the victims, the driver.[111] He visited the driver at the hospital, offered to represent her, and asked her to sign a retainer, but the minor wanted first to discuss the matter with her parents. He then approached the parents, reviewed their insurance policies, and informed them that they could make an uninsured-motorist claim against their own insurer since the other vehicle was uninsured. He was retained by the parents, who identified the other victim whom the attorney then approached but failed to sign up, although the attorney did receive a portion of the client's recovery. The Ohio State Bar Association disciplined the attorney, and the court affirmed, rejecting the claim that his conduct was constitutionally protected as commercial speech under the First Amendment. The highest court emphasized the "conduct" aspect of the solicitation over the "speech component": "Unlike a public advertisement, which simply provides information and leaves the recipient free to act upon it or not, in person solicitation may exert pressure and often demands an immediate response, without providing an opportunity for comparison or reflection." The Court also determined that the substantive evils associated with solicitation—to wit, stirring up litigation, asserting fraudulent claims, debasing the legal profession, and potentially harming the client by overreaching, overcharging, underrepresentation or misrepresentation—were legitimately subject to state regulation or suppression: "The Rules prohibiting solicitation are prophylactic measures whose objective is the prevention of harm before it occurs. The Rules were applied in this case to discipline a lawyer for soliciting employment for pecuniary gain under circumstances likely to result in the adverse consequences the State seeks to avert."

But the U.S. Supreme Court in 1993 in *Edenfield v. Fane*,[112] a case involving an accountant, declared a Florida statute banning solicitation of clients to be unconstitutional on First Amendment grounds. In its 8–1 decision, the Court granted recognition to protection of "commercial speech" in the form of personal solicitation of business. State regulation, however, can properly deal with preventing misrepresentation, overreaching, and invasion of the privacy of potential clients.[113] In *Matter of Avis* the New Jersey case refused to impose "discipline for truthful letters of solicitation sent more than two weeks after . . . a loss became known."[114] Yet a Florida rule requiring lawyers to wait 30 days before sending solicitation letters to accident victims was declared to be unconstitutional. One writer concluded:

> Moreover, while the *Edenfield* court held that *Ohralik* did not relieve states of the obligation to show that the regulation imposed is a reasonably effective method of dealing with the problem, it also noted that the "State's fear of harm from attorney solicitation [is] well founded." The force and effect of Edenfield's treatment of *Ohralik* ultimately will be determined by whether that "fear" is well-founded in general, or only well founded given the facts of *Ohralik*.[115]
>
> Ironically, the very success of the bar in prohibiting lawyer solicitation may necessitate that it argue for a broad construction of *Ohralik*. It is unlikely that any studies exist to demonstrate the dangers of lawyer-client solicitations. Even in the sensitive area of personal injury cases, the information available on client harm from lawyer solicitation is anecdotal and intuitive rather than systematic and empirical. Although *Edenfield* suggests that anecdotal information may suffice, it may be a shaky foundation for a broad prophylactic ban on all commercial speech by lawyers. [citations omitted]

Where legal malpractice results in loss to clients, the several states have established funds to protect clients. In New York, for example, the New York State Lawyers' Fund for Client Protection is important legislation, as delineated in *Matter of Sheridan*.[116] The Fund here won priority over all other unsecured creditors to the estate of a former lawyer who had looted six estates that he had served as executor and attorney, causing the Fund to pay out $371,000 to reimburse 46 individual and charitable beneficiaries. The court invoked the "sovereign prerogative of priority," based on the ancient doctrine that the Crown of England enjoyed a right of priority over its subjects to the remaining assets of an insolvent debtor. The New York Client Protection Fund has been pursuing restitution with increasing success, having recovered a total of $1 million in the past nine years.

A victim's rights act has similar purposes of protecting the victims of crimes. The Model Victims' Rights Act, prepared by the National Conference of Commissioners on Uniform State Laws, seeks to standardize the rights of crime victims.[117] The Model bill covers help and compensation for crime victims and their families and also establishes rights relative to the trial and punishment, including prompt notification after the crime of how a victim-assistance agency works, requires that police and prosecution keep victims current on all phases of the investigation, trial, sentencing, and parole hearings, and mandates the rights of victims to testify on the crime's impact on them, a procedure approved by the U.S. Supreme Court in *Payne v. Tennessee*[118] where victim-impact testimony was admissible in certain death penalty hearings.

Protection of clients from the thievery, fraud, and misrepresentation of lawyers has in recent years come into the fore. Nearly every state has set up client security funds to pay for some, or even all, losses.[119] In New York, for example, the State Client's Security Fund in 1988 reimbursed all but 1 of 202 claimants for the full amount of the money stolen by their lawyers.[120] The New York fund documented $3.8 million in losses in cases involving 54 lawyers and paid out $2.8 million. The fund is financed by a $100 fee from biennial lawyer registration, plus increments from investment income and recoupment by the state attorney general for fraud and misrepresentation. The only client who fell short of full recovery in 1988 was an Austrian baron who lost $1.1 million due to his lawyer's embezzlement, but the Austrian baron did collect $100,000 from the New York fund.[121] The Connecticut Bar Association's Clients' Security Fund is very generous in the sense that it imposes no limit on awards; in 1988 the Connecticut fund approved 47 claims totaling $4.1 million but paid out only 10 percent of that amount to date.[122]

It should be observed that clients' security funds do make diligent attempts to recoup assets from the lawyers charged with the commission of the crime or malpractice. In *Securities Exchange Commission v. Pavarini*,[123] the federal district court ruled that claims by the fund do not have priority over claims by some 300 investors that defendant Pavarini allegedly swindled out of $3.3 million in an investment business that he operated alongside his law practice: "Since no property has been designated as subject to the Fund's lien, its lien is not perfected and it can claim no priority over the [defrauded] investors. . . . [The purpose of the New York fund] is to maintain the integrity of the legal profession . . . not to exercise its authority to protect the rights of its citizens." It was estimated that the New York fund might recoup about 11 percent of the law clients' claims!

Legal malpractice insurance[124] has become very popular in recent days, as more and more lawyers find themselves victims of their client's failure to maintain an effective offense or an effective defense. A lawyer who settles a case without client authority, for example, may be liable to the client for damages if the settlement harms the client's interests.[125] The lawyer who fails to obtain a client's consent to a particular procedure may wind up with the short end of the stick.[126] But a lawyer who doubts the sanity of a client may properly decide that the client cannot determine the client's own best interest, and the lawyer may have to act contrary to the desires of the client.[127] Complex problems arise especially where a disabled client is involved with commitment and/or juvenile delinquency proceedings.[128] About ten bar associations have recently created a multistate corporation called Attorney Liability Protection Society, or ALPS, organized under the Federal Liability Risk Retention Act of 1986, which allows professional groups of lawyers to organize their own malpractice insurance companies.[129]

Attorneys may be disqualified by a court under Canons 4 and 5 of the Code of Professional Responsibility, as shown in *Kempner v. Oppenheimer & Co., Inc.*[130] Here the plaintiff alleged violations of the Securities Exchange Act of 1934 in that the defendant and two of its employees had committed fraud, breach of fiduciary duty, and negligence. The defendant's attorney had originally represented all defendants but had terminated representation of the two employees after learning that the plaintiff's name had been forged on his account documents. The plaintiff, joined by one of the defendant's employees, moved to disqualify the defendant's attorney based upon previous representation of that employee and on the ground that the attorney ought to be called as a witness about the allegations of document destruction and threats or inducements to commit perjury. The federal district court noted that Canon 4 stated that "an attorney may be disqualified . . . if he has accepted employment adverse to the interests of a former client on a matter substantially related to the prior litigation"; but the court rejected the plaintiff's argument because it found that there was simultaneous representation of two clients where each client was aware of the other's relationship and both parties had no reason to believe that confidences of one party would be withheld from the other. The court also rejected the plaintiff's argument that the attorney should be disqualified under Disciplinary Rule 5–105, which provides that a lawyer shall decline proffered employment that represents a conflict of interest and shall discontinue multiple employment if a conflict of interest arises. The attorney, according to the court, had no reason to suspect that a conflict would develop when the lawyer initially agreed to represent both the defendant corporation and its employees.

When the conflict of interests did arise, the attorney moved promptly to disassociate himself.

There is a crime-fraud exception to the attorney-client relationship, tersely stated by Mr. Justice Cardozo in *Clark v. United States:*[131] "The privilege takes flight if the relation is abused. A client who consults an attorney for advice that will serve him in the commission of a fraud will have no help from the law." In short, the attorney-client relationship is designed to protect only the legitimate purpose of the client. In *Sound Video Unlimited, Inc. v. Video Shack, Inc.,*[132] the court found that the client illegally wiretapped his business associates and then turned over the fruits of the wiretaps to his attorneys so that they could initiate litigation. The court ordered the attorneys to testify as to conversations with their client about the use of the wiretaps because of the crime-fraud, despite the attorney-client relationship.[133]

Where there are "intended beneficiaries" the lawyer is more apt to be held liable, as illustrated by *Roberts v. Ball, Hunt, Hart, Brown and Baerwitz.*[134] The defendant law firm prepared an "opinion letter" with respect to its client's status as a partnership, knowing that the client would show the opinion letter to the plaintiff so as to induce the plaintiff to loan the client a sum of money. The California court found no difficulty in predicating liability against the law firm, for "the issuance of a legal opinion intended to secure a benefit for the client, either monetary or otherwise, must be issued with due care, or the attorneys who do not carefully will have breached a duty owed to those they attempted or expected to influence on behalf of their clients." That same year, in *Goodman v. Kennedy*[135] the California Supreme Court, however, found that the defendant lawyers owed no duty to the plaintiffs; the defendant lawyers had allegedly given negligent advice to their clients that certain dividend shares of stock could be issued without jeopardizing a registration exemption, the result being that their clients had sold virtually worthless stock after the registration exemption was lost. The court found no evidence that the lawyers' advice had ever been communicated to the plaintiffs, and therefore the plaintiffs were not intended beneficiaries of the defendant lawyers' negligent advice.[136]

Interestingly, the Securities and Exchange Commission (SEC), as illustrated in *SEC v. Spectrum, Ltd.,*[137] has held the lawyer to an extremely high standard of conduct to protect all investors: "The legal profession plays a unique and pivotal role in the effective implementation of the securities laws. Questions of compliance . . . are ever present and the smooth functioning of the securities markets will be seriously disturbed if the public cannot rely on the expertise proffered by an attorney when he renders an opinion."

But in *Carmel v. Lunney,*[138] the New York Court of Appeals on July 9, 1987, affirmed the nonguilt conviction of a lawyer who represented a party at hearings for violation of the New York Martin Act.[139] It appears that the defendant lawyer had previously appeared at SEC hearings in Washington,

D.C., representing the very brokerage firm for whom the plaintiff worked as a licensed securities salesman.The plaintiff alleged that the defendant attorney counseled him to appear at the Martin Act hearings to inform the attorney general of the state of New York "unreservedly about his activities" at his employer's place of employment. Subsequently, the plaintiff was indicted for grand larceny, scheming to defraud, and conspiracy under the Martin Act. With a new attorney to defend him in the criminal prosecution, the plaintiff pleaded guilty to misdemeanor charges. The plaintiff contended that the defendant was guilty of legal malpractice for not advising him as a client of the possible criminal implications of his testimony, of his privilege against self-incrimination under the Fifth Amendment, and of the possibility of receiving immunity for his testimony in the first place. The plaintiff cited also the potential conflicts of interests stemming from defendant having represented his employer previously. But, according to the court,

> "to state a cause of action for legal malpractice arising from negligent representation in a criminal proceeding, plaintiff must allege his innocence or a colorable claim of innocence of the underlying offense (see *Claudio v. Heller*, 119 Misc.2d 432), for so long as the determination of his guilt of that offense remains undisturbed, no cause of action will lie. Here, because plaintiff's conviction by plea of a misdemeanor violation of the Martin Act has not been successfully challenged, he can neither assert, nor establish, his innocence. He had thus failed to state a cause of action, and his claim was properly dismissed by the Appellate Division. . . . To be sure, a defendant in a criminal proceeding might be able to prove malpractice by establishing that but for the negligent representation he would, for example, have invoked his 5th Amendment rights, or succeeded in suppressing certain evidence conclusive of his guilt. But, because he cannot assert his innocence, public policy prevents maintenance of a malpractice action against his attorney. This is so because criminal prosecutions involve constitutional and procedural safeguards designed to maintain the integrity of the judicial system and to protect criminal defendants from overreaching governmental actions. These aspects of criminal proceedings make criminal malpractice cases unique, and policy considerations require different pleading and substantive rules (see, e.g., Kaus & Mullen, "The Misguiding Hand of Counsel—Reflections on 'Criminal Malpractice,' " 21 UCLA L. Rev. 1191)."

The law had indeed long recognized the sanctity of communication between lawyer and client in order to foster trust and confidence and to promote the free flow of information between lawyer and client. This lawyer-client privilege is, however, subject to the "crime-fraud exception,"[140] which exists to prevent abuse by piercing the privilege if the client seeks advice from the attorney to further a crime or a fraud.[141] In *Bernard D. Morely P.C. v. MacFarlane*,[142] the Colorado Supreme Court held that a trial court may order disclosure of attorney-client communications if there is "some foundation in face" for the allegation, thereby requiring what the court called a "*prima facie* showing" as opposed to the mere establishment of a *prima facie* case. And in *U.S. v. Horvath*,[143] where the clients hired an attorney for the primary purpose of concealing the extent of their financial holdings and sources of income, the Eighth U.S. Court of Appeals deemed the arrangement an "ongoing criminal conspiracy" to conceal funds, and therefore the court denied the attorney-client privilege, compelling the attorney to testify about client communications concerning past criminal acts.

The attorney-client privilege bars the attorney from disclosing information to anyone other than the client, provided that the information is a communication and is made in confidence between a person who is or is about to be a client and a lawyer, for the purpose of obtaining legal advice or legal assistance.[144] The client is the holder of the privilege, and unless the client waives the privilege, its protections will endure forever. A corporation may have such privilege as a client, and any succession in ownership of the corporation or its management does not destroy the privilege.

Claims of misconduct by professionals have in recent years been lodged against lawyers, not only with respect to making misrepresentations in published articles but also with respect to false résumés.[145] The former misconduct is evidenced by plagiarism and data fraud in legal-related work; the latter is evidenced by personal résumés that contain false information.[146] Illustrations of the former are found in the hearings before the Office of Research Integrity of the U.S. Department of Health and Human Services and before a similar office within the National Science Foundation. In *Re Matter of Rameshwar K. Sharma*[147] a researcher was found not to have made false claims in a grant application for research into brain chemistry. And in *Phinney v. Board of Regents*,[148] a civil suit involving plagiarism, the plaintiff won a verdict of more than $1 million from the University of Michigan's Institute of Gerontology because she had been led to believe that she would be given first authorship credit in a number of papers and would be the beneficiary of a number of grant applications if she would share her research and her original ideas. Her suit involved claims of fraud and retaliation against her for complaining that her former mentor plagiarized her work.

On résumé fraud the Sixth U.S. Court of Appeals in *Milligan-Jensen v. Michigan Technological University*[149] opined in favor of the employee, and the case was settled out of court. In *Summers v. State Farm Mutual Automobile Insurance Co.*,[150] the Tenth U.S. Court of Appeals ruled that the trial court had properly dismissed an age-discrimination complaint based on "after acquired" evidence, to wit: a forged signature to document an insurance claim. A year later, another falsification of documents was discovered, and the employer placed the employee on probation before dismissing him due to his poor attitude and similar problems. In short, an employer may avoid all liability for a discharge based solely on unlawful motives by proving that it would have discharged the employee if it had possessed full knowledge of the circumstances existing at the time of the discharge. The Sixth U.S. Court of Appeals in *Johnson v. Honeywell Information Systems, Inc.*[151] found that summary judgment was appropriate only in those résumé fraud cases in which the misrepresentation or omission was material, was directly related to measuring a candidate for employment, and was relied upon by the employer in making the hiring decision.

Part and parcel of the problems of such misconduct is the question of liability of individuals who serve on panels reviewing allegations of misconduct, as seen in *Abbs v. Sullivan.*[152] Here the federal district court evaluated the adequacy of procedures used by the U.S. Public Health Service to investigate whether a federally funded researcher had falsified or fabricated certain published research results.[153] Research institutions generally use peer review committees to investigate allegations of misconduct, and individual liability may result from mistaken beliefs, inadequate investigations, or other misconduct on the part of individuals on the peer review committee.[154] The most likely cause of action against an institution or its misconduct committee members is defamation, followed by wrongful interference with contractual relations, intentional infliction of emotional distress, and discrimination based on age, sex, race, or national origin.[155] In *Gertz v. Robert Welch, Inc.*,[156] the U.S. Supreme Court insisted upon proof of actual harm before the plaintiff is entitled to punitive damages. Plaintiff must prove that the allegedly defamatory statement was indeed false, harmful to plaintiff's reputation and made with intent to defame. Note that the Health Care Quality Improvement Act of 1986[157] was designed to provide uniform minimum protection for activities of professional review organizations and their individual members. The act defines professional review activities and renders the organization and its members "not liable in damages under any law of the United States or of any State."[158] The act specifies that review action may only be taken "(1) in the reasonable belief that the action was in the furtherance of quality health care, (2) after a reasonable effort to obtain the facts of the matter, (3) after adequate notice and hearing procedures . . . , (4) in the reasonable belief that the action was warranted by the facts known after such reasonable effort to obtain facts and after meeting the requirement of paragraph (3)."[159]

Attorneys are very much mindful of the Money Laundering Act,[160] which authorizes the prosecution of attorneys who knowingly accept criminal proceeds as attorney fees. But the act poses such Sixth Amendment problems as the right of the accused to the effective assistance of counsel of his own choice. The act states that the "criminal property" must be valued over $10,000, a theft-by-receipt violation.[161]

A lawyer's liability for fraud and misrepresentation also finds illustration in "lawyer advertising,"[162] which has been sanctioned as recently as June 1988 by the U.S. Supreme Court in *Shapero v. Kentucky Bar Association.*[163] Here the highest court held that defendant's ban on targeted direct-mail solicitation of clients violated the First Amendment. That decision, it should be noted, invalidated Rule 7.3 of the Model Rules of Professional Conduct. Three years earlier, the highest court, in *Zauderer v. Office of Disciplinary Counsel*,[164] had held that nontargeted advertisements containing advice similar to the soliciting letter in the *Shapero* case[165] could not be actionable. But in the Court's 1988 decision, "The First Amendment does not permit a ban on speech merely because it is more efficient; the State may not constitutionally ban a particular letter on the theory that to mail it only to those whom it would most interest is somehow inherently objectionable." The Court in 1988 concluded that the states can regulate "abuses and minimize mistakes through far less restrictive and more precise means, the most obvious of which is to require the lawyer to file any solicitation letters with a State agency . . . giving the State ample opportunity to supervise mailings and penalize actual abuses. . . . [Here there was] no evidence that scrutiny of targeted solicitation letters will be appreciably more burdensome or less reliable than scrutiny of advertisements."[166]

NOTES

1. *See* WARREN FREEDMAN, THE BUSINESS TORT OF FRAUD AND MISREPRESENTATION (1987), at Section 7.4 thereof.

2. *See* WARREN FREEDMAN, INTERNAL INVESTIGATIONS AND THE EMPLOYMENT RELATIONSHIP (1993), at Section 5.03 thereof. Legal experts today advise lawyers to "see a potential malpractice claim as soon as a new client walks in the door," as described in Goldsmith, *By the Letter*, A.B.A.J. (July 1993), at 103. The point is simply that loss prevention starts before the client enters the law office. Once the potential client faces the attorney, the screening procedure is in force: Was the client turned down by another attorney, or did the client fire previous counsel? Does the client have reasonable expectations for the outcome of the case? Does the client want to proceed on principle, regardless of costs? Has the client contacted numerous governmental agencies or done extensive legal research? These are but a few of the "red flags" during the initial interview that can steer the attorney away from a potentially difficult client who might later be inclined to file a malpractice claim.

The decision whether or not to take a case should be made in writing to the potential client. If there is nonengagement, the letter should advise the client to seek other counsel, even though the attorney is not judging the merits of the case.

3. *See* 46 BUS. LAWYER (Dec. 30, 1990), at 518–538. The American Bar Association, located at 750 North Lake Shore Drive, Chicago, Ill. 60611, comprising more than 36,000 attorneys, judges, court administrators, educators, law students, legal assistants, criminal justice professionals, governmental officials, and business executives, has enacted the Model Rules of Professional Conduct. The ABA Standing Committee on Lawyers' Professional Liability in 1992 published its practical guide to preventing legal malpractice and obtaining the most favorable malpractice insurance. The first half of THE LAWYER'S DESK GUIDE TO LEGAL MALPRACTICE includes explanations of how to avoid the ten primary traps that result in malpractice claims. The second half of the book covers malpractice insurance, including a directory of insurers in each state.

Also see LEGAL OPINIONS IN INTERNATIONAL TRANSACTIONS: FOREIGN LAWYERS' RESPONSE TO US OPINION REQUESTS, Report of Subcommittee E-1 on Legal Opinions of SBL Committee E (Banking Law) of the International Bar Association (2d ed. 1989), at 5. The validity of this justification for third-party opinions, that is, that a party to an agreement is estopped from raising a defense against the validity of such agreement if such defense contradicts an opinion previously delivered by such party's counsel, has been seriously questioned at the proceedings of the Subcommittee on Legal Opinions during its session at the IBA's 24th Biennial Conference in Cannes, Oct. 19, 1992. *Note* Gruson, *Legal Opinions: Response to the ABA's Opinion Accord*, INT'L BUS. LAWYER (Mar. 1992), at 125–132.

The Federal Bar Association, 1815 H Street, N.W., Washington D.C. 20006–3697, comprising more than 15,000 private and public sector attorneys, currently or formerly in government service, has a most detailed MODEL RULES OF PROFESSIONAL CONDUCT FOR FEDERAL LAWYERS, reproduced in Appendix B with express permission of the Federal Bar Association (1990).

4. Two recent Connecticut cases illustrate the myriads of problems involved in attorney malpractice: In Cole v. Cummings & Lockwood and Rodenbach, 8 C.S.C.R. 1023 (Oct. 18, 1993), the grieving plaintiffs alleged that the testator's attempt to protect the trust corpus from taxation will fail because the will creates a general power of appointment in plaintiff M and makes the trust corpus includable in her gross estate at death, rather than skipping to the estates of her descendants. Plaintiffs further alleged that they have the ability to enforce the contract as third-party beneficiaries of their father's will. The court refused to strike the complaint, pointing out that defendants' contention that any duty they may owe to plaintiffs ended upon the death of their father is without merit since the facts show that defendants had "assumed a relationship with the intended beneficiaries." The court also found the claim that the Internal Revenue Service (IRS) will interpret the will to create a general power of appointment to be credible.

In the other Connecticut case, Klingeman v. Sakal, 8 C.S.C.R. 928 (Sept. 20, 1993), plaintiff alleged that her lawyers did not fully inform her of the offered settlement by the defendants in her underlying wrongful death action, thereby depriving her of the chance to win or settle her suit. The court ruled that the Connecticut Unfair Trade Practice Act, or CUTPA, is applicable to attorney malpractice, to wit: Defendant's failure to inform plaintiff of a substantial settlement offer, in light of the progression of the trial, may establish an unfair trade practice!

Bad advice given by a lawyer in Matter of Da Silva, 545 N.Y.S.2d 348 (Nassau County Jan. 25, 1993) prompted the New York court to order the refund of almost $5,000 to his clients because the advice amounted to malpractice. The lawyer had advised the coconservators of the estate of an 11-year-old child that they could withdraw more than $34,000 in commissions without court approval. He also advised that they could pay him more than $4,900 in fees without court approval. And in Brust v. Newton, ______ P.2d ______ (Unreported, Wash. 1992), the Washington court found for the client who had sued his lawyers for drafting improperly a prenuptial agreement that the court declared to be void. Lawyers have not generally had a duty toward nonclients as interested third parties, except for the Washington Supreme Court holding in Bohn v. Cody, 832 P.2d 71 (Wash., Dkt. 57579–7, Feb. 27, 1992), where the lawyer was found liable to the nonclients when he helped arrange a loan to his client from the nonclients. *See* Hazard, *Ethics*, N.L.J. (Jan. 20,

1993), at 15–16, quoting from the opinion of the Ninth U.S. Court of Appeals in FDIC v. O'Melveny & Myers, 969 F.2d 744 (9th Cir. June 29, 1992): "No California cases advise us of an exception to the general rule that a lawyer has to act competently to avoid public harm when he learns that his is a dishonest *client.*"

See generally Cohen and Bloch, *Can Lawyers Be Prosecuted for the Advice They Give?* N.Y.L.J. (July 23, 1991), at 1, 5 and 6, concluding:

> Many believe that when it comes to enforcement of the criminal law, lawyers should be treated the same as everyone else. Where attorneys stop being lawyers and engaged in illegal conduct, few will disagree with that position. But where counsel, who have acted in good faith, face the prospect of criminal prosecution for giving legal advice (correct or not) to clients, there are sound policy reasons why prosecutors should move cautiously and should treat counsel differently.

Also note Arnoff and Klampert, *Professional Liability: The New York Law*, N.Y.L.J. (Aug. 30, 1991), at 3 and 4, citing, *inter alia*, such recent cases as Santulli v. Englert Reilly & McHugh, 563 N.Y.S.2d 548 (App. Div., 3d Dept., 1990), wherein the court dismissed the action against the attorney on the basis of the statute of limitations; Brown v. Samakub & Bock, 563 N.Y.S.2d 426 (App. Div., 2d Dept., 1990), where the plaintiff lawyer "did not adequately oppose the motion for summary judgment with the expert evidence which the issues warranted"; and in contrast thereto, Gerard Lollo & Sons v. Stern, 563 N.Y.S.2d 442 (App. Div., 2d Dept., 1990), where the court put the burden on the attorney to present convincing proof in opposition to a motion for summary judgment, especially where the position he was asserting in the litigation against him was different from the position that he had previously advocated in the underlying case. The authors concluded:

> For attorneys to obtain some guidance in the area of attorney professional liability in New York, a review of the current decisions should always lead to the conclusion that attorneys are subject to suit and liability not only in those cases where their conduct falls below the minimally appropriate standard, but also where exceedingly bad professional judgment, and not mere error, causes real economic injury to clients to whom they owe a duty of due care. In addition, such a review should always lead to the conclusion that attorneys will be fairly judged and properly protected in the true exercise of their professional judgment and not challenged for trivial mistakes, unfulfilled and unrealistic client expectations and conduct that does not cause any real economic loss. Above all, the review should demonstrate that lawyers and the judges who judge them should never seek to apply an unseemly double standard to lawyers as against other professionals, thus belying the sign on the courthouse door, "Equal Justice under the Law."

5. 73 N.Y.2d 417 (1992).

6. *See generally* Field, *Change in Legal Opinion Practice Expected as a Result of "Gilmartin" Decision*, N.Y.L.J. (Feb. 5, 1993), at 3 and 4.

7. *See* 46 Bus. Lawyer (Aug. 1991), at 1407–1448.

8. 172 N.Y. 147 (N.Y. 1931).

9. 265 Cal. Rptr. 330 (1989).

10. 791 P.2d 755 (Mont. 1990).

11. *Cf.* Nichols v. Ach, 447 N.W.2d 220 (Neb. 1989), where the Nebraska Supreme Court held that the cause of action for attorney negligence accrued when the former client knew or should have known of the alleged negligence. In Granquist

v. Sandberg, 268 Cal. Rptr. 109 (1990), it was held that the attorney could be liable for failing to set preferentially his elderly client's lawsuit for trial!

12. 579 N.E.2d 165 (Mass. 1991). In Gulf Coast Investment Corp. v. Brown, 813 S.W.2d 218 (Tex., Dkt. D-1518, Dec. 4, 1991), the statute of limitations was tolled until all appeals on the underlying claim are exhausted. Here plaintiffs filed suit against Gulf for wrongful foreclosure due to improper notice, and judgment was rendered in their favor; whereupon Gulf sued its former attorneys for legal malpractice. The Texas Supreme Court held that when an attorney's malpractice in conducting a nonjudicial foreclosure sale of real property results in a wrongful disclosure action against the client, the statute of limitations on legal malpractice in Texas is tolled until the wrongful foreclosure action is finally resolved. To the same effect is Hughes v. Mehaney and Higgins, 822 S.W.2d 63 (Tex., Dkt. D-0678, Nov. 20, 1991).

13. *See* Santulli v. Englert, Reilly & McHugh, 586 N.E.2d 104a (N.Y. 1992).

14. *See* Fischer, *Legal Malpractice: Timing Is Everything*, N.L.J. (Apr. 5, 1993), at 33.

15. *Id.*

16. The distinction between attorneys and accountants as recognized in Crossland Savings PSB v. Rockwood Ins. Co., ______ F. Supp. ______ (Unreported, S.D.N.Y. 1988). Here the court reaffirmed the New York position that an attorney may not be held liable in negligence by one with whom he is not in contractual privity, relying on Michalic v. Klat, 128 A.D.2d 505, 512 N.Y.S.2d 436 (2d Dept. 1987); National Westminster Bank v. Weksel, 124 A.D.2d 144, 511 N.Y.S.2d 636 (1st Dept. 1986); Grenoble Mills Inc., v. Drinker, Biddle & Reath, ______ F. Supp. ______, No. 84 Civ. 3514 (S.D.N.Y. July 30, 1986).

The Seventh U.S. Court of Appeals in Greycas, Inc. v. Proud, 826 F.2d 1560 (7th Cir. 1987) readily upheld the lower court's decision that the attorney was liable for negligent misrepresentation when he lied about conducting a title search on equipment to be used as collateral for a loan. Defendant-attorney was a brother-in-law of the debtor-farmer! Applying Illinois law, the court sanctioned the finding that when an attorney supplied information to a lender that the attorney knows the lender will rely on before deciding whether to grant a loan, the attorney has negligently misrepresented and is liable to the lender-creditor.

Probably the most common example of the "missed deadline" for the practicing lawyer is the "blown statute of limitations," whether from failure to file timely a notice of claim or to commence an action or to move for a new trial or to appeal within time limits. However, the disgruntled client, in order to recover against his or her lawyer, must prove that the underlying action was meritorious, as illustrated in Hickox v. Holleman, 502 So.2d 626 (Miss. 1987), where the Mississippi Supreme Court reversed a trial court's directed verdict for the defendant, holding that his failure to bring a medical malpractice action within the statutory period was negligence.

17. 661 So.2d 1059 (La. Ct. App. 1987).

18. *See* ch. 12 of Warren Freedman, The Tort of Discovery Abuse (1989).

19. *Note* Prosser and Keeton, Law of Torts (1988 Supp.), at 140–142.

20. 738 P.2d 1210 (Kans. 1987).

21. *Id.* at 239–240. *See* 32 A.T.L.A. L. Rev. (Aug. 1989), at 231–233.

22. 100 U.S. 195 (1925).

23. *Id.* at 199.

24. *See* Raymark Industries, Inc. v. Stemple, unreported, _____ N.W.2d _____ (Unreported, Kans. 1988), where two lawyers were defendants; they had founded the Tire Workers Litigation Project and were sued by a former asbestos product manufacturer who had been paying tire workers' negotiated asbestos injury claims that the plaintiff alleged were fraudulent. In the suit for $48 million, the plaintiff also sued three medical experts, approximately 5,700 injured tire workers in 12 states, and dozens of other local attorneys. *See* NAT'L L.J. (Feb. 22, 1988), at 21. *See* DEF. COUNS. J. (Oct. 1987), at 511 *et seq.* n.36: "Eisenberg v. Gagnon, 766 F.2d 770 (3rd Cir. 1985) (tax shelter investors were deceived by attorney in business transaction in which he had a pecuniary interest); Bonavire v. Wampler, 779 F.2d 1011 (4th Cir. 1985) (a classic sting; attorney induced nonclient investors to participate in investment scheme through false representations); Excalibur Oil Inc. v. Sullivan, 616 F. Supp. 458 (N.D. Ill. 1985) (nonclient investor misled by attorney's representation concerning encumbrances); In re Flight Transportation Corp. Securities Litigation, 593 F. Supp. 612 (D. Minn. 1984) (purchasers of securities relied on representations of law firm representing underwriters; cause of action stated); Arnold v. Weck, 388 So.2d 269 (Fla. App. 1980) (adversary settled case in reliance on attorney's false representation that he had settlement authority); A.S.J. Drugs, Inc. v. Berkowitz, 459 So.2d 348 (Fla. App. 1984) (detrimental reliance on misrepresentation); LaFountaine v. State Farm Mutual Auto Ins. Co., 698 P.2d 410 (Mont. 1985) (clerk issued default judgment on misrepresentation by attorney to clerk of court that default judgment had been reinstated); Malewich v. Zacharias, 196 N.J. Super. 372, 482 A.2d 951; (1984) (husband's attorney made false representations to wife's attorney on which latter relied, resulting in default judgment against wife and her attorney's liability to her for malpractice); Nappe v. Anschelewitz, Barr, Ansell and Bonello, 189 N.J. Super. 347, 460 A.2d 161 (1983) (fraudulent representations in loan transaction); Riverside Finance Corp. v. Coniglio Builders Inc., 73 A.D.2d 1039, 425 N.Y.S.2d 433 (1980) (attorney participated in sale of mortgagor's lot notwithstanding his full knowledge of mortgagee's interest)."

The apparent dichotomy regarding a lawyer's liability to nonclients is seen in Vereins-Und Westbank AG v. Carter, 692 F. Supp. 704 (S.D.N.Y. 1988) and in Benedek v. Heit, 531 N.Y.S.2d 266, *appeal denied*, 534 N.E.2d 328 (1988). In the former case, it was held that nonclients may sue a lawyer for negligent misstatements if the lawyer made the misstatement knowing that the third-party nonclient would rely upon it and if the benefit to the lawyer's client is directly related to that reliance. Here the alleged misstatements were made in opinion letters sent by the attorney to a bank and to the insurer who had issued surety bonds guaranteeing payment obligations of limited partners. It was shown that the attorney knew that the bank and the insurer would rely on his opinion. On the other hand, in the latter case, the New York appellate court overturned a jury's $600,000 award against the defendant attorney on the ground that the defendant attorney's obligation to the plaintiff investor was only one of fair dealing: "Nothing was done deliberately to harm plaintiff and it was his own refusal to go ahead with the TV station deal which led to the law suit, which he prudently settled. It is because of this breach that the federal suit was brought and is the 'loss causation.' . . . At no time was the defendant retained as plaintiff's attorney and there was no billing of the plaintiff by the defendant for any legal services." Furthermore, plaintiff had his own counsel, and defendant attorney "cannot be considered to have any obligation to the plaintiff other than one of fair dealing with an investor." *See* N.Y.L.J. (Aug. 12, 1988), at 1.

See RESTATEMENT (SECOND) OF TORTS § 552, which sets forth the rule regarding recovery by third parties for negligent misrepresentations by any person in a business or professional relationship:

(1) One who, in the course of his business, profession or employment, or in any other transaction in which he has a pecuniary interest, supplies false information for the guidance of others in their business transactions, is subject to liability for pecuniary loss caused to them by their justifiable reliance upon the information, if he fails to exercise reasonable care or competence in obtaining or communicating the information.
(2) Except as stated in Subsection (3), the liability stated in Subsection (1) is limited to loss suffered:
  (a) by the person or one of a limited group of persons for whose benefit or guidance he intends to supply the information or knows that the recipient intends to supply it, and
  (b) through reliance upon it in a transaction that he intends the information to influence or knows that the recipient so intends or in a substantially similar transaction.
(3) The liability of one who is under a public duty to give the information extends to loss suffered by any of the class of persons for whose benefit the duty is created, in any of the transactions in which it is intended to protect them.

In short, an attorney making a negligent misrepresentation in the course of representing a client is liable for damages suffered by a third party by reason of such negligent misrepresentation if the attorney intended his representation to influence the action of the third party and if the third party justifiably relied on the representation. *See* Treece and Hall, *Attorney's Liability: Negligent Misrepresentations to Third Parties—a Growing Threat*, FOR THE DEFENSE (July 1989), at 18–23. In Greycas Inc. v. Proud, 826 F.2d 1560 (7th Cir. 1987), *cert. denied*, 108 S.Ct. 775 (1988), the federal appellate court affirmed a judgment against an attorney for $833,000 because he gave a wrong assurance of the favorable financial status of his brother-in-law, the borrower. The plaintiff here had agreed to lend $1.3 million subject to a letter from the borrower's attorney that there were no prior liens on the machinery being pledged as security for the loan. The borrower subsequently defaulted on the loan, and the plaintiff lender discovered that most of the machinery had previously been pledged to other creditors. The attorney had simply relied on statements of the borrower–brother-in-law and had not made any search for prior liens.

A contrary view is seen in the California case of Schick v. Bach, 238 Cal. Rptr 902 (1987). There the lawyer advised his client, a psychologist, that he might properly release certain confidential information regarding a patient. The patient thereon sued the attorney, claiming that his legal opinion was erroneous, contrary to law, and had caused the plaintiff to suffer damages. The court, in denying recovery for the patient against the psychologist's lawyer, found a lack of privity between the parties; furthermore, the attorney did not intend his legal opinion to influence the actions of the patient, for he had made the representation as to law solely for the benefit of his client, the psychologist. An earlier California case, Roberts v. Ball, Hunt, Hart, Brown & Baerwitz, 128 Cal. Rptr. 901 (1976), had set forth six principles governing the conduct of an attorney and a third party, to wit:

(1) the extent to which the transaction between the lawyer and the second party was intended to affect the third party;
(2) the foreseeability of harm to the third party;
(3) the degree of certainty that the third party did in fact suffer harm;

(4) the closeness of the connection between the conduct of the attorney and the injury;
(5) moral blame attachable to the lawyer's conduct; and
(6) the policy of preventing future harm.

Balancing these factors, it becomes clear that there are exceptions to the rule that the attorney owes no duty to nonclient third parties, as seen in Harad v. Aetna Casualty & Surety Co., 839 F.2d 979 (3d Cir. 1988), where the intentional act of the attorney amounted to fraud and other wrongs; and in Guy v. Liederbach, 459 A.2d 774 (Pa. 1988), where claims are asserted by beneficial heirs who alleged injury due to negligent acts or omissions of the decedent's attorney.

Section 12 of the Securities Act of 1933 provides:

Any person who—

(1) offers or sells a security in violation of § 5, or

(2) offers or sells a security [whether or not exempted by the provisions of § 3, other than paragraph (2) of subsection (a) thereof], by the use of any means or instruments of transportation or communication in interstate commerce or of the mails, by means of a prospectus or oral communication, which includes an untrue statement of a material fact or omits to state a material fact necessary in order to make the statements, in the light of the circumstances under which they were made, not misleading (the purchasers not knowing of such untruth or omission), and who shall not sustain the burden of proof that he did not know, and in the exercise of reasonable care could not have known, of such untruth or omission, shall be liable to the person purchasing such security from him, who may sue either at law or in equity in any court of competent jurisdiction, to recover the consideration paid for such security with interest thereon, less the amount of any income received thereon the tender of such security, or for damages if he no longer has the security.

The U.S. Supreme Court in Pinter v. Dahl, 188 S.Ct. 2068 (1988) broadened the liability of attorneys and other professionals by substituting a negligence for a scienter standard but diminished the liability of attorneys by stating that when the attorney acts solely as an attorney, there is no liability under Section 12 of the act. *See* Brodsky, *Liability of Attorneys and Other Professionals*, N.Y.L.J. (May 31, 1989), at 3 and 6.

25. *See* Schmid v. National Bank of Greece, 622 F. Supp. 704 (Mass. 1985), Fidelity & Guaranty Co. v. Byrnes, 497 N.Y.S.2d 719 (1986). As set forth in Applegate v. Dobrovir, Oakes & Gebhardt, 628 F. Supp. 378 (D.C. 1985), found on an attorney's part means that plaintiff can establish a false representation, in reference to a material fact, made with knowledge of its falsity, with the intent to deceive, causing one to act on the representation. Note that in De La Maria v. Powell, Goldstein, Frazier & Murphy, 612 F. Supp. 1507 (Ga. 1985), an attorney may be liable for negligent recommendation of one client to another client for business transactions.

Clients in Florida may disclose grievances against Florida lawvers, as indicated in Doe v. Supreme Court of Florida, ______ F. Supp. ______ (Unreported, Fla., Dkt. 88–8477-DIV, Jan. 1990). This landmark case removed the "gag rule" that had prohibited anyone filing a grievance against a Florida lawyer from publicly discussing the complaint. Indeed, Florida is the only state other than Oregon to allow disclosure of complaints against a lawyer before the fact-finder or court issues a probable cause finding. *See* A.B.A.J. (June 1990), at 22–23.

A law firm in New York can be sued for negligence stemming from advice it gave on a governmental bond deal to a company other than its client, according to Financial Guaranty Insurance Co. v. Drexel Burnham Lambert Inc., ____ N.Y.S.2d ____ (Unreported, New York County Apr. 12, 1990):

Recovery may be had for pecuniary loss arising from negligent presentations where there is actual privity of contract between the parties or where there is a relationship so close as to be the functional equivalent of contractual privity. Professionals owe a duty of due diligence, despite the lack of contract privity, to those parties with whom they have direct contact and communication when those professionals know or should know that the information they impart will be relied upon and when the objective of those professionals is to shape the conduct of those parties (Ossining School v. Anderson, 73 NY2d 417).

26. 621 A.2d 459 (N.J. 1993).
27. 828 P.2d 691 (Cal. 1992).
28. 169 Cal. Rptr. 136 (Cal. App. 1980).
29. 607 N.E.2d 1185 (Ill., Dkt. 70325, Oct. 31, 1991).
30. _____ N.Y.S.2d _____ (Kings County, Civil Ct., Nov. 12, 1991).
31. *See* Johnson v. DeLay, 809 S.W.2d 552 (Tex. App. 1991).
32. *See* Bridge Products, Inc. v. Quantum Chemical Corp., ____ F. Supp. ____ (Unreported, N.D. Ill. 1990).
33. *See* Garwin, *Beware of Beauty Contests*, A.B.A.J. (Jan. 1991), at 84.
34. *See* DCA Food Industries, Inc. v. Tasty Foods, Inc., 626 F. Supp. 54 (W.D. Wis. 1985).
35. *Note* Comment to Rule 1.7 of ABA Formal Opinions 90–358 (Sept. 13, 1990).
36. *Infra* note 11. An attorney with a client has special legal responsibilities arising under the law of Agency such as loyalty but not an unqualified obligation simply to do the client's bidding. *See* Note, N.L.J. (Jan. 20, 1992), at 17–18, which article points out that under Section 348 of Restatement (Second) of Agency "an agent who fraudulently makes representations . . . or knowingly assists in the commission of tortious fraud . . . by his principal . . . is subject to liability in tort to the injured person." However, in Schatz v. Rosenberg, 943 F.2d 485 (1991), the Fourth U.S. Court of Appeals declined to hold attorneys liable as agents; attorneys are said to have a license permitting them to do with impunity what for everyone else is tortious fraud! *Cf.* Greycas v. Proud, 826 F.2d 11560 (7th Cir. 1987).

In Cresswell v. Sullivan & Cromwell, 771 F. Supp. 580 (S.D.N.Y., Dkt. 87–2685, July 1991), four fraud claims charging that in a 1983 securities fraud case the defendant law firm failed to disclose documents damaging to its client were dismissed. Plaintiff investors failed to establish that their own lawyer's negligence was not responsible for neglecting to uncover the information.

37. 40 N.Y.2d 1 (N.Y. 1990). *See* Cooper v. Equity Insurance Co., 268 Cal. Rptr. 692 (1990), finding that the attorneys were not liable for conspiring to violate their client's duty of good faith and fair dealing. The California appellate court observed that an attorney acting solely as an insured's agent could not be liable for conspiring unless it is shown that the attorney acted in furtherance of his own financial gain and violated a duty owed to the client.

In Ulrich v. Hearst, 809 F. Supp. 229 (S.D.N.Y., Dkt. 92–1320, Nov. 13, 1992), a former labor lawyer for the Hearst Corp. was barred from handling three discrimination suits against Hearst because of the very likelihood the lawyer would unavoidably use confidential information. The lawyer was thus barred even without proof that Hearst had disclosed specific, relevant confidences to him.

Also in Santa Clara County Counsel Attorneys Assn. v. Woodside, _____ Cal. Rptr. 2d _____ (Unreported, 6th Dist., Dkt. H008865, Jan. 29, 1993), the California appellate court barred government attorneys from suing their clients: The obligations of loyalty to the client prohibit members of the office from suing the office in wage disputes! *See* N.L.J. (Feb. 15, 1993), at 3 and 37.

Note that federal prosecutors are exempt from a Pennsylvania Supreme Court rule requiring prosecutors to obtain court approval before calling defense counsel before a grand jury for information about current or former clients, as seen in Baylson v. The Disciplinary Board, etc., 975 F.2d 102 (3d Cir., Dkt. 91–1425, Sept. 16, 1992); for lower court, 764 F. Supp. 328 (E.D. Pa. 1992). Emotional distress damages were not recognized in Smith v. Superior Court, 13 Cal. Rptr. 2d 133 (Cal. App. 1992). According to the court, the possibility of serious emotional harm to the client and the degree of certainty that the client suffered such injury following the claim of economic loss are tenuous. There was no evidence of intentional misconduct on the part of the attorney.

Incidentally, reliance on a lawyer's advice in California is reasonable, as shown in the appellate court's overturning of a $40 million verdict in Greenwood & Co. Real Estate v. C-D Investment Co., ____ Cal. Rptr. 2d ____ (Unreported, 2d Dist., Dkt. B048638, Jan. 29, 1993). The court ruled that the jury should have been instructed that reasonable reliance on reasonable legal advice is a defense to the torts of interference with contractual relations and interference with prospective economic advantage.

Note that legal malpractice awards are not dischargeable in bankruptcy, as seen in In Re Stokes, 142 B.R. 908 (N.D. Cal., Dkt. 91–46756 NR, July 23, 1992).

38. *But* as illustrated in Lynch v. Deaconness Medical Center, 7765 P.2d 681 (Wash. 1989), an attorney cannot recover fees from an incidental beneficiary of his services under theories of unjust enrichment or equitable subrogation. The court observed that enrichment was unjust only if, in equity and good conscience, a defendant should not retain the recovery. Here the hospital had merely obtained payment for services it had rendered and for which it had the right to be compensated.

39. Note that the relationship between an attorney hired by insurer to defend its insured and the insurer is not one of attorney-client, as seen in Atlanta International Insurance Co. v. Bell, 475 N.W.2d 294 (Mich., Dkt. 87914, Sept. 18, 1991).

40. 746 F. Supp. 375 (S.D.N.Y., Dkt. 89-CIV 402, Sept. 28, 1990).

41. _____ F. Supp. _____ (Unreported, La., Dkt. 90–2456, 1991), *cert. denied*, 111 S. Ct. 2123 (1991).

42. *See* Coyle, *Is Court's Fee Power Inherent?* N.Y.L.J. (Feb. 25, 1991), at 3 and 27.

43. 561 N.Y.S.2d 519 (Queens County Oct. 25, 1990).

44. 108 S. Ct. 2063 (1988). According to the N.Y. Times, Nov. 4 1990, at 31, federal regulators, combing through the savings and loan wreckage, are increasingly filing lawsuits against lawyers who represented savings and loan institutions, accusing the lawyers with negligence or malpractice. The caseload runs the gamut from simple collection of delinquent loans to fraud. *See* Wilkins, *Who Should Regulate Lawyers?* 105 HARV. L. REV. 801 (1992). *See* Valente and Michaels, *Attor-*

neys-in-Fact: Accountability, N.Y.L.J. (Oct. 30, 1990), at 3 and 7. *See* Lupel, *Attorney Discipline: Too Much of a Good Thing?* TRIAL MAGAZINE (Sept. 1993), at 71, concluding that lawyers today are walking on eggshells and that the growth of attorney discipline has dramatically altered relationships between attorneys and clients as well as among attorneys themselves. *Also see* Schwartz, *Lawyer Discipline: Defining Its Role*; TRIAL MAGAZINE (Sept. 1993), at 74–75. Also see INSIGHT MAGAZINE (Feb. 25, 1991), at 51, on "the tough case of attorney theft" delineating the disappearance of New York attorney Steven J. Romer with $15.5 million in client funds!

45. 764 F. Supp. 1304 (N.D. Tex. 1988).

46. 858 F.2d 1104 (5th Cir. 1988), *judg. vac. on other grounds*, 109 S. Ct. 3236 (1989).

47. 713 F. Supp. 1019 (W.D. Mich. 1989).

48. 546 N.Y.S.2d 324 (App. Div., 1st Dept., 1989).

49. 815 F.2d 206 (2d Cir. 1987). *See generally* Feldman, *The Breakdown of Securities Fraud Aiding and Abetting Liability: Can a Uniform Standard Be Resurrected?* 19 SECUR. REG. L.J. (1991), at 45, pointing out that until recently the traditional standard for imposing aiding and abetting liability for fraud on those professional service firms involved in a securities transaction but not directly involved in the sale of securities has uniformly been applied in almost all federal courts. But in recent years there has been a divergence among the appellate courts as to the standard.

50. *See* Note, A.B.A.J. (Dec. 1990), at 92. Note the preservation of the attorney's lien in bankruptcy in Federal Land Bank of Jackson in Receivership v. Federal Intermediate Credit Bank of Jackson, 128 F.R.D. 182 (1989).

51. _____ N.E.2d _____ (Unreported, Ill. 1991). Attorney liability to third parties was delineated in Prudential Insurance Co. v. Dewey, Ballantine, et al., 573 N.Y.S.2d 981 (App. Div., 1st Dept., Aug. 15, 1991):

> Our examination of the complaint indicates that the plaintiff alleges that the proximate cause of United's challenge to the subject mortgage was the defendants' legal malpractice, causing that mortgage to incorrectly reflect that plaintiff's interest as $92,885 instead of $92,885,000. Since the mortgage was documented and recorded with the Coast Guard, United contended, in the Bankruptcy Court, "that the reduced amount . . . constitutes the extent to which Prudential's First Mortgage is properly recorded under the Ship Mortgage Act . . ." (*see*, RA, at 991). Further, plaintiff alleges in the complaint that, "if . . . [plaintiff] had not settled the dispute with . . . [United], . . . [plaintiff] would have incurred substantial additional legal fees in litigating the dispute, risked the loss of any recovery from the Lancer Vessels, and further delayed its receipt of proceeds from the sale of the ships to its further financial loss . . ." (*see*, RA, at 108) [material in brackets added]. . . .
>
> The fact pattern herein is unlike that found in the usual legal malpractice action, since plaintiff does not claim that defendants mishandled litigation and lost a case, which should have been won. Rather plaintiff claims that defendants' legal malpractice caused third parties, United and GECC, to bring legal challenges against the $92,885,000 mortgage interest of plaintiff. Regardless of the legal malpractice fact pattern, the triable issue of fact is the same: did the defendant's conduct fall "below the ordinary and reasonable skill and knowledge commonly possessed by a member of his [or her] profession . . ." (Grago v. Robertson, *supra*) [material in brackets added].
>
> Based upon our review of the proceedings in the Federal Courts, relative to the challenges of United and GECC to the mortgage, we find triable issues of fact are presented, as to whether it

was reasonable for plaintiff to settle, rather than further litigate, for the purpose of minimizing damages, and whether that settlement was reasonable.

See generally Samet, Walker, Meehan, and Lubega, *The Attack on the Citadel of Privity: The Expanding Liability of Attorneys to Non-Clients for Professional Negligence*, BRIEF MAGAZINE (Winter 1991), at 9 *et seq.* The writers cite Sooy v. Peter, 220 Cal. App. 3d 1305 (1990), at 1313, wherein the California appellate court held that an attorney had no liability to third parties who were not intended beneficiaries of his legal services. The writers nevertheless concluded:

> The citadel of privity is under grave attack. The potency of the attack is rooted in modern tort law's goals of providing maximum recovery to injured parties and placing the risk of loss among those thought to be most able to bear the cost. However, the attack on privity threatens to impose upon the attorney more than just increased exposure to liability; he or she increasingly faces a real ethical dilemma.
>
> When lawyers must be concerned about their potential liability to third parties, the resultant self-protective tendencies may deter vigorous representation of the client. Attention to third-party risk might cause the attorney improperly to consider "personal interests" or "the desires of third parties" above the client's interests. This would contravene the lawyer's duty of loyalty to the client.
>
> At a minimum, the uncertainty of liability to non-clients—at least in states applying California's balancing test—is a factor that may give pause to the well-informed practitioner. The consequences of potential liability to third parties may be profound, interfering with the lawyer's "professional responsibility . . . of assisting members of the public to secure and protect available legal rights and benefits."
>
> The unavoidable tension between these ethical standards on the one hand, and the fear of exposure to malpractice liability to non-clients on the other, is an issue that must be confronted and dealt with squarely even in the heat of battle in the inexorable attack on privity. [Footnotes omitted]

52. *See* Anderson v. Aspelmeier Fisch Power Warner & Engberg, 461 N.W.2d 598 (Iowa 1990), holding that a partner does not engage in conduct detrimental to his law firm when he leaves the firm, even if most of his clients follow him. Obviously, if he had left the firm and none of his clients had followed him, his act of leaving would not have been considered detrimental to the firm; so why should it be different simply because clients did follow him?

An attorney was absolved from liability in a suit brought by a bank from whom his client was borrowing money; the attorney had prepared certain documents and sent them to the bank, which documents contained the mistaken fact that the house that was part of the collateral for the loan was in a land trust and hence not a subject for collateral. *See* First National Bank of Moline v. Califf, Harper, Fox & Dailey, 548 N.E.2d 1361 (Ill. App. 1989). In a similar vein is Sooy v. Peter, 270 Cal. Rptr. 151 (1990), where the court determined that no liability existed in a suit brought by a senior mortgagor's attorney against a junior mortgagor's attorney for statements made by the former to the effect that the senior mortgagor's attorney would advise the junior's of a pending mortgage foreclosure action. For a collection of similar cases, *see* DEFENSE COUNSEL J. (Jan. 1991), at 138.

53. *See* Schlomer v. Perina, 473 N.W.2d 8 (Wis. App. 1991).

54. *See* WARREN FREEDMAN, THE BUSINESS TORT OF FRAUD AND MISREPRESENTATION (1989) at ch. 2 thereof.

55. 113 S. Ct. 1163 (1993).

56. *See* Bank of America National Trust & Savings Assn. v. Touche Ross & Co., 782 F.2d 966 (11th Cir. 1986). *Note* Seamons, *So, My Adviser, Were You Calling the Shots?* BUS. LAW TODAY (Nov.–Dec. 1933), at 10 *et seq*.

57. _____ F.2d _____ (3d Cir., Dkt. 91–1889, June 22, 1993).

58. 504 N.Y.S.2d 188 (New York County, Apr. 23, 1991).

59. People v. Szabo, 497 N.E.2d 995 (Unreported, Ill., Dkt. 69284, Oct. 17, 1991). Another important defense to legal malpractice is the doctrine of *in pari delicto* as illustrated in Pantely v. Garris, Garris, & Garris, P.C., 447 N.W.2d 864 (Mich. App. 1989). Here defendant law firm successfully represented the plaintiff in a divorce action in which plaintiff testified that she had been a resident of the Michigan county wherein the action was filed for the requisite period of 10 days. About a year after the judgment of divorce was entered, the plaintiff's ex-spouse moved to modify or set aside the divorce on the ground that plaintiff had fraudulently misrepresented the duration of her residency. Plaintiff readily admitted so doing, explaining that the defendant law firm had counseled her to do so. Plaintiff subsequently sued the law firm for improper advice to misrepresent her residency, and both parties raised the defense of *in pari delicto*. The Michigan appellate court acknowledged the admission of perjury by the plaintiff and held that plaintiff's action was barred by the doctrine of *in pari delicto*. Supportive cases cited by the court included Feld & Sons Inc. v. Pechner, Dorfman, Wolfe, Rounick & Cabot, 458 A.2d 545 (Pa. Super. 1983) and Evans v. Cameron, 360 N.W.2d 25 (Wis. 1985). *See* Note, DEFENSE COUNSEL J. (July 1991), at 423.

60. *See* Laird v. Blacker, 279 Cal. Rptr. 700 (1991). *See* Boles v. Somonton, 791 P.2d 755 (Mont. 1990) to the effect that a cause of action for negligence in contract drafting by the lawyer accrued on the date the parties read and signed the contract.

61. _____ N.Y.S.2d _____ (Unreported, New York County Sept. 5, 1991).

62. Claims against attorneys by clients and by nonclients are increasing, as reported in the BUS. LAWYER UPDATE (Nov.–Dec. 1990), at 7 *et seq*., in an article by Voyles and Teeter, *Section 12 Liability: Attorneys Not Completely Off the Hook*. The authors delineate suits based on the sale of securities and violations of Sections 12, 15, and 17(a) of the Securities Act of 1933 and Section 10(b) and 20(a) of the Securities Exchange Act of 1934 but focus on Section 12, which provides, in part, that a person who "offers or sells a security" in violation of registration requirements or by means of fraudulent statements or omissions "shall be liable to the person purchasing such security from him." The U.S. Supreme Court in Pinter v. Dahl, 108 S. Ct. 2063 (1988), limited the potential liability of attorneys and other nonbroker professionals. However, "attorneys should remain wary of communications with potential investors. Direct attorney solicitation, and even limited attorney communication, may increase the potential for Section 12 liability."

63. 555 N.Y.S.2d 148 (App. Div., 2d Dept., 1991). *See generally* Barker, *Suing Lawyers for Malpractice*, N.Y.L.J. (Mar. 23, 1992), at 3 and 5, highlighting the 1993 New York Court of Appeals decision in Santulli v. Englert Reilly, 78 N.Y.2d 700 (1992), where the defendant drafted a mortgage for plaintiff to secure payments from the sale of commercial property. The mortgage was supposed to cover property owned by the buyer's father, but the description was in error and did not include that part of the property containing the improvements of value. This errant description did not come to light until several years had elapsed and the buyer had defaulted in his payments.

See Hughes v. Mahaney & Higgins, 821 S.W.2d 154 (Tex. 1991), where the Texas Supreme Court held that the statute of limitations on lawyer malpractice was tolled until all appeals on the underlying action were exhausted.

A lawyer was held liable in malpractice for lost punitive damages, as illustrated in Merenda v. Superior Court, 286 Cal. Rptr. 28 (1991). The plaintiff client recovered as compensatory damages the amount she would have received as punitive damages in a failed action against a third party. Plaintiff hired the defendant attorney to represent her in a sexual assault and battery action against her former employer, who subsequently filed a Chapter 7 petition in bankruptcy. Her claim would have been nondischargeable, but defendant attorney failed to file a timely adversarial action with the bankruptcy court, and as a result, she could not pursue her claim for damages against her former employer. *See* Cox, *Legal Malpractice:, Punies KO'd*, N.L.J., (Feb. 17, 1992), at 3 and 54, pointing out that she could not recover emotional damages even if she succeeds in her malpractice suit.

Note The Bar Plan v. Campbell, _____ S.W.2d _____ (Unreported, Mo. App. Sept. 17, 1991), holding that a legal malpractice insurance policy covers Rule 11 sanctions against attorneys since sanctions meet the definition of damages contained in the policy.

See Kagesoff v. Montejano, _____ Cal. Rptr. _____ (Unreported, Dkt. 572373, 1991), where the attorney was hit with damages totaling $1.75 million for two cases he handled for a single client. He apparently failed to meet statutory deadlines in one case and then in the second case misappropriated an $11,000 judgment!

The doctrine of equitable subrogation permitted an insurer to bring a legal malpractice action against defense counsel retained by it to defend an insured in Atlanta International Insurance Co. v. Bell, 475 N.W.2d 194 (Mich. 1991). The insured employer was sued by an employee who was killed in a construction accident, and the insurer hired the defendant law firm to defend the employee. The defendant failed to raise the comparative negligence defense, and the insured employer suffered a judgment that the insurer was required to pay. The lower court ruled that no attorney-client relationship existed between the insurer and defendant law firm, and therefore the insurer could not sue the defendant. But the Michigan Supreme Court reversed, ruling that equitable subrogation permits one party to stand in the shoes of another party, as does the insurer stand in the shoes of the insured who was defended by defendant. Indeed, the insurer-defense counsel relationship presents special circumstances that are most effectively and justly resolved on the principle of equitable subrogation, according to the court.

In Wysocki v. Reed, 583 N.E.2d 1139 (Ill. App., Dkt. 1–90–2266, Nov. 15, 1991), the court applied the alternative liability theory to a case against two product manufacturers of a drug product that injured the plaintiff; and because the plaintiff could have sued the drug companies, she is entitled to pursue a legal malpractice action against a law firm that allegedly mishandled her products liability suit.

Note the California disciplinary rule that presumes that an attorney who has sex with a client is incompetent; *see* A.B.A.J. (July 1991), at 26, and A.B.A.J. (Feb. 1992), at 90:

> The biggest setback to restricting sex between attorneys and their clients came Oct. 4, when members of the Oregon State Bar narrowly voted down a disciplinary rule proposed by a unan-

imous bar Board of Governors. Opponents said the draft rule was an ambiguous and unneeded invasion of privacy.

Oregon has had a formal ethics opinion since 1982 that requires "disclosure and consent" before a divorce lawyer may have sex with a client. The opinion also prohibits any sexual relations that would "prejudice or damage" the client.

When the state bar revised and trimmed all its ethics opinions last year, however, governors decided they wanted a clearer, broader ban.

"A lawyer shall not have sexual relations with a current client or representative of a client," said their proposed new rule. Excluded would be spouses or other pre-existing lovers and peripheral employees of business-entity clients.

But Oregon lawyers attending the state bar's annual business meeting in October rejected the rule 107–139. Many said it was unnecessary. "We do not need to do this so folks can say we are taking [on] an issue here," Max Rae of Salem argued at the meeting.

64. 762 F. Supp. 1553 (Conn. 1991). *See generally* Tuite, *Passing the File*, A.B.A.J. (Nov. 1990), at 100, citing the case of Monaco v. Rosamund, _____ A.2d _____ (Unreported, N.J., Bergen County, July 19, 1989), where a woman was in business with her brother to whom she conveyed her stock. When the brother died, she requested payment for the stock from his estate. A lawyer friend agreed to write a demand letter to the estate, but there was no written agreement establishing an attorney-client relationship with the woman. Over the years, she wrote to the lawyer eight times, asking about the action against the estate and the applicable statute of limitations. On each occasion, the lawyer advised her that he would not litigate the case and that she should get another lawyer. Finally, the woman hired another attorney who won her claim against the estate, but the decision was reversed on the grounds of the statute of limitations. Suit for malpractice was brought against the first lawyer, and the jury found in her favor because the first lawyer had failed to make a clear and concise statement in writing that he did not represent her!

65. 139 F.R.D. 384 (N.D. Cal., Dkt. 90–20233JW, Oct. 28, 1991).

66. _____ Cal. Rptr. _____ (Unreported, Dkt. A049391, 1992).

67. 813 S.W.2d 400 (Tenn. 1991). *See* Beatie v. DeLong, 561 N.Y.S.2d 448 (App. Div., 1st Dept., Nov. 8, 1990) on the issue of lawyer immunity for erroneous advice. In the course of the trial, the court charged the jury as follows:

> There is a general principle embodied in the law of the State of New York that attorneys should be free to advise their clients without fear of liability [to] third parties. However, the mere fact one is an attorney acting in a professional capacity does not make him absolutely immune from responsibility for his wrongful acts. An attorney may be held personally liable to a third party who sustains an injury in consequence of his wrongful act of improper exercise of authority, where the attorney has been guilty of fraud, collusion or of a malicious or tortious act. To find tortious interference against defendant Durkin you must also determine whether or not he acted in good faith, and to determine whether he acted in good faith you should decide whether the advice was based on reasonable legal ground. *If you find that defendant Durkin did not have reasonable legal ground to offer the advice he gave, you should find for the plaintiff.* [Emphasis added]

The court concluded:

> The jury's verdict that the Beatie contingency fee agreement was reasonable and enforceable, was not against the weight of the evidence. While Beatie had the burden of showing the contingency fee agreement was fair and reasonable, considering the nature of the services, the time,

amount and controversy involved, and the results obtained, and that the terms thereof were fully disclosed to the clients (Jackson v. Sassower, 66 N.Y.2d 991), plaintiff met his burden in these respects. The matter was complex. However, as to the $250,000 damage award against Durkin for tortious interference with contract, Durkin's conduct would be immunized from liability under the shield afforded attorneys in advising their clients, even when such advice is erroneous, in the absence of fraud, collusion, malice or bad faith (RESTATEMENT 2D TORTS, § 772; Hahn v. Wylie, 54 A.D.2d 629; Gifford v. Harley, 62 A.D.2d 5; D & C Textile Corp. v. Rudlin, 41 Misc.2d 916; Kasen v. Morrell, 18 Misc.2d 158, 162, *aff'd*, 6 A.D.2d 816). While defendants contend that this issue is to be determined under New Jersey law, as Durkin acted solely within New Jersey, and, does not have a New York office, the choice of law is largely irrelevant as defendants fail to demonstrate that New Jersey law is any more favorable on this issue than New York law. Mere negligence by an attorney giving advice to his client is insufficient to give a right of action to a third party injured thereby (Kasen v. Morrell, *supra*).

In Lightron Corp. v. J. S. M. Holdings, Inc., 567 N.Y.S.2d 976 (Nassau County Jan. 25, 1991), the cocounsel acting as a mail drop had sanctions against him lifted by the New York court. The co-counsel pointed out that he knew nothing about the case! However, the court cautioned that attorneys who accept a fee and appear officially as co-counsel must be prepared to accept the concomitant responsibilities.

68. 544 A.2d 683 (D.C. App. 1988). *See* Silberberg, *Allocation of Liability for Rule 11 Sanctions*, N.Y.L.J. (Nov. 14, 1991), at 3, focusing on Estate of Northern J. Calloway v. Marvel Entertainment Group, 111 F.R.D. 637 (S.D.N.Y., Dkt. 82 Civ. 8697, Sept. 17, 1991), which imposed Rule 11 sanctions against the individual attorney who signed the documents that are the basis of the violation, rather than the law firm of which he was a member. (*Aff'd and rev'd in part*, 854 F.2d 1452 [2d Cir. 1993], *rev'd in part*, 110 S. Ct. 456 (1992]).

See generally Arnoff and Klampert, *Lawyers' Professional Liability Litigation*, N.Y.L.J. (Mar. 5, 1991), at 1 and 6, citing three recent New York cases, to wit: Beatie v. Delong, 562 N.Y.S.2d 448 (App. Div., 1st Dept., 1990); Prudential Insurance Co. v. Dewey Ballentine Bushby Palmer & Wood, N.Y.L.J. (Dec. 10, 1990), at 25, col. 2; and Campagnola v. Mulholland Minion & Roe, 555 N.E.2d 611 (N.Y. 1990). The Beatie case raised the question of whether predecessor counsel has a cause of action against a successor counsel when the successor's legal malpractice destroyed the present counsel's fee, and responded in the negative. The Prudential case confronted the issue arising from the effect of a settlement before the loss caused by malpractice actually occurs and attorney work-sharing on the legal malpractice cause of action. And the Campagnola case addressed the issue whether defendant attorneys can seek to offset the fees they have earned against the recoverable action if they were successful in the underlying action, and responded in the negative.

In a unique case, the U.S. Supreme Court in Antoine v. Byers & Anderson, Inc., 113 S. Ct. 2167 (1993) held that a court reporter may be liable for failing to produce a trial transcript that was needed for a criminal appeal.

69. *See* DEFENSE COUNSEL J. (Oct. 1991), at 543 et *seq.*

70. 523 A.2d 1003 (Md. 1987).

71. *See* Walsh v. Foley, ______ A.2d ______ (Unreported, Md. App., Dkt. 145, Oct. 19, 1990).

72. 111 S. Ct. 922 (Dkt. 89–1500, Mar. 10, 1991).

73. 468 N.W.2d 38 (Iowa 1991).

74. 947 F.2d 611 (2d Cir., Dkt. 90–9026, Oct. 22, 1991); lower court opinion at 132 F.R.D. 147 (S.D.N.Y. 1990).

75. *Id.*

Though there is thus perhaps some small measure of efficiency to be gained in combining consideration of sanctions with consideration of the merits, we conclude that the interest in efficiency is not sufficiently compelling in the context of a claim that turns on the plaintiff's credibility. In such a case it is highly disadvantageous to the plaintiff for both sets of arguments to be pressed simultaneously, for it can only reduce a plaintiff's chances of prevailing on the merits if simultaneously with asking the court to believe his testimony and thereby find his claim meritorious, he must urge that his claim is "at least not frivolous." . . . While we do not mean to imply that an attorney automatically gains immunity from Rule 11 sanctions whenever he has successfully fended off a motion for summary judgment, we cannot, in light of the pretrial record here, uphold the district court's ruling that counsel should have known Healey's trial testimony would be deemed so incredible that his claims would be found frivolous.

76. *See* Arnoff and Klampert, *Sanctioning and Responsibility*, N.Y.L.J. (Oct. 22, 1991), at 3 and 8:

In professional liability litigation involving attorneys, these considerations suggest that, before commencing a suit, an attorney not only should consult with an expert, but also should meet with the potential defendant to give him or her a chance to explain the conduct being questioned. Professional liability litigation involves, by necessity, questions of conformity with professional standards, expert identification of those standards, and, especially where substantial economic loss has occurred, an explanation of why the professional pursued one course of conduct rather than another. The requirement that an attorney should consult with an expert before filing a malpractice action is not an onerous one. The legal profession has articulated appropriate standards of conduct and there are a number of experts available who can help the attorney perform this pre-filing duty of investigation.

77. 566 N.Y.S.2d 462 (Suffolk County 1991).

78. *Id.*:

Significantly, the proof required to establish liability in a . . . malpractice case differs from the proof required to prove a case of ordinary negligence. . . . "[W]ithout expert assistance a jury will often have no understanding of what constitutes reasonable behavior in a complex and technical profession. . . .' *Thus, facts and circumstances which may, to one unschooled in the . . . profession, appear to constitute a breach of duty or malpractice . . . may involve conduct which is well within the accepted standards of care by the . . . [professional] in question.* This matter provides a clear example of the need for expert testimony to establish . . . malpractice liability.

79. 78 N.Y.2d 227 (1991).

80. How does a lawyer shift the blame to his client without violating confidential communications? The obvious solution, according to International Business Counselors Inc. v. Bank of Ikeda Ltd., ______ F. Supp. ______ (Unreported, S.D.N.Y., Dkt. 89 Civ. 83873, Apr. 5, 1991), is to allow the lawyer to submit confidential documents from a client for in-camera inspection by the court. In the context of a sanctions motion the client here admitted that the correspondence had misled counsel: In the client's affidavit it was stated that "it was due solely to misleading representations made by IBC and IBC's insistence upon filing suit immediately."

81. 433 U.S. 350 (1977).

82. *See* Hornsby, *The Complex Evolution of Attorney Ad Regs*, N.L.J. (Aug. 6, 1990), at S4 and S12, which sets forth an index to state regulations on lawyer advertising:

Alabama: Code of Professional Responsibility, Rules of Disciplinary Enforcement (adopted 1985, amendments effective Jan. 1, 1986), Secs. DR 2–101 through DR 2–104.

Alaska: Code of Professional Responsibility, Rules of the Court, Secs. DR 2–101 (amended July 1, 1979), DR 2–102 (amended April 1, 1979), DR 2–103 (amended April 1, 1978), DR 2–104 (amended April 1, 1979) and DR 2–105 (amended April 1, 1979).

Arizona: Rules of Professional Conduct, Arizona Rule of the Supreme Court 42, Rules 7.1–7.5 (7.2 and 7.3 amended Aug. 1, 1989).

Arkansas: Rules of the Court Regulating Professional Conduct (adopted Jan. 1, 1986), Rules 7.1 and 7.3.

California: Rules of Professional Conduct (effective May 27, 1989), Rule 1–400.

Colorado: Code of Professional Responsibility, Colorado Court Rules (amendment effective Jan. 1, 1990), Secs. DR 2–101 through DR 2–105.

Connecticut: Rules of Professional Conduct (effective Oct. 1, 1986), Rules 7.1 through 7.5.

Delaware: The Delaware Lawyer's Rules of Professional Conduct (effective 1985), Rules 7.1 and 7.5.

District of Columbia: Rules of Professional Conduct (adopted March 1, 1990), Rules 7.1 and 7.5.

Florida: Florida Rules of Professional Conduct, Rules 4–7.1through 4–7.6 (Rule 4–7.3 amended effective Jan. 1, 1988).

Georgia: Georgia Bar Rule 4–102, Standards 5 through 19 (1987).

Hawaii: Code of Professional Responsibility (Rules of the Supreme Court of the State of Hawaii), Secs. DR 2–101 through DR 2–105 (Sec. DR 2–102 (B) amended effective Nov. 23, 1988; Sec. DR 2–103 amended effective July 3, 1989).

Idaho: Rules of Professional Conduct, Rules 7.1 through 7.4 (amended March 15, 1990).

Illinois: Rules of Professional Responsibility (Rules of the Supreme Court of Illinois), Rules 7.1 through 7.4 (Rule 7.3 amended effective Jan. 19, 1989).

Iowa: Iowa Code of Professional Responsibility for Lawyers, Secs. DR 2–101 through DR 2–105 (Secs. DR 2–101, DR 2–102 and DR 2–105 amended effective June 1, 1989).

Kansas: Rules Relating to Discipline of Attorneys (adopted March 1, 1988), Rules 7.1 through 7.5.

Kentucky: Rules Relating to Discipline of Attorneys (adopted March 1, 1988), Rules 7.1 through 7.5.

Louisiana: Rules of Professional Conduct, Rules 7.1 through 7.5 (amended June 15, 1989).

Maine: Code of Professional Responsibility, Maine Bar Rule 3 (Maine Rules of Court), Sec. 3.9 (amended 1986).

Maryland: Rules of Professional Conduct (Maryland Register, Vol. 13, Issue 11, May 23, 1986), Rules 7.1 through 7.5.

Massachusetts: Canons of Ethics and Disciplinary Rules Regulating the Practice of Law (Supreme Judicial Court Rules 3:07), Secs. DR 2–101 through DR 2–105 (amended effective July 16, 1986).

Michigan: Rules of Professional Conduct, Rules 7.1 through 7.5 (amended Jan. 1, 1990).

Minnesota: Rules of Professional Conduct (Minnesota Supreme Court Rules, effective Sept. 1, 1985), Rules 7.1 through 7.5.

Mississippi: Rules of Professional Conduct (Mississippi Rules of Court, effective July 1, 1987), Rules 7.1 through 7.5.1.

Missouri: Code of Professional Responsibility (Supreme Court Rule 4, effective Jan. 1, 1986), Rules 7.1 through 7.5.

Montana: Rules of Professional Responsibility, Secs. DR 2–101 through DR 2–105 (amended 1977).

Nebraska: Code of Professional Responsibility, Secs. DR 2–101 through DR 2–105 (amended 1977).

Nevada: Supreme Court Rules, Rules 195 through 198 (amended effective Aug. 15, 1988).

New Hampshire: Rules of Professional Conduct, Rules 7.1 through 7.5 (adopted 1986).

Washington: Rules of Professional Conduct (Title 7), Rules 7.1 through 7.5 (amended Sept. 1, 1988).

West Virginia: Rules of Professional Responsibility, Rules 7.1 through 7.5 (amended effective Jan. 1, 1989).

Wisconsin: Supreme Court Rules (Wisconsin Court Rules and Procedure adopted effective Jan. 1, 1988), SCR 20:7.1 through SCR 20:7.5.

Wyoming: Rules of Professional Conduct for Attorneys at Law (adopted Jan. 12, 1987), Rules 7.1 through 7.4.

83. 486 U.S. 466 (1988).

84. 110 S. Ct. 2281 (1990).

85. *See generally* Stewart, *The Rights of Lawyers*, A.B.A.J. (Aug. 1990), at 34 *et seq*., wherein the Peel case is delineated in terms of its 5–4 decision reversing sanctions against a lawyer whose letterhead stated that he held a "Certificate in Trial Advocacy" from the National Board of Trial Advocacy. The dissenting opinions found the letterhead statement to be potentially misleading and "inherently likely to deceive the public. . . . Not only does the certification claim lead the consumer to believe that this lawyer is better than those lawyers lacking such certification, it also leads to the conclusion that the State licenses the lawyer's purported superiority. . . . Claims of certification may well lead the ordinary consumer to conclude that the State has sanctioned such a claim."

86. *See* N.Y.L.J. (May 15, 1991), at 1 and 7. In *Capoccia v. Committee on Professional Standards*, ____ F. SUPP ____ (Unreported, N.D.N.Y. Dec. 20, 1990), the attorney was exonerated because defendant had failed to demonstrate a substantial government interest that would justify restricting his advertisement.

87. ____ S. Ct. ____ (1993). The states of Florida and Texas allow sensitive files from civil litigation to be open to the public, mainly because of the efforts of the Association of Trial Lawyers of America, the plaintiff lawyers' group, according to INSIGHT MAGAZINE (Nov. 5, 1990), at 56–57. The new rules were handed down by the Texas Supreme Court and by the Florida legislature in order to open up files primarily in products liability, medical malpractice, and environmental torts. Protective court orders preventing outside persons from gaining access to information obtained during the discovery period of litigation are being discouraged. But disclosure of the information means disclosure of everything from a company's trade secrets to a person's sexual orientation. The New York State Lawyers' Fund for Client Protection during the first six months of 1990 paid out a total of $1,666,250 in benefits to 88 clients for thefts committed by New York lawyers. *See* N.Y.L.J. (Sept. 17, 1990), at 1 and 2. The New York legislature appropriated $5 million to the fund, and all New York lawyers have been biennially assessed $60 each.

Insecure client security funds for clients bilked by lawyers are described in A.B.A.J. (Mar. 1992), at 17–18. As a result, many states have been forced to "cap" amounts payable, especially in face of the growing number of demands from clients:

California had 571 claims filed in 1987 versus 821 in the first nine months of 1991. It paid out $10 million in '87 and $24.2 million in '91. Pennsylvania's claims went from 107 in 1987 to 285 in 1991; total payouts were $1.4 million in '87 and $4 million from January to September 1991. New Jersey was the only exception among the 20 largest funds that responded to the survey. Claims there did go up between 1987 and the first three quarters of '91, from 132 to 193. But the total paid dropped from $5.6 million to $4.6 million. New York's total valid claims swelled from $5.7 million in 1987 to $28 million in all of 1991. Fully $7 million of the '91 figure arose from the crimes of just one lawyer. North Dakota had to close up shop because just two lawyers' misdeeds produced all six of the fund's claims, totaling $110,000. There was $15,000 in the bank.

Is there a right to specialize on the part of lawyers? Judging by the decisions in Ex Parte Howell, 487 So.2d 848, (Ala. 1986) and in In Re Johnson, 341 N.W.2d (Minn. 1983), it would appear that the First Amendment does not permit a categorical ban on truthful statements by attorneys claiming certification as civil trial specialists by the National Board of Trial Advocacy. However, at least 28 states and the District of Columbia ban such advertising, according to Gibbons, *The Right to Specialize*, A.B.A.J. (May 1990), at 57–60, wherein a tabulation on lawyer advertising sets forth (a) an absolute ban except for exempt areas of patent, trademark, and admiralty law; (b) no ban on advertising certification except for the requirement that all statements be true; (c) state certification of legal specialties; and (d) state approval of certifying organizations. In category (a) are 28 states and the District of Columbia; in category (b) are 7 states; in category (c) are 11 states; and in category (d) are 4 states. *See* Smolla, *Specialist Advertising and the First Amendment*, TRIAL MAGAZINE (Aug. 1990), at 18–20. *Also note* A.B.A.J. (Sept. 1990), at 14, pointing out:

The states affected by Peel include the 28 that ban lawyer-certification advertising. Also, 11 states that operate their own certification programs will have to decide what to do about certification programs offered by private groups. Only Alabama, Connecticut, Georgia and Minnesota have systems to approve private certification programs. Seven states do not ban certification advertising, merely requiring ads to be truthful. States that certify legal specialties themselves are just beginning to grapple with how to review certification programs offered by private groups. "It's something that we'll have to go to our supreme court with," says Gary McNeil, executive director of the Texas Board of Legal Specialization. Texas, which certifies 4,500 lawyers, operates one of the nation's most comprehensive certification programs.

See Gibson v. Florida Bar Assn., 906 F.2d 624 (11th Cir., Dkt. 90–1101, Nov. 6, 1991), holding that First Amendment interests are satisfied where bar association members are permitted to object on a case-by-case basis to specific instances of political advocacy by the bar association, or to receive a postcollection refund of a portion of his or her dues to the bar association. *Note* Keller v. State Bar Assn., 110 S. Ct. 2228 (1990), stating that a unitary bar association cannot compel its members to fund political activities unless those activities are reasonably related to regulating the legal profession and improving the quality of legal services.

See Virginia Citizens Consumer Council Inc. v. Board of Pharmacy, 373 F. Supp. 683 (Va. 1974), *aff'd*, 425 U.S. 748 (1976), holding unconstitutional a Virginia statute prohibiting price advertising concerning prescription drugs. And in Consumers Union v. American Bar Assn., 433 U.S. 350 (1977), the highest court struck down a prohibition against lawyers listing their names and fees in a directory prepared by Consumers Union. *See generally* Merhige, *Professionalism, Credibility, and Public Trust*, TRIAL MAGAZINE (Oct. 1991), at 30 *et seq.*

88. As Chief Justice Rehnquist in the Keller case opined, "Precisely where the line falls . . . will not always be easy to discern . . . the extreme ends of the spectrum are clear." *See generally* A B.A.J. (Sept. 1990), at 16–17, pointing out:

There has been one puzzling result of that program. A number of former Wisconsin bar activists have taken advantage of the checkoff, even though they presumably are interested in the bar's lobbying efforts. Officials speculate that secretaries or administrators are filling out the dues forms and saving their bosses a little money. Montana and Florida both give partial refunds to members who object to lobbying. Montana returns between 10 cents and 20 cents per bill. Executive Director George Bousliman said no one has requested a refund in the last three legislative sessions, partly because the bar focuses its lobbying efforts narrowly. Florida has been refunding its dissenters a *pro rata* share of the full legislative budget, not the estimated costs of lobbying for the bills a member finds objectionable. Last year, that share was $7.63 out of the $140 total dues per lawyer.

89. The New York State Bar Association Committee on Professional Ethics on December 4, 1990, ruled that New York lawyers may use client testimonials in their advertising. Opinion 614 is set forth hereinafter in its entirety:

OPINION 614 TOPIC: Advertising: client testimonials. DIGEST: It is proper to advertise client testimonials provided reasonable disclaimers are expressed about any statements or results the lawyer has achieved. CODE: DR 2–101(A), (B), (C)(2); EC 2–10. QUESTION: May a lawyer advertise on radio or television by using client testimonials? OPINION: A lawyer proposes to advertise on radio and television by using client testimonials in which actual clients whose cases have been completely resolved will state certain objective facts concerning the client's case and express the client's satisfaction with the law firm's services and the result obtained. The U.S. Supreme Court had an opportunity recently to answer the proposed question, but declined to do so after hearing oral argument. Oring v. State Bar of Cal., 109 S. Ct. 858 (1989). It is common knowledge that word-of-mouth endorsements and recommendations by former clients are an effective way to build a legal practice. DR 2–101(C)(2) permits advertising by the use of "names of clients regularly represented, provided that the client has given prior written consent." The inquirer asks, however, whether a lawyer can also provide client endorsements and testimonials in the advertisement itself, rather than simply listing the names of previous clients. Although the Committee believes that this particular type of advertising has the potential to be misleading to an unsophisticated potential client, we decline to adopt a per se rule prohibiting this type of advertising. Since 1977, the U.S. Supreme Court has recognized the value of legal advertising (commercial speech) in facilitating well informed consumer decisions in the selection of an attorney. Bates v. State Bar of Arizona, 433 U.S. 350 (1977). "It is a matter of public interest that . . . [private economic] decisions, in the aggregate, be intelligent and well informed. To this end, the free flow of commercial information is indispensable." Virginia State Board of Pharmacy v. Virginia Citizens Consumer Counsel, 425 U.S. 748, 765 (1976) .A recent survey report stated that almost one-third of all lawyers now engage in some form of advertising. Reidinger, *Law Poll*, 73 A.B.A.J. 25 (1987). The right of a lawyer to advertise, however, is not plenary, and the lawyer can be restricted from commercial speech that is false or misleading. DR 2–101(A) states, "A lawyer . . . shall not use or disseminate or participate in the preparation or dissemination of any public communication containing statements or claims that are false, deceptive, [or] misleading . . ." EC 2–10. DR 2–101(B) proscribes claims that are puffery, self-laudatory claims regarding the quality of the lawyers' legal services, and claims that cannot be measured or verified. The Supreme Court has stated that advertising claims regarding the quality of legal services "are not susceptible of measurement or verification; accordingly, such claims may be so likely to be misleading as to warrant restriction." Bates v. State Bar of Arizona, 433 U.S. 350, 383–84 (1977). Although not adopted in New York, a review of the ABA Model Rules may be helpful in understanding the permissible scope of restrictions on lawyer advertising. Rule 7.1(a) states that a communication is false or misleading if it "contains a material misrepresentation of fact or law, or omits a fact necessary to make a statement considered as a whole not materially misleading." If the advertisement is "likely to create an unjustified expectation about the results the lawyer can achieve," then Rule 7.1(b) proscribes it. In this respect, the official comment to Model Rule 7.1(b) offers guidance. It states that claims of past success "may create the unjustified expectation that similar results can be obtained for others without reference to the specific factual and legal circumstances." It further states that this limitation "would ordinarily preclude advertisements about the results obtained on behalf of the client, such as the amount of a damage award or the lawyer's record in obtaining favorable verdicts, and *advertisements containing client endorsements.*" (Emphasis added.) DR 2–101(B) prohibits advertising that contains "claims regarding the quality of the lawyers' legal services or claims that cannot be measured or verified." Accordingly, a lawyer may not directly or through selected edited utterances present former clients' testimonials describing prior results in a manner that: 1. Fails to contain sufficient information to allow an informed decision on whether to seek the lawyer's services; 2. Creates unjustified expectations or "false hopes." In Re R.M.J., 455 U.S. 191, 200 n.11 (1982); or 3. Offers overblown assurances of a client's satisfaction. Shapero v. Kentucky Bar Ass'n, 486, 479 (1988). Notwithstanding the penumbra of protection afforded by the First Amendment, valid and legal restrictions, other than a total ban, on lawyer advertisement and solicitation remain. We decline, however, to adopt a per se prohibition on any client endorsement, as some states have opted to do. See, e.g., D.C. Code of Professional Responsibility DR 2–101(C)(2) (1988); Indiana Rules of Professional Conduct Rule 7.1(d)(3)(1988) (prohibiting lawyer advertising which "contains testimonial about or endorsement of a lawyer"); Conn. Bar Ass'n Op. 88–3 (1988), summarized in Law Man. ABA/BNA 901: 2057 (restricting distribution of an article which "compares one lawyer with another lawyer and includes a client endorsement"); Penn. Bar Ass'n Op. 88–143 (1988), summarized in Law. Man. ABA/BNA 901: 7313 (prohibiting brochures containing client endorsement). Instead, we prefer to adopt a narrower rule "designed to prevent the potential for deception and confusion [that is] no broader than reasonably necessary to prevent a perceived evil." Shapero v. Kentucky Bar Ass'n, 486 U.S. 466, 472 (1988) (citing In re R.M.J., 455 U.S. 191, 203 [1982]). Thus, we hold improper those client endorsements describing prior results that are potentially misleading in the various ways described herein, e.g., statements of "Overblown assurances of client satisfaction," statements that create unjustified expectations or "false hopes" or statements that fail to contain sufficient information, thus rendering the statement false, deceptive or misleading. Additionally, some disclaimer should be joined with client endorsements describing prior results to the effect that the endorsement does not guarantee or predict a similar outcome with respect to any future matter on which the lawyer may be retained. The U.S. Supreme Court has sanctioned the use of disclosure requirements reasonably related to protecting the public from misleading or deceptive advertisements or from misunderstanding the significance of a stated fact. Zauderer v. Office of Disciplinary Counsel, 471 U.S. 626 (1985). See also, Peel v. Attorney Disciplinary Comm., ____ U.S. ____, n.17, S. Ct. 2281, 2292 (1990). Disclosure requirements are constitutional as long as they are reasonably related (and not necessarily the least restrictive means available) to protecting consumers from deceptive or misleading advertising. Zauderer v.Office of Disciplinary Counsel, 471 U.S. at 651052 n.14. "[D]isclosure requirement[s] trench much more narrowly on the advertiser's interest than do flat prohibitions of speech." *Id.* at 651. On the issue of whether the lawyer's advertisement may include client statements on the outcome of the concluded case, we refer the reader to N.Y. State 539 (1982). An ad that makes no distinction among various legal and factual nuances in each *sui generis* case has the potential to mislead the public. To a layperson of average education and intelligence, unaware of these nuances, such an ad may suggest that a similar substantial recovery or result may be obtained in every such case. Thus to avoid unjustified expectations or false hopes by the consumer, a disclaimer should be inserted in the advertisement that facts and prior results in an earlier case do not guarantee or predict a similar outcome with respect to any future matters on which the lawyer may be retained. CONCLUSION: A lawyer may advertise by using client testimonials provided reasonable disclaimers with respect to description of prior results obtained are inserted where necessary to avoid unjustified expectations by the consumer and provided the advertisement otherwise complies with existing disciplinary rules and opinions. (1) Our opinion is necessarily limited to ethical issues under the Code of Professional Responsibility, which must be interpreted in the light of controlling constitutional authority developed in such cases as Peel v. Attorney Disciplinary Comm., ____ U.S. ____ n.17, S. Ct. 2281, 2292 (1990); Oring v. State Bar of Cal., ____ U.S. ____ ,109 S. Ct. 858 (1989); Shapero v. Kentucky Bar Ass'n, 486 U.S. 466 (1988); Zauderer v. Office of Disciplinary Counsel, 471, U.S. 626 (1985). In re R.M.J., 455 U.S. 191 (1982); Bates v. State Bar of Arizona, 433 U.S. 350 (1977).

90. *Note* The Florida Bar: Petition to Amend the Rules Regulating the Florida Bar—Advertising Issues, 571 So.2d 451 (Fla. Dec. 21, 1990), which document imposes new restrictions on lawyers who advertise in Florida as a way to publicize their services and solicit clients. Some of the new rules have been summarized in TRIAL MAGAZINE (Apr. 1991), at 20. *Also see* A.B.A.J. (Mar. 1991), at 22, stating that the new Florida rules "take the flamboyance out of lawyer advertising." In Peel v. Attorney Registration and Disciplinary Commission of Illinois, 110 S. Ct. 2281 (Mar. 11, 1991), the highest court held that a state may not prohibit a lawyer from advertising himself or herself as a "certified specialist" unless that statement is false or deceptive. *Note* these excerpts from the Editorial in N.J.L. (Jan. 21, 1991):

Most of us are bombarded from every quarter, including law firms, to the apparent consternation of the Florida Supreme Court. Now that court has promulgated strict limits on the tone and content of broadcast ads for lawyers, and other states are thinking of emulating Florida's example. Yes, some of the ads tend to the vulgar, and seeing numbers flash across the screen such as "1-800–ABOGADO" makes some of us wince. But the partial regulation of ads is either an ineffective halfway measure, if you just plain dislike the spectacle of lawyers advertising, or a wrongful intrusion into free speech. It seems inescapable that the new rules are trying to do what the nation's high court has unequivocally forbidden states from doing: banning legal advertisements. The restrictions, such as barring dramatizations, professional actors and the like, gut a lawyer's ability to take his or her message to potential clients. And professions wanting to protect an impressionable public from the horrors of broadcast ads smack of elitism. Many critics of the new rules point out that for many people, lawyer ads are the only way to gain access to the profession. After all, the group of people and companies with long-established links to firms is, however influential, probably not the majority. Like it or not, the profession has become a business, with all that that entails. With the economy in such dire straits, some lawyers and firms may need all the help they can get. Yes, misleading or fraudulent ads are wrong. But the profession has a wealth of mechanisms to deal with them. The movement toward restricting lawyer advertisements, while perhaps admirable from an aesthetic standpoint, ignores reality and undoubtedly favors those (i.e., large firms) that apparently do not need to advertise. We hope more states do not rush to restrict ads.

Also note N.L.J. (Jan. 21, 1991), at 1 and 22, setting forth excerpts from the Florida Supreme Court's opinion in The Florida Bar: Petition to Amend the Rules Regulating the Florida Bar—Advertising Issues, Dkt. 74,987: "The proposed rule constitutionally restricts those methods which, through clever manipulation, could be used to deceive the public. . . . The unique characteristics of electronic media, including the pervasiveness of television and radio, the ease with which these media are abused, and the passiveness of the viewer or listener, make the electronic media especially subject to regulation in the public interest." A dissenter contended that "the majority, out of frustration and annoyance, is swatting at a troublesome and persistent Bar fly with a sledgehammer."

The Florida Supreme Court In Re Florida Bar Advisory Opinion on Non-Lawyer Preparation of Pension Plans, Dkt. 74,479 (1990), opined that accountants, actuaries, life insurance agents, and other nonlawyers may draft pension plans in Florida without illegally practicing law. Furthermore, the drafting of pension plans is regulated by federal laws.

91. Bodine, *Advertising Acumen*, N.L.J. (Aug. 13, 1990), at 9.

92. *See* A.B.A.J. (Oct. 1991), at 28, reporting that lawyers who ran TV commercials fared poorly in Las Vegas courts.

93. *See* DEFENSE COUNSEL J. (Oct. 1991), at 574 *et seq.*

94. 571 N.E.2d 572 (Ind. App. 1991).

95. 591 A.2d 1286 (D.C. App. 1991).

96. *See* A.B.A.J. (Dec. 1991), at 98.

97. *See* Matter of Burtch, 770, P.2d 174 (Wash. 1989). The contingent percentage fee is a child of the "American rule," which by contrast with the English practice refuses to tax attorneys' fees against the losing party. The CODE OF PROFESSIONAL RESPONSIBILITY historically has permitted the contingent fee; *see* DR2–106(B)(8) *but note* that in criminal cases the contingent fee is prohibited in DR2–106(C). *See* MACKINNON, CONTINGENT FEES FOR LEGAL SERVICES (1964). A salient economic feature of the contingent percentage fee is that it represents a binding contract not readily challengeable as unfair compensation. To require payment of a fee regardless of the outcome of the case is said to bar poor potential litigants from access to the legal system; *see* Clermont and Currivan, *Improving on the Contingent Fee*, 63 CORNELL L. REV. 529 (1978). The contingent fee system is also justifiable on the basis that defendants win more tort trials than plaintiffs, according to SPEISER, LAWSUIT (1980), at 120. On the other hand, the contingent fee system makes the attorney financially interested in the result of litigation, and therefore his or her incentives may be skewed, as pointed out in Note, *The Contingent Fee: Disciplinary Rule, Ethical Consideration, or Free Competition?* 1979 UTAH L. REV. 547, at 561: "[T]he relatively minimal expense of the trial may not outweigh the advantage to the lawyer of a gamble on an increased recovery, whereas the client's interest . . . may lie in accepting settlement rather than in risking the possibility of obtaining no recovery at all." Also of concern is that the contingency fee system encourages the filing of groundless speculative lawsuits. A "cap" of attorneys' fees has been upheld by the New Jersey Supreme Court in ATLA v. New Jersey Supreme Court, 330 A.2d 350 (N.J. 1974): "Attorneys have never had the right to enforce contractual provisions for more than a fair and reasonable fee . . . they are not businessmen entitled to charge what the traffic will bear."

Selected Additional Readings on Legal Malpractice

Third Party Legal Opinion Report, Including the Legal Opinion Accord, of the Section of Business Law, American Bar Assn., 47 BUS. LAWYER (Nov. 1991), at 167–234.

Wilkins, *Who Should Regulate Lawyers?* 105 HARV. L. REV., 801 (1992), delineating the many arguments for and against particular enforcement systems, both compliance and independence, in terms of a matrix of lawyer-client interactions.

Martyn, *Peer Review and Quality Assurance for Lawyers,* 20 TOLEDO L. REV. 295 (Winter 1989), pointing out that lawyers lag behind most professionals in articulating and implementing criteria for quality professional services.

On the admission of non-German lawyers to practice in Germany, *see* 26 INT'L LAWYER (1992), at 236:

> In an effort to liberalize the professional services market in Germany for citizens of EC Member States, the German Bundestag amended the Federal Attorneys' Act in 1989 to allow lawyers admitted in other EC Member States to open offices in Germany and practice EC law and the law of their home jurisdiction. Lawyers from other states may also practice EC law and their home country's law if reciprocity with that state is assured.* Effective January 1, 1991, EC citizens may now obtain full admission to the German bar without going back to school if they pass a fitness examination testing basic knowledge of German law.** The new Act, which transforms the Council Directive on the Recognition of High School Diplomas*** into German law, applies to members of the bars of Member States such as avocats in Belgium and France and barristers and solicitors in the United Kingdom. It gives details of the topics to be covered in the examination such as knowledge of the German Civil Code (BGB), the Commercial Code, and labor, constitutional, and criminal law. It also contains provisions on the administration of the examination and elaborates on the principle that a foreign attorney who passes the examination will be treated as a fully qualified attorney and may become a member of a local attorneys' chapter. As mentioned above, the Act does not apply to non–EC citizens, who will be limited to practicing EC and their home law.

---

*Act of Dec. 13, 1989, BGB1. I, 2135 (amending, §§ 206–207 of the Federal Attorneys Act). However, a lawyer may not solicit new clients by inviting nonclients to attend a practice presentation, BGH, July 4, 1991, BB 1991, 1735.

**BGB1.I [1990] 1349.

***Council Directive 89/48, 1989 O.J. (L 19) 16.

98. 565 N.E.2d 107 (Ill. App. 1990). Civility in professional relationships was the subject of a timely article by Aspen, *A Renewed Commitment to Civility,* TRIAL MAGAZINE (Sept. 1993), at 67–68. The writer, as chairperson of a Seventh U.S. Court of Appeals committee, defined "civility" as "professional conduct in litigation proceedings of judicial personnel and attorneys." In short, abrasive confrontations, as delineated in 143 F.R.D. 371, 432–435 (1991) and 441 (1992), were found to frequently prevail. The article cited Malautea v. Suzuki Motor Co., 987 F.2d 1536 (11th Cir. 1993) on reconciliation of the duty to represent a client zealously with the attorney's professional obligations as an officer of the court: "All attorneys, as officers of the court, owe duties of complete candor and primary loyalty to the court before which they practice. An attorney's duty to a client can never outweigh his or her

responsibility to see that our system of justice functions smoothly. This concept is as old as common law jurisprudence itself."

99. *See* Barbara A. v. John G., 193 Cal. Rptr. 422 (1983), where the California court stated that whether it should be an actionable breach of ethics for an attorney to induce a client to have sexual relations during the course of representation was a decision better left to the state bar association for disciplinary action. *Also see* DEFENSE COUNSEL J. (Oct. 1991), at 556–557.

See Jorgenson and Sutherland, *A Breach of Trust: Attorney-Client Sexual Contact*, TRIAL MAGAZINE (Sept. 1993), at 68–69, pointing out that a client who puts trust in a lawyer has the right to expect that the lawyer will act only in the best interests of the client. Note that client is often vulnerable and comes to depend a great deal on the lawyer. In August 1992 the ABA Standing Committee on Ethics and Professional Responsibility adopted this no-binding ethical Opinion #364: "A sexual relationship between lawyer and client may involve unfair exploitation of the lawyer's fiduciary position, and/or significantly impair a lawyer's ability to represent a client competently, and therefore may violate both the Model Rules of Professional Conduct and the Model Code of Professional Responsibility."

See generally Feldman-Summers and Jones, *Psychological Impacts of Sexual Contact Between Therapists or Other Health Care Practitioners and Their Clients*, 52 J. CONSULTING CLIN. PSYCH. 1054 (1984).

100. 504 N.Y.S.2d 188(App. Div., 1st Dept., Mar. 21, 1991).

101. *See generally* Tuite and Corboy, *Attorney Discipline: Do We Need an Ethical Rule Restricting Sexual Relations with Clients?* A.B.A.J. (Jan. 1992), at 34–36. The former responded yes, declaring that a separate rule regulating sexual relations with clients is necessary to set clear standards of behavior; and the latter responded no because existing rules offer adequate protection. *Note* A.B.A.J. (Oct. 1990), at 34, spelling out the fact that the legal profession must confront sexual harassment, "the dirty little secret of the legal profession," affecting women at all levels, from judges and lawyers to paralegals, secretaries, and law students.

102. 751 F. Supp. 1175 (E.D. Pa. 1990), *rev'd*, 983 F.2d 509 (3d Cir. 1992).

103. *See* WARREN FREEDMAN, INTERNAL COMPANY INVESTIGATIONS (1994) at ch. 6 thereof.

104. *See* International Brotherhood of Teamsters v. U.S., 431 U.S. 324 (1977).

105. *See* 106 HARV. L. REV. 2039 (1993), *generally* at 2044:

> In order to prevent the courts from becoming review boards for partnership committees, the Third Circuit refused to expand the role of the trier of fact in title VII disparate-treatment cases. Rather than allow triers of fact to substitute their own subjective judgments of an associate's qualifications for partnership for those of the firm, the court's holding in Ezold recognizes that subjective promotional decisions should not be scrutinized more strictly than objective entry-level employment decisions. In the short run, the Third Circuit thus prevented trial courts from becoming a "second chance" for all members of protected classes who are denied partnership. In the long run, the Third Circuit's refusal to adopt a rule that would provide a strong incentive for employers to rely solely on objective criteria in making upper-level employment decisions may well offer much greater promise to women and minorities that they will achieve partnership and other high levels of employment.

106. 510 A.2d 56 (N.J. 1986).

107. *See* Hubbard and Johnson, *Avoid Malpractice Automate,* A.B.A.J. (Sept. 1993), at 88 *et seq.*

108. ___ F.2d ___ (Unreported, 9th Cir. 1992).

109. FDIC v. Ernst & Young, 967 F.2d 166 (5th Cir. 1991); and Shrader & York v. FDIC, 991 F.2d 216 (5th Cir. 1991). *See* Fox, *OTS v. Kaye, Scholer: An Assault on the Citadel,* 48 Bus. Lawyer 1521 (Aug. 1993).

110. 436 U.S. 447 (1978).

111. *See* Fischer, *Justices Revisit the Solicitation Question*, N.L.J. (Sept. 27, 1993), at 38 *et seq.*

112. 113 S. Ct. 1792 (1993).

113. *Infra* note 111.

114. 599 A.2d 1265 (N.J. 1992).

115. *Infra* note 111.

116. 566 N.Y.S.2d 845 (Yates County Surrogate 1991).

117. *See* Woo, *Victim's Rights Guide Is Drawn by Legal Group,* Wall St. J., Aug. 7, 1992, at B1.

118. 111 S. Ct. 2597 (1991).

119. *See generally* Arkin, *Business Crime: The Press as Weapon for Both Defense and Prosecution*, N.Y.L.J. (Apr. 13, 1989), at 3 and 4.

120. *See* Clarke, *Krulewitz Case Highlights Meagerness of Client Fund,* 15 C.L.T. 23 (June 12, 1989), at 5, delineating the case of a Connecticut resident who lost his life savings of $395,149 to a gambling-addicted lawyer. The attorney Krulewitz admitted his guilt, but the Connecticut Bar Association's Client's Security Fund could not handle the debt except for a 20 percent downpayment.

121. *See* N.Y.L.J. (Apr. 24, 1989), at 1 and 2.

122. Most attorneys who bilk their clients share several characteristics, according to executives of the New York fund. They are typically middle-aged men who practice alone. Gambling, alcoholism, and drug abuse are often involved. And a substantial number are attorneys who have advertised low-cost legal services, taken clients' money, and then failed to complete their work. Indeed, while the Schmidt cases are noteworthy for the large amounts involved, the more typical awards made by the fund are for much smaller sums arising from routine business transactions.

123. ___ F. Supp. ___ (Unreported, S.D.N.Y. Apr. 25, 1989).

124. *See* Trial Magazine (Dec. 1987), at 36 *et seq. See* Phoenix Ins. Co. v. U.S. Fire Ins. Co., 235 Cal. Rptr. 15 (1987), where the California court reviewed the respective rights and duties of primary and secondary or excess insurers of legal malpractice.

See Note, *Lawyer Deep Pocket*, A.B.A.J. (Jan. 1990), at 34, delineating that fact that lawyers are sued for letting clients do wrong! "More and more, people injured in dubious financial deals are suing the lawyers who represented the deal makers. And more and more, courts are letting them do it." As pointed out in Greycas Inc. v. Proud, 826 F.2d 1560 (7th Cir 1986), law firms have been held liable for writing letters encouraging banks to lend clients money. In Seidel v. Public Serv. Co., 616 F. Supp. 1342 (N.H. 1985), a lawyer was held liable under securities law as a "controlling person" because of the influence the lawyer wielded over a corporate board of directors that approved documents to be given to potential investors.

Lawyers are apparently finding new ways to sue other lawyers, according to the N.Y. Times, June 16, 1989, at B4. Courts in at least six states, including Massachusetts and Texas, have held lawyers accountable under state consumer protection statutes prohibiting deception with respect to consumer goods and services. RICO cases predominate, especially where fraud in the sale of securities is alleged.

See also Mallen, *Avoiding Partnership Liability*, TRIAL MAGAZINE (Jan. 1990), at 93–95, pointing out that the liability of the partnership extends beyond actual authority; liability for a tortious act or omission exists if a partner acted with ostensible or apparent authority, as illustrated in Phillips v. Carson, 731 P.2d, 820 (Kans. 1987).

See also Note, *Evaluating the New Director Exculpation Statutes*, 73 CORNELL L. REV. 786 (1988); and Demott, *Limiting Directors' Liability*, 66 WASH. U.L.Q. 295 (1988).

125. *Note* Miotk v. Rudy, 605 P.2d 587 (Kans. 1980).

126. *See* Quesnell v. State, 517 P.2d 568 (Wash. 1973).

127. *See* State v. Aumann, 265 N.W.2d 816 (Iowa 1978).

128. *Note* Neely, *Handicapped Advancing Against Barriers and Partial Solutions in the Representation of Disabled Children,* HASTING L.J. 1359 (1982).

129. *See* A.B.A.J. (Dec. 1, 1987), at 82 *et seq.*

130. 622 F. Supp. 1271 (S.D.N.Y. 1987).

131. 289 U.S. 1 (1932).

132. 661 F. Supp. 148 (N.D. Ill. 1987).

133. *See* Note, 98 HARV. L. REV. 1450 (1985); and Note, 23 AM. CRIM. L. REV. 366 (1986).

134. 128 Cal. Rptr. 901 (1976).

135. 556 P.2d 737 (Cal. 1976).

136. *See* TRIAL MAGAZINE (Apr. 1987), at 28 *et seq.*

137. 489 F.2d 535 (2d Cir. 1973).

138. ____ N.E.2d ____ (Unreported, N.Y. 1987).

139. *See* Wilson v. Saintine Exploration & Drilling Corp., 872 F.2d 1124 (2d Cir. 1989), where a dissolved New York City law firm escaped liability for alleged errors in a prospectus for a securities offering that it prepared and distributed for a client. In short, the court held that the law firm could not be liable under Section 12(2) of the Securities Act of 1933, which protects defrauded investors against mistakes in offerings by sellers of securities. (Note that the case was reconsidered as the U S. Supreme Court had ruled in Pinter v. Dahl, 108 S. Ct. 2063 [1988] that a real estate broker who had recommended an investment to friends and associates could not be held liable under Section 12[1] of the Securities Act of 1933 because the real estate broker did not stand to make any financial gain for himself or anyone else other than the investors.) The federal appellate court opined:

> Persons who are not in privity with the plaintiff but who would have been collateral participants under our former caselaw will now be statutory sellers within the meaning of Pinter if they solicited the sales in question for a financial gain. Such persons may now be liable under § 12 whether or not scienter or loss causation is shown. For example, in Mayer v. Oil Field Systems Corp., 803 F2d 749 (2d Cir., 1986), a partnership's general partners fulfilled their pay-out obligation to limited partners by exchanging all shares of the partnership for stock of another entity. That stock traded at a disappointing price, and the limited partners sued. We held that the general partners were not in privity with the limited partners and

were thus collateral participants. Because they lacked scienter, they could not be liable under § 12(2). 803 F2d at 756. Had Mayer been decided under the Pinter standard, however, we would have had to consider, not whether the general partners had scienter, but whether their causing the exchange for financial gain was the legal equivalent of solicitation of a sale.

In another respect, Pinter contracts the category of persons potentially liable under our § 12(2) caselaw. After Pinter, some persons who are not in privity with the plaintiff but who would have been collateral participants under our prior caselaw are now not statutory sellers because they did not solicit the sales in question. Such persons are no longer subject to any liability under § 12.

It is clear that Ruffa & Hanover falls within the category of participants whose potential liability is contracted rather than expanded by Pinter. Wilson expressly concedes that the firm's participation in the sale consisted solely of the ministerial act of mailing a copy of the private placement memorandum to Wilson at Rodolfy's request. That cannot under any view be considered the kind of solicitation necessary under Pinter. It is clear from the Court's opinion that its concern had to do with persons such as brokers who might act on the seller's behalf for a profit. See Pinter, 108 S. Ct. at 2082. Moreover, Pinter expressly cautioned that the draconian provisions of § 12 must not be extended to include lawyers, such as Ruffa & Hanover, who have performed only their usual professional functions in preparing documents for an offering. 108 S. Ct. at 2081. Indeed, Justice Blackmun's opinion expressly disapproved of the rationale of the leading decision of this circuit, Katz v. Amos Treat & Co., 411 F2d 1046, 1053 (2d Cir., 1969), holding a lawyer liable under § 12(l), in circumstances in which the lawyer had actual contact with the purchasers. *Id.* at 2081, n27. Of course, it does not follow that lawyers are exempt from the concept of a "seller" under § 12 where they earn a commission from an actual seller for persuading their clients to make a particular investment. *Cf.* Brady v. duPont, 828 F2d 75, 77 (2d Cir., 1987).

Wilson seeks support from footnote 24 of the Pinter decision, which states that the Court did not rule upon the existence of aider and abettor liability under § 12, citing the decision in Mayer and In re Caesar's Palace Securities Litigation, 360 F. Supp. 366 (SDNY 1973). Our prior caselaw, however, made no distinction under § 12 between liability based on aiding and abetting and liability based on collateral participation. Indeed, it treated the terms as synonymous and used them interchangeably, as the Caesar's Palace opinion stated. 360 F. Supp. at 380. We agree with the amicus brief filed by the SEC that persons who do not meet the Pinter test for statutory sellers may not be held liable under § 12 as aiders and abettors.

The lone dissenting opinion was critical of the majority's conclusion that the law firm never solicited the offer for financial gain.

In view of the critical lack of clarity with respect to the law firm's role in the instant case, I should have thought it not only prudent but mandatory to remand to the district court for specific findings as to the extent of the law firm's participation in the solicitation of sales, including particularly the following:

(1) What the law firm's role was in Saintine, including its fee arrangement.
(2) Whether the law firm itself sent the false statement to prospective investors.
(3) Whether the law firm acted as an "agent" of the seller.
(4) Who generated the list of prospective purchasers, i.e., did the list come from the law firm?
(5) Whether the law firm earned a fee from the actual seller for putting out a false and misleading private placement memorandum which enabled, or indeed was a sine qua non for, the seller to induce buyers to buy.

Finally, the panel majority makes much of the fact that at oral argument appellant's attorney stated that a remand was unnecessary because he could think of no further evidence he could offer as to the law firm's participation in the solicitation of Wilson. That both parties and the panel majority would like to avoid a remand, is of no moment. Leaving aside the fact that there are critical aspects of the relationship between the law firm and Saintine that remain unexplored (see the specific areas set forth above as to which the district court should make findings of fact), the parties cannot by agreement dispense with the requirement that a judgment be founded on proper findings of fact. Swanson v. Levy, 509 F2d 859, 861 (9 Cir., 1975) ("The requirement that the district court find the fact specially and state separately its conclusions of law must be fairly observed and may not be waived by the parties."); Waialua Agr. Co. v. Maneja, 178 F2d 603, 606–07 (9 Cir., 1949) (same) (citing Kelley v. Everglades Drainage Dist., *supra*, 319 U.S. at 421), *cert. denied*, 339 U.S. 920 (1950).

To summarize: From the majority's refusal either to affirm or to remand to the district court to make appropriate findings of fact and conclusions of law in the light of Pinter, I respectfully but emphatically dissent.

140. *See* Salomon and Bock, *Privilege Exception Flourishes*, N.L.J. (June 28, 1993), at 27 *et seq.*

141. *See* Clark v. U.S., 289 U.S. 1 (1933), which required *prima facie* evidence of a crime or fraud.

142. 647 P.2d 1215 (Colo. 1982).

143. 731 F.2d 557 (8th Cir. 1984).

144. *See* 8 WIGMORE, EVIDENCE, Section 7292 (1961).

145. *See* Slind-Flor, *Scientific Fraud and the Law*, N.L.J. (Oct. 25, 1993), at 7 *et seq.*

146. *See* Wieder and Addas, *Justices Likely to Address Resume Fraud,* N.L.J. (Oct. 25, 1993), at 23 *et seq.*

147. Dkt. A–93–50 (1993).

148. Dkt. 90–13030 CM (6th Cir. 1933).

149. 975 F.2d 302 (6th Cir. 1992).

150. 864 F.2d 700 (10th Cir. 1988). *Cf.* Wallace v. Dunn Construction Co., 968 F.2d 1174 (11th Cir. 1992): – "The employer is at risk of suits for harm to the public on respondeat superior or negligent hiring grounds and for workmen's compensation liability to other employees and the employee herself."

151. 955 F.2d 409 (6th Cir. 1992).

152. 756 F. Supp. 1172 (W.D. Wis. 1990), *vacated*, 963 F.2d 918 (7th Cir. 1992).

153. *See* Note, 37 VILLANOVA L. REV. 1361 (1992).

154. *Cf.* Mazart v. New York, 441 N.Y.S.2d 600 (Ct. C1. 1981).

155. *See* infra note 152 at 1368.

156. 418 U.S. 323 (1974).

157. 42 U.S.C. §§ 11101–11152 (1988).

158. *See* 42 U.S.C. § 11111.

159. *See* 42 U.S.C. § 11112.

160. 18 U.S.C. § 1957.

161. *Id.*

162. *See generally,* Stewart and Nelson, *Hawking Legal Services,* A.B.A.J. (Aug. 1, 1988), at 44. *See* Reynoldson, *The Case Against Lawyer Advertising*, A.B.A.J. (Aug. 1, 1989), at 60 *et seq. See* Wagner, *Lawyer Advertising*, TRIAL MAGAZINE (April 1989), at 5–6, where the president of the Association of Trial Lawyers of America,

or ATLA, pointed out: "The consumer of legal services lives in a better world today. Almost everyone would agree that advertising has contributed to the improvement. . . . [But we] should encourage the type of regulation of advertising that will ensure that the public will receive the benefits."

163. 708 S. Ct. 1916 (1988).

164. 471 U.S. 626 (1985).

165. *Infra* note 162.

166. *Id.* According to the majority opinion of Mr. Justice Brennan:

Lawyer advertising is in the category of constitutionally protected commercial speech. *See* Bates v. State Bar of Arizona, 433 U.S. 350 (1977). The First Amendment principles governing state regulation of lawyer solicitations for pecuniary gain are by now familiar: "Commercial speech that is not false or deceptive and does not concern unlawful activities . . . may be restricted only in the service of a substantial governmental interest, and only through means that directly advance that interest." Zauderer, *supra*, at 638 (citing Central Hudson Gas & Electric Corp. v. Public Service Comm'n of New York, 447 U.S. 557, 566 [1980]). Since state regulation of commercial speech "may extend only as far as the interest it serves," Central Hudson, *supra*, at 565, state rules that are designed to prevent the "potential for deception and confusion . . . may be no broader than reasonably necessary to prevent the perceived evil. In re R.M.J., 455 U.S. 191, 203 (1982)."

In Zauderer, application of these principles required that we strike an Ohio rule that categorically prohibited solicitation of legal employment for pecuniary gain through advertisements containing information or advice, even if truthful and nondeceptive, regarding a specific legal problem. We distinguished written advertisements containing such information or advice from in-person solicitation by lawyers for profit, which we held in Ohralik v. Ohio State Bar Assn., 436 U.S. 447 (1978), a State may categorically ban. The "unique features of in-person solicitation by lawyers [that] justified a prophylactic rule prohibiting lawyers from engaging in such solicitation for pecuniary gain," we observed, are "not present" in the context of written advertisements. Zauderer, 471 U.S., at 641–642.

Our lawyer advertising cases have never distinguished among various modes of written advertising to the general public. *See*, e.g., Bates, *supra* (newspaper advertising); *id.*, at 372, n.26 (equating advertising in telephone directory with newspaper advertising); In re R.M.J., *supra* (mailed announcement cards treated same as newspaper and telephone director advertisements). Thus, Ohio could no more prevent Zauderer from mass-mailing to a general population his offer to represent women injured by the Dalkon Shield than it could prohibit his publication of the advertisement in local newspapers. Similarly, if petitioner's letter is neither false nor deceptive, Kentucky could not constitutionally prohibit him from sending at large an identical letter opening with the query, "Is your home being foreclosed on?", rather than his observation to the targeted individuals that "It has come to my attention that your home is being foreclosed on." The drafters of Rule 7.3 apparently appreciated as much, for the Rule exempts from the ban "letters addressed or advertising circulars distributed generally to persons . . . who are so situated that they might in general find such services useful." . . .

Like print advertising, petitioner's letter—and targeted, direct-mail solicitation generally—"poses much less risk of overreaching or undue influence" than does in-person solicitation, Zauderer, 471 U.S., at 642. Neither mode of written communication involves "the coercive force of the personal presence of a trained advocate" or the "pressure on the potential client for an immediate yes-or-no answer to the offer of representation." *Ibid.* Unlike the potential client with a badgering advocate breathing down his neck, the recipient of a letter and the "reader of an advertisement . . . can 'effectively avoid further bombardment of [his] sensibilities simply by adverting [his] eyes,' " Ohralik, *supra*, at 465, n.25 (quoting Cohen v. California, 403 U.S. 15, 21 (1971). A letter, like a printed advertisement (but unlike a lawyer), can readily be put in a drawer to be considered later, ignored, or discarded. In short, both types of written solicitation "conve[y] information about legal services [by means] that [are] more conducive to reflection and the exercise of choice on the part of the consumer than is personal solicitation by an attorney." Zauderer, *supra*, at 642. Nor does a targeted letter invade the recipient's privacy any more than does a substantively identical letter mailed at large. The invasion, if any, occurs when the lawyer discovers the recipient's legal affairs, not when he confronts the recipient with the discovery.

Admittedly, a letter that is personalized (not merely targeted) to the recipient presents an increased risk of deception, intentional or inadvertent. It could, in certain circumstances, lead the recipient to overestimate the lawyer's familiarity with the case or could implicitly suggest that the recipient's legal problem is more dire than it really is. *See* Brief for ABA as *Amicus Curiae* 9. Similarly, an inaccurately targeted letter could lead the recipient to believe she has a legal problem that she does not actually have or, worse yet, could offer erroneous legal advice. *See, e.g.*, Leoni v. State Bar of California, 39 Cal. 3d 609, 619–620, 704 P.2d 183 (1985), *summarily dism'd*, 475 U.S. 1001 (1986).

But merely because targeted, direct-mail solicitation presents lawyers with opportunities for isolated abuses or mistakes does not justify a total ban on that mode of protected commercial speech. *See* In re R.M.J., 455 U.S., at 203. The State can regulate such abuses and minimize mistakes through far less restrictive and more precise means, the most obvious of which is to require the lawyer to file any solicitation letter with a state agency, *id.*, at 206, giving the State ample opportunity to supervise mailings and penalize actual abuses. . . .

The record before us furnishes no evidence that scrutiny of targeted solicitation letters will be appreciably more burdensome or less reliable than scrutiny of advertisements. *See* Bates, 433 U.S., at 379; *id.*, at 387 (Burger, C.J., concurring in part and dissenting in part) (objecting to "enormous new regulatory burdens called for by" Bates). As a general matter, evaluating a targeted advertisement does not require specific information about the recipient's identity and legal problems any more than evaluating a newspaper advertisement requires like information about all readers. If the targeted letter specifies facts that relate to particular recipients (e.g., "It has come to my attention that your home is being foreclosed on"), the reviewing agency has innumerable options to minimize mistakes. It might, for example, require the lawyer to prove the truth of the fact stated (by supplying copies of the court documents or material that lead the lawyer to the fact); it could require the lawyer to explain briefly how she discovered the fact and verified its accuracy; or it could require the letter to bear a label identifying it as an advertisement; *see id.*, at 384 (dictum); In re R.M.J., *supra*, at 206, n.20, or directing the recipient how to report inaccurate or misleading letters. To be sure, a state agency or bar association that reviews solicitation letters might have more work than one that does not. But "[o]ur recent decisions involving commercial speech have been grounded in the faith that the free flow of commercial information is valuable enough to justify imposing on would-be regulators the costs of distinguishing the truthful from the false, the helpful from the misleading, and the harmless from the harmful." Zauderer, *supra*, at 646.

The dissent of Justice O'Connor pointed out the Court's reliance on the Zauderer case:

States may not prohibit a form of attorney advertising that is potentially more pernicious than the advertising at issue in that case. I agree with the Court that a line of cases built on defective premises and flawed reasoning. As today's decision illustrated, the Court has been unable or unwilling to restrain the logic of the underlying analysis within reasonable bounds. The resulting interference with important and valid public policies is so destructive that I believe the analytical framework itself should now be reexamined. . . . [F]airly severe constraints on attorney advertising can continue to play an important role in preserving the legal profession as a genuine profession. Whatever may be the exact appropriate scope of these restrictions at a given time and place, this Court's recent decisions reflect a myopic belief that "consumers," and thus our nation, will benefit from a constitutional theory that refuses to recognize either the essence of professionalism or its fragile and necessary foundations. Compare, e.g., Bates, 433 U.S. at 370–372, with *id.*, at 400–401, and n.11 (Powell, J., concurring in part and dissenting in part). In one way or another, time will uncover the folly of this approach. I can only hope that the Court will recognize the danger before it is too late to effect a worthwhile cure. . . .

One distinguishing feature of any profession, unlike other occupations that may be equally respectable, is that membership entails an ethical obligation to temper one's selfish pursuit of economic success by adhering to standards of conduct that could not be enforced either by legal fiat or through the discipline of the market. There are sound reasons to continue pursuing the goal that is implicit in the traditional view of professional life. Both the special privileges incident to membership in the profession and the advantages those privileges give in the necessary task of earning a living are means to a goal that transcends the accumulation of wealth. That goal is public service, which in the legal profession can take a variety of familiar forms. This view of the legal profession need not be rooted in romanticism or self-serving sanctimony, though of course it can be. Rather, special ethical standards for lawyers are properly understood as an appropriate means of restraining lawyers in the exercise of the unique power that they inevitably wield in a political system like ours.

It is worth recalling why lawyers are regulated at all, or to a greater degree than most other occupations, and why history is littered with failed attempts to extinguish lawyers as a special class. *See generally* R. Pound, The Lawyer from Antiquity to Modern Times (1953). Operating a legal system that is both reasonably efficient and tolerably fair cannot be accomplished, at least under modern social conditions, without a trained and specialized body of experts. This training is one element of what we mean when we refer to the law as a "learned profession." Such knowledge by its nature cannot be made generally available and it therefore confers the power and the temptation to manipulate the system of justice for one's own ends. . . . Like physicians, lawyers are subjected to heightened ethical demands on their conduct towards those they serve. These demands are needed because market forces, and the ordinary legal prohibitions against force and fraud, are simply insufficient to protect the consumers of their necessary services from the peculiar power of the specialized knowledge that these professionals possess.

Imbuing the legal profession with the necessary ethical standards is a task that involves a constant struggle with the relentless natural force of economic self-interest. It cannot be accomplished directly by legal rules, and it certainly will not succeed if sermonizing is the strongest tool that may be employed. Tradition and experiment have suggested a number of formal and informal mechanisms, none of which is adequate by itself and many of which may serve to reduce competition (in the narrow economic sense) among members of the profession. A few examples include the great efforts made during this century to improve the quality and breadth of the legal education that is required for admission to the bar; the concomitant attempt to cultivate a sub-class of genuine scholars within the profession; the development of bar associations that aspire to be more than trade groups; strict disciplinary rules about conflicts of interest and client abandonment; and promotion of the expectation that an attorney's history of voluntary public service is a relevant factor in selecting judicial candidates.

Restrictions on advertising and solicitation by lawyers properly and significantly serve the same goal. Such restrictions act as a concrete, day-to-day reminder to the practicing attorney of why it is improper for any member of this profession to regard it as a trade or occupation like any other. There is no guarantee, of course, that the restrictions will always have the desired effect, and they are surely not a sufficient means to their proper goal. Given their inevitable anticompetitive effects, moreover, they should not be thoughtlessly retained or insulated from skeptical criticism. Appropriate modifications have been made in the light of reason and experience, and other changes may be suggested in the future.

See Becker, *Shapero—Direct Mail Clarified*, 22 AKRON L. REV. 199, Fall 1988, which also discusses the Zauderer case, . . . In the Shapero case the following letter was sent by the attorney to potential clients.

> It has come to my attention that your home is being foreclosed on. If this is true, you may be about to lose your home. Federal law may allow you to keep your home by ORDERING your creditor [sic] to STOP and give you more time to pay them.
>
> You may call my office any time from 8:30 a.m. to 5 p.m. for FREE information on how you can keep your home.

APPENDIX A

Report on Standards for Opinions of Florida Counsel of the Special Committee on Opinion Standards of the Florida Bar Business Law Section

Florida Bar Opinion Committee

INDEX

D—Mergers, Acquisitions and Bulk Transfers (To be included later)
E—Secured Transactions under the U.C.C. (To be included later)
F—Real Estate Transactions (To be included later)
G—Federal and Florida Securities Laws (To be included later)
H—Opinions relating to Partnerships (To be included later)
I—Opinions relating to limited liability companies (To be included later)

1410 The Business Lawyer; Vol. 46, August 1991

Report on Standards for Opinions of Florida Counsel of the Special Committee on Opinion Standards of the Florida Bar Business Law Section

*Florida Bar Opinion Committee**

This Report establishes standards for opinions of Florida counsel to third parties in commercial transactions, with particular consideration of matters involving Florida law. It does not cover situations or opinions in which counsel gives legal advice to his own client, but only written opinions which are addressed to third parties. This Report is intended to apply only to opinions delivered after the date of its issuance and should not be construed to have retroactive effect.

This Report should not be construed to suggest that legal opinions are necessary in all commercial transactions. There are many transactions in which the parties may decide to eliminate the requirement for delivery of a legal opinion because of the nature of the transaction or because the benefits of the legal opinion would be outweighed by its cost.

This Report is divided into eleven parts:** (1) Introduction; (2) Common Elements of Opinions; (3) Opinions Relating to the Enforceability of Contracts; (4) Opinions Relating to the Issuance and Transfer of Securities; (5) Opinions on Litigation; (6) Opinions in Mergers, Acquisitions and Bulk Transfers; (7) Opinions Concerning Secured Transactions under the Uniform Commercial Code; (8) Opinions in Real Estate Transactions including Loan Transactions; (9) Opinions Concerning Federal and Florida Securities Laws Matters; (10) Opinions Concerning Limited and General Partnerships; and (11) Opinions Concerning Limited Liability Companies. The text of standard forms of opinions, including sample officer's certificates, are Exhibits** to this Report.

This Report covers opinions given by individual lawyers, law firms, lawyers in corporate legal departments and by lawyers employed by other entities. Solely for ease of reference, this Report uses only the masculine gender, which is intended to include the feminine and the neuter.

*Florida Bar Opinion Committee: Chairman—Thomas G. O'Brien III. Members—Gardner F. Davis, Anthony L. Dutton, Jeffrey M. Fuller, Richard M. Leisner, Timothy C. Leixner, Paul S. Singerman, Karen J. Orlin, Philip B. Schwartz, Jeffrey A. Stoops, William L. Thompson, Jr., Gregory C. Yadley.

**As of April 8, 1991, parts 1 through 5 and Exhibit A to this Report have been finalized and approved by the Executive Council of the Business Law Section. Additional parts and exhibits will be added by amendment, but the parts that have been approved by the Executive Council of the Business Law Section are not expected to be amended further.

I. Introduction

A. Scope

A legal opinion is a formal writing expressing the lawyer's informed understanding of the legal principles applicable to a specific transaction or a particular aspect of that transaction. As such, it represents a reasoned judgment by the attorney as to how the highest court in the applicable jurisdiction would decide a legal issue if it were presented with that issue on the date of the opinion. It is not a guarantee that the court would make this decision, but reflects the attorney's informed judgment based upon an analysis of the laws, facts and other matters relevant to the opinion.

B. Goals

This Report is intended to:

(1) establish a uniform understanding among Florida counsel and the recipients of opinions rendered by Florida counsel on the meanings of the terms used in these opinions;

(2) establish standards for due diligence in rendering opinions so that the expectations of recipients of opinions will be consistent with the responsibilities of counsel rendering the opinions;

(3) simplify opinions given by Florida lawyers by allowing them to incorporate standardized assumptions, qualifications and definitions contained in this Report, and thereby reduce the length of opinions and permit addressees to focus more easily on the substance of opinions;

(4) reduce the frictions which can arise in negotiating opinions and reduce costs incurred by clients in connection with the negotiation and issuance of opinions;

(5) reduce the potential for misunderstanding between counsel and his client regarding the issuance of opinions; and

(6) improve the understanding of the public and the bar of the purposes and limitations of opinions.

C. Reasonableness in Opinions

This Report discusses the reasons why some requests for opinions are commercially reasonable and others are not, and is intended to provide reasonable standards as to what opinions Florida lawyers should be asked to give on particular issues. To a great degree, the reasonableness of a requested opinion requires weighing the amount of due diligence required to give the opinion against the benefits to the recipient of the opinion. Accordingly, in setting out due diligence standards which Florida lawyers must satisfy to give these opinions, the Report establishes a "comfort level" for addressees of opinions rendered in conformity with this Report.

In reaching these standards, a balance has been struck between the benefits of receiving an opinion and the costs of providing these benefits. While these standards may, in some cases, result in opinions which are somewhat different from those to which some recipients and opinion-givers have become accustomed, this Report takes the position that these standards should apply in all cases.

D. Plain English; No Implied Opinions

Wherever possible, the proposed opinions attached to this Report are written in "plain English" to eliminate legalese, jargon and the repetition of terms that have the same meanings or less inclusive meanings. In some cases, this Report modifies the traditional language often used in opinions so that opinions will be clearer and more readable.

It is the position of this Report that the recipient of an opinion is not entitled to assume that an express opinion on a particular matter addresses any other matter by implication unless it is unmistakably clear that inclusion of an implied opinion within an express opinion is both essential to the legal conclusion set forth in the express opinion and reasonable under the circumstances.

E. Incorporation by Reference

The proposed standard opinions that are Exhibits to this Report do not contain many of the explicitly stated exceptions, limitations and assumptions commonly found in most opinions. These have been eliminated from the text of the opinions because they are part of the common "ground rules" that are contained in this Report. By incorporating this Report in an opinion by reference, the exceptions, qualifications and assumptions contained in this Report are automatically incorporated into the opinion, and it is not necessary to recite them in the text of the opinion.

This Report recommends that opinions rendered by Florida counsel include a specific statement that this Report has been incorporated by reference into their opinion. Incorporation of a report with extensive ground rules has worked well for over 10 years in the area of responses to requests for information from auditors pursuant to the American Bar Association Statement of Policy Regarding Lawyers' Responses to Auditors' Requests for Information.

This Report also describes the steps to be taken by the attorney in rendering each opinon discussed in this Report and recites the factual data on which the attorney should rely in giving the particular opinion. Accordingly, the forms of opinion that are part of this Report do not recite these steps. In cases in which opinions go beyond the matters covered by this Report, the opinion should specify the additional due diligence, if any, performed that serves as the basis for counsel's additional opinions.

F. Ethical Issues in Rendering Opinions

A Florida attorney issuing a written opinion to a third party is subject to the Rules of Professional Conduct promulgated by the Supreme Court of Florida.

Rule 4-2.3 (Evaluation for Use by Third Persons) applies to the rendering of opinions. It provides:

> A lawyer may undertake an evaluation of a matter affecting a client for the use of someone other than the client if:
>
> (1) The lawyer reasonably believes that making the evaluation is compatible with other aspects of the lawyer's relationship with the client; and
>
> (2) The client consents after consultation.
>
> In reporting the evaluation, the lawyer should indicate any material limitations that were imposed on the scope of the inquiry or on the disclosure of information.

Opinions given on a client's behalf for use by third parties create a tension between an attorney's obligations to his client and his obligations to persons whom he knows will rely upon his opinion. An attorney's ethical duties in rendering opinions can be understood in the following contexts:

(1) Duty of Loyalty. Attorneys owe their clients a duty of loyalty. As long as the client's informed consent is obtained, rendering an opinion to a third party is not a breach of that duty. Before an attorney renders an opinion, he should explain to his client the scope of the opinion and the requirements and consequences which may arise from its issuance. For example, he should advise the client that once his opinion is given, it may become more difficult for the client to argue positions contrary to the legal conclusions contained in the opinion.

This Report takes the position that it is not a conflict of interest for an attorney to render an opinion to the other party in a transaction. For example, a member of the Florida Bar representing a borrower in a loan transaction may properly give an opinion to the lender that the loan agreement is "enforceable" against his client, provided the attorney reaches that opinion after appropriate due diligence and legal research, and provided the opinion is subject to appropriate exceptions and limitations. (See Section III.I. of this Report.) If an attorney representing a borrower concludes that the borrower's obligations under specific provisions of the loan agreement may not be enforceable against his client under applicable law, under the Florida Bar's Standards of Professionalism (Standard 4.4), the attorney is obligated to advise counsel for the lender of this fact. (See Section III.I.)

(2) Conflict Between an Attorney and His Client. If delivery of a particular opinion appears to be in the best interests of the client (where, for example, the addressee will not close the transaction without the opinion), but the attorney is reluctant to deliver the opinion out of concern about his potential liability for the opinion (because of uncertainty about a legal issue, or for other reasons), a conflict can exist between the "zealous representation" obligation of the attorney and his own self-interest. In such a situation, the attorney should discuss with the client the issues which cause him to be unwilling to give a requested

opinion and request the client's support in seeking modifications to the requested opinion.

(3) Confidentiality. The contents of an opinion rendered to a third party are not protected by the attorney-client privilege. Accordingly, attorneys should consider this before rendering opinions and confirm that the client understands this fact and its ramifications.

(4) Good Faith. An attorney should neither ask for, nor advise his client to demand, opinions that an attorney qualified to render such an opinion would not reasonably be willing to give.

(5) Candor. If any attorney involved in the delivery, negotiation or receipt of an opinion knows that the assumptions, facts or law upon which the opinion is based are incorrect, he should advise the attorney rendering the opinion of these matters so that they can be addressed. Similarly, if the attorney involved in the transaction for which the opinion is being delivered knows of facts or circumstances that compel him to conclude that the information or assumptions on which opining counsel proposes to rely are false, the attorney must bring this conclusion to the attention of the opining attorney, and the opining attorney may not rely on the false information or assumptions in rendering his opinion except with the informed consent of the addressee. Similarly, if the opining counsel concludes that an area of law that otherwise would be excluded from the scope of the opinion (See Section II.G.) clearly affects the legality of the transaction, he should bring this fact to the attention of counsel for the addressee.

G. Negotiation of Opinions

Issues relating to opinions are best solved early in the negotiation of the transaction to which they relate. The scope and text of opinions, and the cost and time requirements related to the opinions, should be negotiated at the same time as the agreements between the parties and in the same manner as other material terms.

Forms of opinions and, under most circumstances, factual certificates should be reviewed and approved by counsel for the addressee, and sufficient time should be allowed to research legal principles, investigate facts and identify areas of uncertainty, if any, in the interpretation and application of legal principles.

This Report takes the position that it is not appropriate for the addressee or his counsel to impose the business risks of the transaction on opining counsel by using economic leverage to demand opinions that addressee's counsel would not reasonably be willing to render.

If counsel for the addressee is not a Florida lawyer, opining counsel should send a copy of this Report to addressee's counsel as soon as it becomes apparent that an opinion will have to be delivered as part of the transaction.

The parties may agree, for purposes of an opinion, to arbitrary assumptions, legal interpretations or other facts or circumstances that may not be in accord with reality. These agreements, when described with reasonable particularity in the opinion, will supersede the assumptions contained in this Report to the extent they are inconsistent with or in conflict with them. This type of private agreement is neither endorsed nor disapproved by this Report, and counsel may rely upon such agreements in rendering his opinion.

H. Liability for Opinions

An attorney may be held liable for providing an erroneous legal opinion under theories of negligence, fraud, misrepresentation or breach of fiduciary duty. Historically, Florida courts have required the plaintiff in a negligence action for an erroneous legal opinion to be in privity of contract with the opining attorney. As a result, the attorney's client could successfully sue the attorney for negligently providing an erroneous legal opinion, but no cause of action could be maintained by the addressee of a legal opinion unless the addressee was otherwise in privity of contract with the opining attorney.

Recently, Florida courts have eliminated the privity requirement in negligence actions involving other types of professionals and have adopted the position set forth in the Restatement (Second) of Torts § 552. The Restatement (Second) of Torts provides that a professional will be liable to any person whom he knew would rely on his work product in taking or failing to take a course of action. If this standard is applied to Florida attorneys, an opining attorney will be liable to the addressee of a legal opinion if the opinion was negligently prepared and erroneous, regardless of a claim of a lack of privity between the addressee and the opining attorney.

II. Common Elements of Opinions

A. Date; Proposed Legislation

The date of an opinion should be the date on which it is to be delivered, and is normally the closing date of the transaction. Unless specifically noted, the date of the opinion is the date on which the legal conclusions in the opinion are expressed, and the attorney has no duty to update the opinion. If counsel is relying on documents dated prior to the date of the opinion, this should be explicitly noted in the qualifications to the opinion.

A lawyer giving an opinion has a duty to consider all laws which have been enacted, regulations which have been adopted and decisions which have been published prior to the date of the opinion, including enacted laws and adopted regulations which have effective dates in the future. In rendering an opinion, a lawyer has no duty to investigate whether proposed legislation or regulations will affect the opinion being given, and will not be held to have constructive knowledge of proposed legislation or regulations or their effects. Consistent with a lawyer's overriding duty of good faith, honesty and candor, however, if a lawyer (including counsel for the addressee) giving substantive attention to the transaction for which the opinion is being rendered has actual knowledge that a proposed law or regulation would affect an opinion being given, he should confirm that the opining counsel is aware of the proposal. If an opining counsel has actual knowledge, without investigation, of a proposed law or regulation which counsel concludes would affect his opinion, the proposed law or regulation should be noted in the opinion. The opining attorney in this circumstance does not, however, have a duty to express an opinion on the effect that the proposed legislation or regulation would have on his opinion if the proposal were adopted.

If opining counsel updates his opinion, the updated opinion should be treated as if it were an entirely new opinion. The consent of the opining attorney's client should be obtained before the updated opinion is issued, and the opining counsel should confirm that the opinions expressed are correct as of the date of the updated opinion.

B. Addressee and Reliance

Unless otherwise noted in an opinion, only the addressee of a legal opinion should be entitled to rely on it. This Report assumes that the addressee of an opinion will be aware of the contents of this Report because the opinion will expressly incorporate this Report by reference, and counsel for the addressee is expected to have reviewed this Report on behalf of the addressee.

If an opinion comes into the possession of third persons, these persons are not entitled to rely upon the legal conclusions in the opinion. These third persons should have no claim against the attorney giving the opinion if they suffer damages based on their reliance on the legal conclusions contained in the opinion.

To avoid claims by third parties who are not expressly authorized to rely on an opinion, and because third parties may not be aware of the contents of this Report, opinions should state:

> This opinion is furnished to you by us as counsel for [client], is solely for your benefit [and the benefit of named persons], and is rendered solely in connection with the transaction to which this opinion relates. This opinion may be relied upon only in connection with this transaction and may not be relied upon by any other person[s] without our prior written consent [except that a copy of this opinion may be delivered by you to [insert name(s) of persons to which a copy of this opinion may be delivered] in connection with [describe, with specificity, the circumstances in which this opinion may be delivered] and these persons may rely on this opinion as if it were addressed to them].

C. Role of Counsel

The scope of required due diligence and the meaning of the opinion do not depend on the relation of counsel to the client or counsel's role in the transaction (even if the role is limited solely to rendering the opinion). That is, before counsel gives a particular opinion, counsel must complete the necessary due diligence to give the opinion, regardless of counsel's relationship to the client. The labels "special counsel" or "general counsel" have no significance and should not be used. The forms of opinion contained in this Report merely state that the attorney has acted as counsel to the named person in connection with the particular transaction.

If counsel has a conflict of interest or an appearance of a conflict of interest relating to the client, or if counsel has any special relationship with the client (such as an attorney of the firm or a close relative serving on the client's board of directors or holding a significant ownership interest in the client), or if other facts exist which might affect (or be perceived to affect) counsel's independence, these facts should be disclosed in the opinion.

D. Brief Description of the Transaction

The opinion should include a brief description of the transaction to establish the context in which the principal documents and the opinion are delivered.

E. Requirement for the Opinion

The opinion should state the reason it is being given. Generally, the delivery of the opinion will be required by one of the principal transactional documents as a condition precedent to consummation of the transaction. The opinion should provide: "This opinion is furnished pursuant to Section ________ of the Agreement and is given with the consent of the Company." If the opinion is not required by the agreement, the opinion should state that it is furnished pursuant to the addressee's request.

F. Definitions

Terms defined only in the opinion should be shown in quotation marks at the time they are defined in the opinion. Terms which are defined by referring to the principal transactional or other documents should be defined as follows: "Capitalized terms not otherwise defined in this opinion have the definitions set forth in the Agreement." Whenever a term used in the opinion is taken from a statute, the lawyer should use the term that is used in the statute. For example, the Florida Business Corporation Act uses the terms "articles of incorporation," "shareholders" and "shares" rather than the terms "certificate of incorporation," "stockholders" and "stock" which are used in some other jurisdictions.

G. Limitations to Laws of Specific Jurisdictions or to Substantive Areas of Law; Excluded Areas of Law

Unless limitations as to the specific jurisdictions and substantive areas covered are stated, the opinion will be presumed to cover all of the jurisdictions and all substantive areas applicable to the transaction to which the opinion relates. Except as provided in the next paragraph of this Report, an opinion will be deemed to address (a) all applicable Federal and state statutes, laws, judicial decisions, rules and regulations within the particular jurisdictions that have been published and are available generally to lawyers in the opining counsel's judicial circuit and (b) all substantive areas covered by the opinion, unless the opinion by its terms is limited solely to a review of specifically listed laws or areas of law, or if the opinion specifically excludes listed laws or areas of law. For example, an opinion might state that: "We express no opinion on any matter within the jurisdiction of the Federal Communications Commission." (See Section III.G. for examples of law excluded from some opinions.)

Notwithstanding the foregoing, unless specifically identified in the underlying documents as requiring coverage and specifically identified in the opinion itself, an opinion will not be deemed to cover any of the following types of laws: usury laws; Federal and state securities laws and regulations; Federal Reserve Board margin regulations; pension and employee benefit laws and regulations such as ERISA; Federal and state antitrust and unfair competition laws and regulations; Federal and state regulations concerning filing requirements (such as Hart-Scott-Rodino and Exon-Florio), other than requirements applicable to filings related to articles of incorporation, articles of merger and the like; compliance with fiduciary duty requirements; Federal and state laws and regulations concerning the creation, attachment, perfection, priority or enforcement of security interests; fraudulent conveyance/transfer laws; Federal and state environmental laws and regulations; Federal and state land use laws and regulations; and local laws (including statutes, administrative decisions, and rules and regulations of county, municipal and political subdivisions).

Florida counsel should usually limit their opinions to Florida law and to United States Federal law. If Florida counsel opines on an issue of foreign law (i.e., the law of a state other than Florida or of a foreign country), he is holding himself out as competent on that issue of foreign law. Even if a Florida attorney considers himself qualified to opine on matters of foreign law or other specialized matters, the addressee has the final decision whether to accept the opinion of a Florida lawyer on these matters.

In determining whether to accept the opinion of Florida counsel on a matter of foreign or specialized law, the addressee should consider the complexity of the issue, the cost of retaining local/specialist counsel and the basis for the expertise of Florida counsel. For example, Florida counsel who regularly represent corporations incorporated in other jurisdictions often opine on routine matters of the corporate law of those jurisdictions. Similarly, Florida counsel often opine on other routine and uncomplicated issues of foreign law such as qualification of a corporation to do business in foreign jurisdictions, and base this opinion on certificates of the officials of foreign jurisdictions and certificates of officers of the client. If Florida counsel renders an opinion on a statute of a foreign jurisdiction, the opinion will be understood to cover the statute and all regulations and judicial decisions interpreting it.

This Report takes the position that it is generally not beneficial to the addressee to receive an opinion from Florida counsel that assumes that Florida law will apply to a contract when the contract expressly provides that another jurisdiction's laws will govern it. Although it is not recommended, it is permissible for Florida counsel to give an opinion that hypothesizes that (1) Florida law is identical to the law of another jurisdiction (even if that hypothesis is known by opining counsel not to be correct, provided opining counsel advises the addressee that the hypothesis is not correct), or (2) if a court refuses to apply the law of the jurisdiction that is set forth in the contract, it will apply Florida law.

If this opinion is requested, it should state:

> We note that the Agreement provides that it is governed by the law of the State of __________ (the law stipulated by the Agreement to be the law governing its interpretation and enforcement). We have assumed, with your permission, that the law of ____________ is identical to the law of Florida in all respects material to our opinions. [We advise you, that, to our knowledge, the law of __________ is different from the law of Florida on the matters covered by paragraph _______ of our opinion.]

See Section III.I for a discussion of the impact of the governing law provision on the enforceability opinion.

H. Opinions of Local/Specialist Counsel

If local/specialist counsel ("LSC") is needed to give an opinion on matters of local law or on a specialized area of law, two issues arise: (1) the nature of the duty of the principal opining counsel (the "POC") with respect to the selection of the LSC, and (2) the responsibility of the POC for the opinion of the LSC.

(1) The Duty of the POC in Selecting the LSC.

It is the position of this Report that the addressee has a right to approve or reject all of the counsel from whom the addressee will receive opinions. Obviously, addressees should not reject counsel unless they have a reasonable basis to conclude that counsel does not have the qualifications needed to give the requested opinions. It is the position of this Report that even though the POC often proposes the LSC for the addressee's consideration, the POC does not select the LSC, and the POC does not have a duty to participate in the selection of the LSC. If the POC or his client proposes an LSC for the addressee's consideration, the POC (or his client) has only an obligation to use reasonable care in making the recommendation.

(2) Responsibility of the POC for the Opinion of LSC.

Because the addressee has the right to approve or reject the LSC, it is the position of this Report that the addressee should accept the LSC's opinion without looking to the POC for a confirming opinion. The POC should exclude from the scope of his opinion all matters covered in the opinion of the LSC and should state that these matters are covered by the opinion of the LSC as follows:

"In rendering the foregoing opinion, we have not expressed an opinion on matters of [state or specialized area] law. These matters are covered by the opinion of [LSC] addressed to you and dated ______________."

There are times, however, when the addressee requires that the POC express an opinion on the matters covered by the opinion of the LSC so that the addressee can be sure that all matters for which opinions have been requested are covered in a single opinion. In these instances, (a) the POC should be permitted to express his opinion on the local or specialized laws by relying solely on the opinion of the LSC, (b) the LSC's opinion should be addressed to the addressee rather than the POC and (c) the LSC's opinion should provide that the POC may rely on it to the extent necessary to render his opinion.

The POC does not have a duty to review the accuracy of an opinion on which he proposes to rely, but the POC may not properly rely on an opinion if he has actual knowledge that the opinion is not correct or knows that the facts or law on which the LSC's opinion is based are not correct. If the POC has such knowledge, he should advise the LSC of his conclusion. In addition, even though the LSC is supplying the opinion directly to the addressee, the addressee may properly request that the POC state in his opinion that the lawyers in the POC's firm who have given substantive attention to the transaction have no knowledge of the incorrectness of any fact expressly assumed or relied on by the LSC in giving his opinion.

This Report considers it unreasonable for an addressee to refuse to permit the POC to rely solely on the LSC's opinion by requiring that the POC independently state that the LSC's opinion is satisfactory in form and scope, that he "concurs" in the opinion of the LSC, that the LSC's opinion is "satisfactory in form and substance," or that the addressee is "justified in relying upon the opinion of the LSC." If the POC expresses any of these opinions, it is the position of this Report that the POC must perform the due diligence required to give the opinion, which duplicates the work performed by the LSC. Having two lawyers perform the same due diligence results in unnecessary expense. If the POC does not rely solely on the LSC's opinion and either gives the opinion or expresses any of the opinions contained in this paragraph without actually performing his own due diligence, the POC will be assuming the risk that the LSC's opinion is incorrect.

I. Factual Certificates

Opining counsel customarily obtain from appropriate persons certificates covering factual matters that are not readily verifiable by counsel and upon which counsel must base legal opinions. These matters usually include the identification of material contracts to which the client is a party, locations where the client has offices or employees or maintains inventory or other assets, the existence of liens or judgments affecting the client's assets and pending or overtly threatened litigation.

Counsel should not base an opinion solely on oral discussions with the client or a representative of the client. If an opinion is based on facts supplied by the client, these facts should be contained in a written certificate lest confusion arise concerning the facts disclosed in oral discussions.

Unless counsel has knowledge to the contrary, counsel may also rely upon the accuracy and truthfulness of the objective facts contained in the representations and warranties made by his client in the documents which relate to the transaction for which the opinion is being rendered. Counsel may not, however, rely on the legal conclusions contained in the representations and warranties in rendering his opinion. Counsel should also confirm that all facts required to support an opinion are obtained, whether they are contained in the representations and warranties or a separate certificate to counsel. If additional facts are needed to support the opinion, counsel will need to determine the additional facts that are needed to support the opinion.

Counsel should prepare the certificate for execution by a person whose position gives him knowledge of the facts in question. The certificate should include a statement that it is being delivered to counsel to be relied on in giving the opinion and, if appropriate, that it supplements the factual assertions contained in the documents that underlie the transaction (which factual assertions may be relied upon without written authorization from the client). Care should be taken that the certificate states objective facts (such as "The Company's material agreements are as follows: ________________.") rather than legal conclusions (such as statements that "the transaction does not violate the terms of any material agreement" or that the client "does business" in States A and B). Counsel is not obligated to investigate the accuracy of the matters contained in the certificates, but counsel may not rely on any fact in a certificate that counsel knows is not correct.

The addressee of the opinion will often request that the factual certificates on which the opining counsel relies be attached to the opinion or provided to the addressee. Attaching the certificates to the opinion or providing them to the addressee and his counsel avoids confusion as to the facts on which opining counsel is relying. In some cases, however, the information contained in the factual certificates will be either proprietary or confidential. If the information in the certificate is proprietary, the client will not want to have the certificate attached to the opinion (particularly if the opinion will be filed with a public agency as an exhibit to the agreement), but may be willing to give the addressee a copy of the certificate on a confidential basis. If the information is protected under a claim of privilege (such as counsel's knowledge of an unasserted claim which is possible of assertion), the disclosure to the addressee is likely to waive the privilege. If the addressee is willing to proceed with the transaction without disclosure of the privileged information, the addressee may properly ask opining counsel to confirm (without disclosing the contents of the certificate) that nothing in the certificate causes the opining counsel to be unable to give the opinion.

If the opinion relies on one or more factual certificates, the opinion should state: "In rendering the following opinions, we have relied, with your approval, as to factual matters that affect our opinions, on the matters set forth in the certificates furnished to us by __________________, copies of which are attached as Exhibit _____ to this opinion."

J. Investigation and Knowledge

Counsel is required to take all of the steps and make all of the legal and factual investigations described in this Report which are needed to give the specified opinions. There may be good reasons, however, to limit counsel's factual investigations and the addressee may be prepared to accept the opinion based on a limited factual review. In particular, the costs of a wider investigation must be weighed against the benefits that the addressee of the opinion will obtain from an opinion based on a broader investigation.

As used in this Report, unless otherwise specified, "knowledge" of an attorney means the actual present recollection of the attorney and the other persons in his firm who have given substantive attention to the transaction that is the subject of the opinion. Use of a knowledge qualification limits the opinion and the due diligence responsibility of the opining attorney. The use of a knowledge qualifier, and the selection of the qualifier appropriate for each qualified portion of the opinion will be a result of negotiation between the parties and should be based on the relative importance of the specific matter as to which the opinion will be given and the cost of performing the required factual investigation. The cost of the investigation will depend on the nature of the requested opinion, the size of the firm, the size of the client and the nature and size of the transactions and other matters on which the firm has represented the client.

Although the lawyer's duty to investigate facts may be expressly limited as described below, counsel giving substantive attention to the transaction is always required to advise the addressee if he has actual knowledge of facts which would cause the opinion to be incorrect.

In ascending order of due diligence responsibility, this Report recognizes five levels of factual inquiry:

(1) Counsel's opinion and investigation are limited to specific documents and expressly stated facts;

(2) Counsel is deemed to know only those facts which counsel would learn by performing the steps described below in the "to our knowledge" limitation;

(3) Counsel is deemed to know only those facts which counsel would learn by performing the steps described below in the "to our knowledge after limited investigation" limitation;

(4) Counsel is deemed to know only those facts which counsel would learn by performing the steps described below in the "to our knowledge after investigation" limitation; and

(5) Counsel's investigation is not limited.

Accordingly, the use of other modifying phrases such as "best of our knowledge," "due inquiry," "we do not know of" and "we have no knowledge" is discouraged, since these words do not add to, detract from or otherwise alter the meaning of the specific language of the knowledge qualification phrases recognized by this Report.

(1) Limited To Specified Documents and Facts. If the addressee is willing to accept an opinion based on a limited investigation, the opinion should state: "In rendering the following opinions, we have relied, with your approval, as to factual matters that affect our opinions, solely on our examination of [specified documents] and have made no independent verification of the facts contained in those documents [including the representations and warranties contained in the Agreement]."

(2) "To Our Knowledge." This phrase limits the knowledge of the opining attorney to the actual current recollection of those persons in his firm who have given substantive attention to the transaction that is the subject of the opinion and does not include constructive knowledge of matters or information. The phrase does not imply that the opining attorney or the firm has undertaken any independent investigation within the firm, with the client, or with any other persons to determine the existence or absence of any facts or circumstances, and no inference should be drawn merely from the opining attorney's or firm's past and current representation of the client. Stating that a matter is "to our knowledge" means only that the opining attorney and the attorneys of the firm who have given substantive attention to the transaction do not have a current recollection of any fact or circumstance contradicting the statement and should not imply that the firm knows the statement is correct.

(3) "To Our Knowledge After Limited Investigation." This phrase incorporates the level of knowledge described in "to our knowledge" and means that additional investigation has been made within the firm of those attorneys presently with the firm who have given substantive attention to matters relating to the client's affairs since the beginning of the client's last complete fiscal year, or such other period as the parties negotiate. It also requires that reasonable inquiry be made of those representatives of the client who are, in the judgment of opining counsel, likely to know the facts on which the opinion will be based. The phrase does not include the additional investigation and knowledge encompassed by the phrase "to our knowledge after investigation."

(4) "To Our Knowledge After Investigation." This phrase incorporates the level of knowledge described by the phrase "to our knowledge after limited investigation" and states that an additional investigation has been made with respect to the factual accuracy of the opinions stated. Unless specifically limited in the opinion, "after investigation" includes knowledge of facts contained in written materials in an attorney's or firm's files and encompasses the current recollection of every attorney presently in the firm. It indicates that an investigation, reasonable in light of the facts and circumstances of the transaction and the matters on which opinions are being rendered, has been made of the client's officers and all other persons and entities to whom it is reasonable to expect that

an inquiry be made. For example, it is expected that counsel will make an inquiry of those persons whom he believes are likely to have actual current of knowledge of whether the facts on which the opinion is based are correct. The phrase also implies that the opining attorney has a reasonable basis for believing the opinions expressed are factually correct.

K. Assumptions

Opining counsel is permitted to make assumptions about factual matters that affect the opinion, but as to which he has not made (and which by agreement of the parties is not expected to make) any investigation. Most of the assumptions in an opinion relate to matters involving parties other than opining counsel's client.

Counsel may not make a factual assumption which counsel knows to be incorrect and may not rely on any statement of fact in a document which counsel knows is not correct, unless counsel discloses to the addressee and addressee's counsel that the assumption or statement of facts is not correct and the addressee agrees that counsel may nevertheless make the assumption. Counsel also may not assume a specific legal issue on which counsel has been asked to render an opinion.

The most common assumptions are set forth below, and any additional assumptions made by counsel must be set forth specifically. For example, if counsel is asked to opine that the choice of Florida law will be upheld, counsel may have to assume that the domicile of his client (which depends on intent) is Florida.

Unless one of the following assumptions is specifically excluded from an opinion, all of the listed assumptions will be incorporated by reference into opinions incorporating this Report. Accordingly, the assumptions listed below do not have to be restated in the text of opinions:

(1) the legal capacity of each natural person;

(2) the legal existence of all parties to the transaction other than opining counsel's client;

(3) the power and authority of each person other than the client or person(s) acting on behalf of the client to execute, deliver and perform each document executed and delivered and to do each other act done or to be done by such person;

(4) the authorization, execution and delivery by each person other than the client or person(s) acting on behalf of the client of each document executed and delivered or to be executed and delivered by such person;

(5) the legality, validity, binding effect and enforceability as to each person other than the client or person(s) acting on behalf of the client of each document executed and delivered or to be executed and delivered and of each other act done or to be done by such person;

(6) the payment of all required documentary stamps, taxes and fees imposed upon the execution, filing or recording of documents;

(7) that there have been no undisclosed modifications of any provision of any document reviewed by opining counsel in connection with the rendering of the opinion and no undisclosed prior waiver of any right or remedy contained in any of the documents;

(8) the genuineness of each signature other than that of the client or person(s) acting on behalf of the client, the completeness of each document submitted to opining counsel, the authenticity of each document reviewed by opining counsel as an original, the conformity to the original of each document reviewed by opining counsel as a copy and the authenticity of the original of each document received by opining counsel as a copy;

(9) the truthfulness of each statement as to all factual matters otherwise not known to opining counsel to be untruthful contained in any document encompassed within the due diligence review undertaken by opining counsel;

(10) that the accuracy on the date of the opinion as well as on the date stated in all governmental certifications of each statement as to each factual matter contained in such governmental certifications;

(11) that the addressee has acted in good faith, without notice of adverse claims, and has complied with all laws applicable to it that affect the transaction;

(12) that the transaction complies with all tests of good faith, fairness, and conscionability required by law;

(13) that routine procedural matters such as service of process or qualification to do business in the relevant jurisdictions will be satisfied by the parties seeking to enforce the agreement;

(14) that all statutes, judicial and administrative decisions, and rules and regulations of governmental agencies constituting the law for which opining counsel is assuming responsibility are published (e.g., reported court decisions and the specialized reporting services of BNA, CCH and Prentice-Hall) or otherwise generally accessible (e.g., LEXIS or WESTLAW) in each case in a manner generally available (i.e., in terms of access and distribution following publication) to lawyers practicing in opining counsel's judicial circuit;

(15) that other agreements related to the transaction will be enforced as written;

(16) that no action, discretionary or otherwise, will be taken by or on behalf of opining counsel's client in the future that might result in a violation of law;

(17) that there are no other agreements or understandings among the parties that would modify the terms of the transaction documents or the respective rights or obligations of the parties to those documents;

(18) that with respect to the transaction and the transaction documents, there has been no mutual mistake of fact and there exists no fraud or duress; and

(19) that the constitutionality and validity of all relevant laws, regulations and agency actions unless a reported case has otherwise held or widespread concern has been expressed by commentators as reflected in materials which lawyers routinely consult.

L. Opinion

An opinion letter should state: "Based on the foregoing, and subject to the qualifications and limitations stated in this letter and in the Report, we are of the opinion that . . . ." The words "view," "conclusion" and the like may be acceptable instead of "opinion" when giving advice to one's own client, but not in opinions to third parties.

This Report takes the position that it is not appropriate to ask or to render "quitclaim" opinions stating "to our knowledge, we know of nothing that causes us to be of the opinion that . . . ." or "nothing has come to our attention that causes us to. . . ." In opinions on securities laws matters, however, the underwriters will usually require a "cold comfort" opinion from counsel for the issuer. This practice is unique to underwritten securities offerings and is intended to assist the underwriter to establish that he conducted his required due diligence investigation. Unless counsel has agreed to accept significant investigatory responsibilities in connection with the transaction (for example, as issuer's counsel in an underwritten offering), counsel should not provide (or be asked to provide) negative assurance opinions. (See Section IX.)

M. Reasoned Opinions

If legal uncertainty exists about the conclusion that the highest court in a jurisdiction would reach on a particular issue, only a "reasoned" opinion can be given. The uncertainty may exist for several reasons, including an absence of (or contradictory) statutory, regulatory or decisional law authority, recent transition in the area of law in question or the existence of serious public policy concerns which may affect a court's decision regarding the issue in question.

Typically, a reasoned opinion identifies the uncertain legal issue at hand, articulates the reasons for the uncertainty, analyzes the various plausible conclusions a court could reach in deciding the issue and offers a prediction as to which conclusion is most likely to be reached by the highest court. The manner in which the conclusion is stated depends upon the relative degree of the legal uncertainty presented by the issue at hand. There are three common formulations for the conclusion to a reasoned opinion, which, from most confident to least confident, are as follows: a court "would hold," a court "should hold" and a particular outcome "is more likely than not."

It is the position of this Report that it is generally inappropriate for the addressee of an opinion to ask opining counsel to render a reasoned opinion because the increase in cost outweighs the benefit to the addressee. Even though reasoned opinions sometimes help all parties to a transaction analyze issues and risks attendant to the transaction, this Report considers it the better practice for the addressee to be advised by its own counsel of the legal analysis which would be contained in a reasoned opinion.

If a reasoned opinion is delivered, it should read: "While the matter is not free from doubt, it is our view that, if the matter were properly presented to a court having jurisdiction, and assuming interpretation of the relevant law on a basis consistent with existing authority, [the court would hold ____________] or [the court should hold ______________] or [(a particular outcome) is more likely than not]."

N. Signature

If an attorney practices as an individual, he should sign his own name. If an attorney has formed a professional association or signs an opinion on behalf of a firm (including a firm that is a professional association), any one of the following is acceptable: "Name of attorney/On behalf of Firm," "Firm/By name of attorney," "Firm/Name of Attorney," "Firm/Name of attorney, a Partner or Officer, as appropriate," or the signed name of the firm only, provided the firm maintains an internal mechanism to identify the attorney delivering the opinion. For multi-state firms with offices in Florida, the attorney who signs an opinion on matters of Florida law should be a member of the Florida Bar. Opinions given by inside counsel may be signed in the individual's name or in his official capacity. In either case, inside counsel may be held liable for his own negligence, and the corporation generally will be liable for the authorized act of its agent. See Section I.H. above for a discussion of opining counsel's liability for opinions.

III. Opinions Relating to the Enforceability of Contracts

In transactions that involve contracts, the addressee will generally request an opinion to confirm that the contract will be enforceable against the client of the opining counsel. The "building blocks" of the enforceability opinion are opinions on the existence and organization of the entity entering the contract, its corporate power to enter the contract, the specific authorization of the contract, the execution and delivery of the contract and the absence of conflict between the contract and applicable laws, rules and regulations. This section presents a progression of opinions which culminates in the opinion that the contract is enforceable against the opining counsel's client.

A. Corporate Status

An opinion on the status of a corporation or other entity is given in most transactions. The form of opinion typically requested has been to the effect that the corporation is a corporation, duly incorporated, validly existing and in good standing under the laws of a particular jurisdiction. This Report takes the position that portions of the requested opinion are unnecessary and that some of the terms are unclear. This Report recommends that for a Florida corporation, the appropriate opinion should be: "The Company has been incorporated under the Florida Business Corporation Act [or the Florida General Corporation Act] and its status is active."

Although § 607.0128(2)(b)(1) of the Florida Business Corporation Act ("FBCA") uses the phrase "duly incorporated," the terms "duly" and "validly" are not used in any of the forms of opinion recommended by this Report because there is no clear understanding as to what these terms mean or whether they add to the opinion. Some commentators suggest that the term "validly incorporated" may be used to indicate that the company is a de jure as opposed to de facto corporation. Because the "has been incorporated" opinion will be supported by a certificate of the Secretary of State as to the filing of the articles of incorporation, the corporation will necessarily be a de jure corporation.

The opinion that a corporation "has been incorporated" may be given on the basis of Section 607.0203 of the FBCA and a certificate of the Secretary of State that the corporation's articles of incorporation have been filed by the Department of State. Section 607.0203 of the FBCA states that the Department of State's filing of the articles of incorporation of a corporation is conclusive proof that the incorporator(s) satisfied all conditions precedent to incorporation, except in a proceeding brought by the state to cancel or revoke the incorporation. This Report takes the position that the "has been incorporated" opinion is the appropriate opinion to be given instead of the commonly-given opinion that the entity "is a corporation, duly incorporated."

Section 607.0128 of the FBCA provides for the Department of State to issue a "certificate of status" for a corporation that states, among other things, that (1) the corporation is duly incorporated, (2) all fees and penalties owed by the corporation to the Department have been paid, (3) the corporation's most recent annual report has been delivered to the Department for filing, and (4) articles of dissolution of the corporation have not been filed. To ensure that dissolution proceedings have not been commenced, opining counsel should also determine from a review of the records of the corporation and from a certificate of an officer of the corporation that no steps leading to the corporation's dissolution have been taken.

For example, if counsel is aware that resolutions approving the dissolution of the corporation have been adopted, but articles of dissolution have not been filed, counsel may give the active status opinion, but should disclose the adoption of the resolutions in the opinion and consider the effect of the resolutions on the opinions being given with respect to the transaction.

The Department's form of certificate of status states that the corporation's "status is active." The active status opinion for a Florida corporation replaces the typical opinion that a corporation is "validly existing and in good standing."

B. Organization

An opinion that the corporation was properly organized is often requested in addition to the corporate status opinion. "Organization" is discussed in Section

607.0205 of the FBCA, and refers to the actions taken in the initial stages of a corporation's existence. Organization under the FBCA requires the adoption of bylaws and the election of directors and officers.

To render this opinion, counsel must review the minute books of the corporation to confirm that the organizational steps were taken in conformity with Florida corporate law in effect at the time the corporation was organized. Counsel should, at a minimum, require the client to adopt bylaws and to elect directors and officers if it is not clear from the corporate records that all of these actions were taken. It may also be necessary to ratify or confirm those prior corporate actions for which complete records do not exist.

The opinion should read: "The Company was organized under the Florida Business Corporation Act [or prior law, as applicable]."

C. Qualification and Good Standing in Foreign Jurisdictions

Opinions on qualification to do business have generally been requested in one of three forms: The corporation is qualified and in good standing (1) in each jurisdiction in which it owns or leases property or conducts business; (2) in each jurisdiction in which the nature of its business or properties requires it to be qualified; or (3) in each jurisdiction which requires qualification except to the extent that failure to qualify would not have a material adverse impact on the corporation.

This Report requires instead that counsel render an affirmative opinion on this issue as follows: "To our knowledge after limited investigation, the Company is required to be qualified as a foreign corporation in the States of _______________, _______________ and _______________. Based on the Certificates of Good Standing [or other appropriate names of certificates] issued by the States of _______________, _______________ and _______________, the Company is qualified as a foreign corporation to conduct business in these States."

To give an opinion on qualification, counsel will have to determine the activities that are carried on and the assets that are owned by the corporation in various jurisdictions. This will require a certificate from an officer of the corporation that describes the actual activities and assets of the corporation in other jurisdictions. Based on these facts, counsel must make a legal judgment as to whether or not qualification is required in each jurisdiction. Counsel may not rely on an officer's certificate that merely contains a legal conclusion reciting the jurisdictions in which the corporation is "doing business" (a legal concept which is defined differently in different states).

If counsel determines that qualification is required, counsel should assist the client in qualifying and should obtain a certificate from the appropriate public official(s) of each relevant state to confirm that the corporation is qualified or authorized. In determining which are the agencies from which public authority documents and certificates should be obtained in a particular jurisdiction, opining counsel may properly rely on advice from a corporation service company that regularly does business in that jurisdiction. For most states, the Department of State (or another government office or agency, or a private organization that has access to government files) issues a certificate (sometimes called a Subsisting or Good Standing Certificate) that may be relied upon by counsel as the sole basis for his opinion, but in other states a certificate from taxing or other authorities will also be required. This reliance on certificate(s) of governmental authorities should be explicitly stated, and the text of the opinion should explicitly track the language of the certificates ("validly subsisting" or "validly existing" or the like).

This Report takes the position that, provided Florida counsel considers himself qualified to opine on this specific matter of foreign law, it is reasonable for Florida counsel to give opinions that qualification to do business in foreign jurisdictions is not necessary or to give an opinion based on the certificate of public officials that the corporation is qualified in the foreign jurisdiction. In this regard, the discussion in Section II.G. of this Report (relating to opinions by Florida counsel on matters of foreign law and the right of the addressee to require an opinion of local counsel on matters of foreign law) is relevant.

The issuance of a certificate by the appropriate official in a foreign jurisdiction and the delivery of an opinion based upon it that the corporation is validly subsisting or validly existing in a foreign jurisdiction is limited to the corporate qualification to do business in the foreign jurisdiction and is not an opinion that the corporation has paid all taxes and otherwise complied with all laws of the foreign jurisdiction.

D. Corporate Power

Corporate power of a Florida corporation is derived from the FBCA, other applicable statutes and the corporation's articles of incorporation and bylaws. The recommended form of opinion for Florida corporations is: "The Company has the corporate power to conduct its business and to execute and deliver the Agreement and to perform its obligations under the Agreement."

The words "own its properties" are not needed in the opinion because to "conduct its business" includes all of the actions which are part of the business of the corporation, including the ownership of property. It is also unnecessary to state that the corporation has "full," "all" or "all necessary" corporate power and authority. These terms do not add to the opinion. Similarly, the opinion does not speak of power to "enter into" or "consummate" the agreement because these terms are ambiguous and are otherwise covered by the recommended form of opinion.

To render this opinion, counsel should review the FBCA and, if the corporation is in a regulated industry, other Florida and Federal laws which define the powers of entities such as the corporation. Counsel should examine the powers (and limits, if any) stated in the articles of incorporation and the bylaws of the corporation to confirm that the corporation has the power to conduct its businesses. To confirm that the bylaws are complete and are in effect, counsel should either (1) review the minute book to confirm their adoption, completeness and effectiveness or (2) obtain a certificate from an officer of the corporation (to which the current bylaws should be attached) confirming the date on which the bylaws were adopted by the Board of Directors or the shareholders, as applicable, and that the bylaws are complete and current.

E. Authorization by the Corporation

The reasonable expectation of the addressee is that counsel will confirm that he has no reason to doubt that the person(s) now acting on behalf of the corporation have proper authority to do so and that all necessary approvals by the Board of Directors and shareholders have been taken or obtained. In rendering this opinion, counsel should rely on the affirmative acts of the corporation and its officers, directors and agents and not on principles of estoppel, apparent authority, waiver and the like as the basis for his opinion regarding approval of the Agreement. The recommended form of opinion is: "The Company has authorized the execution, delivery and performance of the Agreement by all necessary corporate action."

To determine whether the corporation has authorized the transaction, counsel should review the applicable statutes, the articles of incorporation and bylaws, the minutes of the meeting (or other corporate action) at which the specific resolutions relating to the transaction were adopted by the Board of Directors and shareholders, and any shareholder agreements, voting trusts or other agreements of which the corporation or counsel is aware that may affect the authorization of the transaction. Opining counsel should request and rely on a certificate from an officer that the corporate documents made available to him constitute all of the documents which may affect the authorization of the transaction and that these documents (other than the articles of incorporation supplied by the Department of State) are true and correct and have not been rescinded or repealed.

In theory, rendering this opinion would also require verification that all the steps in the chain of the elections of directors, transfers of shares, all amendments to the bylaws, and all comparable matters since the corporation's formation were performed in accordance with the corporate law in effect when the actions were taken. For non-publicly owned corporations and corporations that have not existed for a long period, counsel should examine the records of the corporation's proceedings to confirm that the person(s) now acting on behalf of the corporation have authority to do so.

The cost of this due diligence may be disproportionately high in relation to the benefit obtained, however, if the corporation has been active for a long time or if it is publicly-owned. In addition, corporate records may be missing for valid reasons, and it may not be possible to locate these missing records after diligent search. In each of these circumstances, this Report takes the position that counsel may rely on the so-called "presumption of regularity and continuity" as the basis for concluding that all steps in the chain of the election of directors presently in office have all been properly taken. The presumption of regularity and continuity, which is not a legal doctrine, but rather a practical expedient under these circumstances, also permits counsel to assume facts that customarily would be reflected in the historical records of a corporation.

Counsel may not rely on the presumption of regularity and continuity if he becomes aware through his review of the corporate documents authorizing the transaction, or the bylaws, certificates, or any other document furnished to him by the corporation, that there is likely to be a problem with the facts on which he proposes to rely (i.e., questions as to the presence of a quorum at a particular meeting, the completeness of meeting notices, the vote taken on the election of directors by the shareholders, or other historic activities). Similarly, he may not assume facts that missing documents would customarily show if he has any reason to believe that the missing records would show anything contrary to the presumed facts.

If counsel relies on the presumption of regularity and continuity regarding all or parts of the minutes of the Board of Directors' meetings and shareholders' meetings or to assume historical facts, this reliance must be expressly disclosed in the opinion.

F. Execution and Delivery of the Contract

The signing of a contract is a physical act which counsel can observe. If not observed, counsel should obtain an officer's certificate stating the name of the person(s) who signed the document and confirming the identity of these persons and the genuineness of their signatures. Counsel should confirm that the person(s) executing the agreement was authorized to do so in the resolutions authorizing the agreement itself.

Delivery of a contract is a matter of the intention of the parties and does not require any specific physical act. In rendering an opinion that the contract has been "delivered," opining counsel must satisfy himself (by an officer's certificate or otherwise) that the corporation does not have any unfulfilled conditions or other contingencies that must be satisfied before the corporation intends for the contract to be effective. This officer's certificate would state that the corporation has given possession of the document to the addressee with the intent to form an immediately binding agreement.

The recommended form of opinion is: "The Agreement has been executed and delivered by the Company."

G. No Breach or Default

The following opinion is recommended: "The execution and delivery of the Agreement, the performance by the Company of its obligations under the Agreement and the exercise by the Company of the rights created by the Agreement do not (i) violate the Company's articles of incorporation or bylaws;

(ii) to our knowledge [as limited pursuant to Section II.J. of this Report] constitute a breach of or a default under any agreement or instrument to which the Company is a party or by which it or its assets are bound or result in the creation of a mortgage, security interest or other encumbrance upon the assets of the Company (except as set forth in the Agreement); (iii) to our knowledge [as limited pursuant to Section II.J. of this Report], violate a judgment, decree or order of any court or administrative tribunal, which judgment, decree or order is binding on the Company or its assets; or (iv) violate any Federal or Florida law, rule or regulation."

The due diligence required to opine that a contract does not violate the corporation's articles of incorporation and bylaws requires opining counsel to review appropriately identified copies of those documents.

The opinion as to whether the proposed transaction violates, constitutes a breach of, or a default under, other agreements is more difficult, especially if the corporation is large or is a party to many agreements. Often, counsel will want to discuss the scope of his investigation with the addressee's counsel and agree upon appropriate materiality standards for his review. (See Section II.J. above). To complete the investigation needed to give this opinion, all agreements must be identified for counsel. To support his due diligence, counsel should obtain a certificate from the corporation setting forth that the agreements being reviewed are all of the corporation's agreements that meet the agreed-upon materiality criteria, and he must review each of these agreements. If any of the agreements is an oral agreement, the terms of it must be set forth in full in the certificate. In reviewing these disclosed agreements, counsel may assume that each of these agreements will be performed and enforced in accordance with its terms. Opining counsel is not obligated to resolve a factual issue (such as meeting a debt to equity ratio) that is not readily apparent. If counsel identifies such an issue, he should request a certificate from the appropriate person on the identified factual issues.

Opining counsel may rely upon the certificate unless he has actual knowledge of agreements incorrectly excluded from the certificate. Counsel for the addressee should be willing to allow opining counsel to exclude from his opinion all matters requiring financial information or relating to compliance with financial covenants, and should instead rely on certificates from the corporation or its accountant as to these matters. In these cases, counsel should identify these matters to the addressee's counsel so that addressee's counsel can receive appropriate assurances from the corporation and its accountants on these issues.

Similar problems of due diligence exist for an opinion as to violations of judgments, decrees or orders. In these cases, agreements as to materiality and the scope of investigation should be agreed upon with addressee's counsel. Counsel should generally not have to conduct an independent investigation on these issues and should be permitted to rely on a certificate as to outstanding orders, judgments and decrees applicable to the corporation. If such an investigation is performed by opining counsel, this should be noted in the opinion.

With respect to the opinion that the execution, delivery and performance of the contract will not violate any law, rule or regulation, this Report takes the position that this opinion covers only provisions of law that prohibit specified conduct and that impose fines, penalties or other sanctions for a violation of these provisions. Common law doctrines, such as those of contracts or torts, are not encompassed by this opinion. Hence, if performance of the contract violates another contract to which the opining counsel's client is a party or if performance tortiously interferes with another person's rights, this kind of violation or tortious interference would not be a "violation of law" covered by this opinion (although it might be a violation of an agreement and therefore be discloseable in another part of the opinion).

Counsel must be familiar with the cases, laws, statutes and regulations affecting the contract and the client's business relating to the contract. Counsel should consider his ethical obligation to be knowledgeable in the law in the area to which the contract relates (Section 4-1.1 of the Rules of Professional Conduct). In appropriate circumstances, specialist counsel with expertise in the areas of law relating to the contract or the client should be selected. (See Section II.H. regarding opinions of specialist counsel and the relationship between the role of principal opining counsel and the role of specialist counsel.) Unless otherwise agreed, the opinion described in this section analyzes only the entering into and performance of the agreement in determining if these acts violate any laws. In this regard, it is generally inappropriate to request an opinion to the effect that the client is in compliance with all laws or "material" laws of a jurisdiction.

Finally, counsel may want to discuss with addressee's counsel the types of laws to be covered by the opinion and the types of laws to be excluded from the opinion. For example, in a real estate financing of a hotel, it may be appropriate to agree to limit the investigation of applicable statutes, laws or regulations to an investigation of the zoning on the property, but not to include an investigation to determine whether the restaurant located in the hotel is in compliance with local health and safety laws. (See Section II.G. for a discussion of laws that are presumed excluded unless specifically included.)

The extent of these limitations should be agreed upon by opining counsel and addressee's counsel as early in the transaction as possible.

H. No Required Consents

An opinion is usually requested that, except as specified, no notice, report or other filing or registration with, and no consent, approval or authorization of, any Federal, Florida or local governmental authority is required to be submitted, made or obtained in connection with the execution and delivery of the contract and the performance of the fundamental obligations that are central to the contract.

To give this opinion, counsel must consider which governmental authorities have jurisdiction over the client and the matters contemplated by the contract.

These authorities will vary among transactions and the participants in the transactions. Governmental authorities include Federal, state and local authorities, bureaus, commissions, agencies, boards or other subdivisions. After determining which governmental authorities have jurisdiction, counsel must then investigate whether consents or registrations will be required from these authorities. If required, counsel should advise the client and assist him in obtaining these consents. Counsel should discuss with the addressee's counsel the scope of required consents, and the opinion may be limited, if agreed upon by the addressee's counsel, to consents and approvals of governmental authorities which, if not obtained, could have a material adverse impact on the transaction contemplated by the contract.

I. Valid, Binding and Enforceable (The Remedies Opinion)

As noted in the introduction to this Section, the culmination of the opinions concerning the corporation, the authorization, execution and delivery of the contract and the contract itself, is that the contract is valid, binding on the corporation and enforceable against it. The addressee wants the assurance that it will be able to obtain, in an appropriate forum, the "benefit of its bargain." The recommended opinion is:

> Subject to the limitations contained in the next paragraph, the Agreement is a valid and binding obligation of the Company enforceable against the Company under the law of Florida and the Federal law of the United States.

Some opinions state that a contract is "a legal, valid and binding obligation enforceable in accordance with its terms." This Report takes the position that the term "legal" adds nothing of substance to the opinion and should be deleted and that the words "in accordance with its terms" makes the opinion virtually impossible to render. Many commentators have discussed the term "enforceable" or "enforceable in accordance with its terms," and considerable conflict exists as to their scope. It is the position of this Report that a contract is enforceable if an ultimate remedy is available to the addressee (barring the corporation's insolvency) to obtain the benefit of its bargain. "Enforceable" does not mean that a court will enforce every provision of the contract exactly as it is written. As a result, opining counsel may include (and addressees should accept) the general limitations on and exceptions to the enforceability opinion that are contained in the form of opinion set forth below and in Exhibit A.

If the contract provides that it is governed by Florida law or does not contain a governing law provision, the term "valid" means that the contract is of a type that may be enforced generally under Florida and Federal law and that there are no laws or regulations that prohibit the making or performance of the contract. (See the discussion below regarding contracts governed by the law of another jurisdiction.) For example, various types of indemnification contracts sometimes are held to be invalid on the ground that they are contrary to public policy. To be satisfied that the contract is not invalid, the opining attorney should conduct all legal investigations necessary to be familiar with the particular laws and public policies that relate to each aspect of the contract.

For example, if a contract contains a non-competition provision, it is necessary to review the specific Florida Statutes relating to non-competition agreements. Similarly, if the transaction involves a loan, it will be necessary to review the Florida Statutes relating to usury if an opinion is given as to that issue.

A contract is "binding" upon a particular party if a court concludes that it should be enforced in some manner and to some extent because all necessary conditions have been met. Some of the necessary conditions are that the contract (a) was made by a person with legal capacity, (b) is binding upon the other parties, and (c) was made for consideration. The statute of frauds also should be considered as a potential defense against the existence of some oral contracts. In rendering opinions, counsel may make the assumptions set forth in Section II.K. of this Report, including those relating to the legal capacity of all individuals and the legal existence of all parties other than his client and the binding effect of the contract on parties other than his own client. He must, however, conduct the legal and factual investigation needed to satisfy himself that all other necessary conditions have been met that may affect whether his own client is bound by the contract.

The limitation proposed in this Report recognizes that opining counsel can assure the addressee that an enforceable contract has been made, but cannot provide assurance, directly or by implication, as to how any particular provision of the contract will be treated by a particular court. This Report also recognizes the common "equitable principles" limitation, including limitations commonly imposed by courts that contracts must be commercially reasonable and conscionable and that the parties must have acted in good faith. This Report also rejects the practice of listing numerous limitations followed by an opinion to the effect that notwithstanding the stated limitations, the addressee will be able to obtain the benefit of its bargain. Structuring the opinion in this manner fails to acknowledge that some limitations (such as insolvency) may act as an absolute bar to enforcement of all or part of the contract.

Accordingly, this Report recognizes that in addition to limitations as to how a contract will be enforced, there are circumstances under which the entire contract or parts of it may not be enforced at all. The most common exception to enforceability is the bankruptcy or insolvency exception. Because this exception could be applied to all contracts, it almost always is stated as an exception in the remedies opinion. Similarly, this Report excludes compliance with fraudulent conveyance and fraudulent transfer statutes because the determination as to whether a transaction is a fraudulent conveyance or fraudulent transfer is entirely factual and can affect enforceability of all or part of the contract.

Many courts may refuse to enforce certain contract provisions in specific fact situations. As a result, many attorneys have included additional exceptions to enforceability covering oral modifications, specific performance, non-competition, usury and arbitration, to name only a few. As a practical matter, it is impossible to list every possible exception that may exist to enforceability of a contract "in accordance with its terms," especially if that phrase means that each and every term would be enforceable as it is written. It is the position of this Report, therefore, that it is appropriate for an attorney to give the broad enforceability opinion set forth above, followed by the following general limitations and exceptions:

> Our opinion concerning the validity, binding effect and enforceability of the Agreement means that (a) the Agreement constitutes an effective contract under applicable law, (b) the Agreement is not invalid in its entirety because of a specific statutory prohibition or public policy and is not subject in its entirety to a contractual defense and (c) subject to the last sentence of this paragraph, some remedy is available if the Company is in material default under the Agreement. This opinion does not mean that (a) any particular remedy is available upon a material default or (b) every provision of the Agreement will be upheld or enforced in any or each circumstance by a court. Furthermore, the validity, binding effect and enforceability of the Agreement may be limited or otherwise affected by (a) bankruptcy, insolvency, reorganization, moratorium, fraudulent conveyance or other similar statutes, rules, regulations or other laws affecting the enforcement of creditors' rights and remedies generally and (b) the unavailability of, or limitation on the availability of, a particular right or remedy (whether in a proceeding in equity or at law) because of an equitable principle or a requirement as to commercial reasonableness, conscionability or good faith.

In giving opinions on agreements pursuant to Federal securities laws, it also is appropriate to exclude indemnity provisions from the scope of the enforceability opinion.

If the contract contains a governing law provision, the remedies opinion will cover the enforceability of that provision, unless the governing law provision is expressly excluded from the opinion. If the contract provides that it is governed by Florida law, the remedies opinion means that a Florida court will give effect to the governing law provision and apply Florida law. If the contract states that it is governed by the law of another jurisdiction, however, the remedies opinion means that a Florida court will apply the internal law of the other jurisdiction. If counsel is asked to give an opinion on the assumption, contrary to the express terms of the contract, that Florida law applies for purposes of his remedies opinion, counsel should exclude the governing law provision from his opinion.

This Report recognizes that in particular circumstances there may be one or more provisions in a contract that are of special importance to the addressee and on which the addressee wants express assurance. The addressee may want assurance, for example, as to whether a contract provision calling for arbitration of disputes will be enforced, or whether a court will enforce a venue provision, whether a court will enforce a choice of law provision, or whether the addressee will be able to foreclose a mortgage on real property or take possession of and sell personal property that is subject to a security interest. It is not improper for the addressee to seek opinions on such matters, and opining counsel must do the legal investigation necessary to permit him, to the extent possible, to give such opinions. If, following his investigation, counsel concludes that any specifically requested opinion is contrary to applicable law, he should advise the addressee's counsel and decline to give the opinion.

IV. Opinions Relating to the Issuance and Transfer of Securities

When securities are issued by a corporation or are transferred, the purchaser generally will request a series of opinions regarding the corporation and its securities.

A. Capitalization

The recommended opinion on the capitalization of a corporation is: "The Company's authorized capitalization consists of ____________ common shares [and other securities as appropriate], of which ____________ common shares [and other securities as appropriate] are outstanding."

The total authorized capitalization of a corporation is stated in its articles of incorporation. To give this opinion, counsel needs to review a certified copy of the articles of incorporation (as amended) and use the information taken from the articles in rendering his opinion.

The opinion regarding outstanding securities covers all issuances of securities by the corporation. Because this analysis is central to counsel's ability to give an opinion on the issuance of securities, counsel must review the articles of incorporation, the bylaws and the actions of the Board of Directors each time securities were issued. Counsel must then compare these actions with the requirements of the governing corporate law in effect at the time of issuance.

Counsel will also have to be satisfied that preemptive rights do not exist for any of the shares (or that they were complied with) and that the consideration paid for the shares was adequate under Florida law. If shares were issued as a stock dividend prior to July 1, 1990, counsel should satisfy himself by reviewing the resolutions authorizing the dividend or obtain a certificate from the appropriate officer stating that adequate retained earnings existed at the time the stock dividend was declared.

The word "duly" has not been included in this opinion, or in the opinions on corporate status and organization, because it does not add to the opinion.

In rendering this opinion, counsel should obtain data on issued and outstanding securities from the transfer agent for publicly traded securities. For non-publicly traded securities, counsel should obtain a certificate from the officer of the corporation responsible for the books and records relating to stock issuances that the books and records are complete. Counsel should then review these records to determine the number of each class of issued and outstanding securities. Counsel should also obtain a certificate regarding other agreements or rights to purchase the corporation's securities (i.e., options, warrants, subscription rights, conversion rights, etc.) and disclose these rights in the opinion. It is not appropriate to rely on the corporation's financial statements as to the number and type of outstanding securities because changes may have occurred since the date of these financial statements.

If a Corporation has treasury shares and this fact is relevant to the opinion, counsel should obtain a certificate as to the number of treasury shares from the corporation's registrar or transfer agent (if the securities are publicly traded) or the officer who maintains the corporation's stock records (if it is not publicly traded). The words "and [number] shares are held in the treasury" should be added after the word "outstanding." Under the FBCA, treasury shares automatically revert to authorized but unissued shares unless otherwise provided in the articles of incorporation.

Just as in the opinion regarding authorization by the corporation (See Section III.E.), if the corporation has been active for a long time or if it is publicly owned, or if its records are missing for valid reasons, the presumption of regularity and continuity will permit opining counsel to assume (unless he knows of a reason to doubt the correctness of the assumption) that the shares of a corporation were issued for value and were issued pursuant to proper authority. The presumption of regularity and continuity is not a legal doctrine, but is a practical expedient to avoid the expense in limited circumstances of reviewing each stock issuance, the minutes of each meeting at which the issuances were authorized, the circumstances of the issuances and the underlying authority of the persons who authorized and issued the securities. If counsel relies upon the presumption of regularity and continuity, this reliance must be expressly stated in the opinion.

It is the position of this Report that, if the records of the corporation show that a specified number of shares are outstanding, and provided counsel does not know that there may have been some flaw in any of the issuances and no one has raised a question concerning the validity of any issuance, counsel may assume that the shares were properly issued.

B. Fully Paid and Nonassessable

The recommended opinion is: "The Shares are fully paid and nonassessable."

Shares may be issued under Florida law even if they are not fully paid, provided the holder has a continuing obligation to pay the balance of the purchase price. An opinion that shares are "fully paid" is factual and counsel may rely on a certificate of an officer of the corporation that no consideration for the shares remains unpaid.

C. Additional Securities

The recommended language is: "There are no agreements or other documents, except as identified in ____________, pursuant to which the Company may be required to authorize or issue additional securities." Counsel should obtain a certificate from an appropriate officer of the corporation identifying all contracts relating to the issuance of additional securities and counsel must review these contracts.

D. Title to Shares and Freedom from Restrictions

A "title" opinion is usually sought by a purchaser acquiring securities in a secondary sales transaction. Generally, an opinion is requested that the purchaser is receiving good title to the securities being sold, free and clear of liens and encumbrances. The primary weakness with this language is that it uses "title concepts" borrowed from real property law for a situation in which real property law does not apply.

This Report takes a different approach to this issue. The law governing securities transfers, Chapter 678 of the Florida Statutes, does not use the term "title," but speaks instead of rights in a security. Under the Uniform Commercial Code, the formulation of the concept of "good title" is an acquisition "free of any adverse claim," in which "adverse claim" is defined as "a claim that a transfer was or would be wrongful or that a particular adverse party is the owner of or has an interest in the security." See F.S. § 678.301.

It is problematic for seller's or the pledgor's counsel to give an opinion on the quality of the title that the purchaser will acquire in a security, because the opinion will depend, in part, on the purchaser's knowledge of adverse interests against the seller's ownership interest in the security. For example, the seller may have acquired his rights in the security as a bona fide purchaser, cutting off adverse claims for as long as he owns the security, but when he subsequently transfers the security to a purchaser who has notice of these claims, these claims will once again attach. In rendering this opinion, counsel may assume that the purchaser is not aware of any claims relating to the ownership of the securities to be acquired.

This Report recommends the following opinion: "Upon delivery of the Shares [or other securities] to the purchaser and payment in accordance with the Agreement, the purchaser will acquire the ownership rights to the Shares [or other securities] free, to our knowledge [as limited in accordance with Section II.J. of this Report], of all adverse claims of which the purchaser did not have notice."

To give this opinion, counsel should examine each certificate representing the securities to be transferred to determine the name of the record owner, the endorsements required to transfer the securities and all restrictions against transfer identified on the certificate. A certificate from the seller should also be obtained that the seller has no knowledge of any claims asserted against his ownership, or the ownership of these securities generally, and that, except as disclosed, there are no encumbrances or liens against his interest in the security. The seller should also represent that there are no agreements which restrict his ability to transfer the securities. Further, counsel should examine the articles of incorporation and bylaws for restrictions on transfers of securities.

E. Reservation of Shares

The recommended language is: "The Company has reserved the shares of [security] issuable upon conversion of the [preferred stock, debentures, etc.] at the conversion prices and under the other terms and conditions provided for in [the appropriate instrument]."

If the adjustment provisions relating to dilution and recapitalization will cause the number of shares or other units of the security to change (rather than the more customary adjustment to the conversion price), counsel should add: "We express no opinion, however, on the number of [securities] reserved if adjustment in that number is required under the terms of [specified section of the controlling document]."

F. Preemptive Rights

Counsel must review the original articles of incorporation and all amendments to them to give an opinion as to whether preemptive rights exist for specified securities. If a corporation was formed before January 1, 1976, preemptive rights existed unless the articles otherwise provided. Thereafter, unless the articles provided for preemptive rights, none existed. If preemptive rights existed at the time of issuance, that fact should be noted in the opinion, and counsel must review the corporate records to determine if the rights were exercised and honored, or if they were waived in prior issuances of securities.

V. Opinions on Litigation

In numerous transactions, the addressee will want a confirmation from opining counsel that no litigation exists or is overtly threatened that would jeopardize the ability of counsel's client to perform under the agreement or diminish the value of that which is being sold (such as assets or securities) to the addressee.

A litigation opinion actually is not a legal opinion but is a representation by counsel that, based on his described investigation, he knows of no litigation except that which is disclosed. Because the opinion constitutes a statement of counsel's knowledge, the scope of counsel's due diligence should be defined by using one of the limitations in Section II.J. of this Report.

This Report takes the position that in most cases, the appropriate due diligence will be reflected by the phrase "to our knowledge after limited investigation." This level of due diligence requires counsel to ask for information about pending or overtly threatened actions and proceedings from (1) all attorneys presently with his firm who have given substantive attention to matters relating to the client's affairs since the beginning of the client's last complete fiscal year or for such period as is agreed upon, and (2) those representatives of the client who are, in counsel's opinion, likely to know about pending or overtly threatened litigation. Based on this inquiry, counsel should prepare a list of all outstanding litigation matters that meet the agreed-upon criteria, and should attach this list as a schedule to his opinion.

Unless specifically agreed to by opining counsel, it is not necessary for opining counsel to search public records to determine whether or not litigation is ongoing against his client. If court records are examined (such as the records of courts sitting in the location of the corporation's principal office), the scope of the examination should be disclosed.

The recommended form of opinion is: "To our knowledge [after limited investigation, or after investigation] and except as set forth on Schedule—to this opinion, we have no knowledge of any pending or overtly threatened actions, claims, investigations or other proceedings against the Company."

In this Report, the term "overtly threatened" has the meaning set forth in the American Bar Association *Auditor's Letter Handbook* (1975). It has the meaning that a potential claimant has manifested to the client an awareness of and present intention to assert a possible claim.

"Proceedings" are actions of an adjudicatory nature, as opposed to actions merely involving the filing of reports or other information with a governmental body. A governmental investigation generally will constitute a "proceeding" if the corporation has been designated as a "target" of an investigation. If an agency institutes formal proceedings only after an investigation is concluded, a "proceeding" will not be pending, but may have been overtly threatened and should be included in the litigation schedule.

The schedule attached to the opinion should contain (1) the name of the action or proceeding, (2) the court or authority in which it is pending (if a claim has not been filed, the schedule should note that the claim is overtly threatened), and (3) the name of counsel representing the corporation in the matter. The opinion and the schedule should not discuss the substance and status of the litigation, even if opining counsel's firm is handling the matter. Although additional information on litigation is generally contained in attorneys' responses to auditors' inquiries, the information provided in opinions should be more restricted because the addressee does not have the same obligation to the corporation as its auditor.

Opining counsel should exercise extreme caution if requested to opine upon the existence of "material" litigation or to opine on litigation that would have a material adverse effect on the corporation. These requests require counsel to evaluate the probable outcome of litigation, the possible amount of the loss and its effect on the financial condition of the corporation. These evaluations are generally beyond the ability and knowledge of the opining counsel. This Report takes the position that opining counsel should list all pending or overtly threatened litigation against the corporation of which he learns through his due diligence and should avoid attempting to determine materiality. The parties may, of course, agree that only litigation in which potential damages exceed a given amount are required to be listed.

If the addressees' due diligence includes inquiries regarding the matters disclosed on the schedule attached to the opinion, counsel may discuss pending or threatened litigation with the addressee and addressee's counsel only if opining counsel's client consents. Unless expressly authorized, however, counsel should not discuss litigation with the addressee or addressee's counsel in a way that would waive the attorney/client privilege or give confidential information to the addressee.

1444 The Business Lawyer; Vol. 46, August 1991

EXHIBIT A

Date: *[(Date of closing of captioned transaction)]*

Addressee(s)
[(address)]

Re. *[Insert brief description of transaction such as "Transaction [between/among]ABC Company, Addressee"*[1]*]*

Ladies and Gentlemen:

We have acted as counsel to the ABC Company (the "Company") in connection with the referenced transaction. In that transaction, the Company entered into the *[(insert name of agreement)]* dated *[insert date] [between/among]* the Company and ______________________________ (the "Addressee") (the "Agreement"[2]) in which *[insert brief description of transaction]*. This opinion is furnished pursuant to *[your request—See Section II.E. of the Report]* Section _____ of the Agreement, and is given with the consent of the Company. Capitalized terms not otherwise defined in this opinion have the definitions set forth in the Agreement.

We do not express any opinion concerning any law other than the law of Florida *[If the opinion involves opinions on the general corporate law of another state, add: the General Corporation Law of the State of __________]* and the Federal law of the United States.

This opinion has been prepared and is to be construed in accordance with the Report on Standards For Florida Opinions dated April 8, 1991 issued by the Business Law Section of The Florida Bar (the "Report"). The Report is incorporated by reference into this opinion. *[By incorporating the Report, the issuer of the opinion is required to complete the due diligence required for each opinion rendered in the opinion.]*

[If the parties to the transaction and their counsel have agreed that the opinion may be based solely on limited documents and facts (See Section II.J. of the Report), the following paragraph should be included. Section II.J. of the Report discusses the five levels of factual inquiry which may apply to specific opinions prepared and construed in accordance with the Report. It is unlikely that a single level of inquiry will be appropriate for all opinions given in the opinion. Instead, different levels of factual inquiry may be appropriate for the various opinions which are given in the opinion.]

---

1. The italicized portions of the text throughout this form of opinion are informational only and should not be included in the opinion.
2. If no agreement is involved, provide a brief description of the principal transaction documents.

In rendering the following opinions, we have relied, with your approval, as to factual matters that affect our opinions solely, on our examination of the following documents and have made no independent verification of the facts asserted to be true and correct in those documents, including the factual representations and warranties contained in the Agreement: *[List documents with specificity. If factual certificates are relied upon to support any of the opinions, those certificates should be included in the list of documents, and the next paragraph (regarding certificates) should be omitted.]*

[If the opinion includes opinions on factual matters or opinions on matters that are both factual and legal and opining counsel is relying on certificates for these factual matters, the following paragraph should be included.]

In rendering the following opinions, we have relied, with your approval, as to factual matters that affect our opinions, on the matters set forth in the certificates furnished to us by ____________, copies of which are attached as Exhibit _______ to this opinion.[3]

In rendering the following opinions, we have made no assumptions other than those set forth in the Report. *[Or: In addition to the assumptions contained in the Report, we have, with your consent, assumed (stated assumption(s) with specificity).]*

Based on the foregoing, and subject to the qualifications and limitations stated in this letter and in the Report, we are of the opinion that:[4]

1. The Company has been incorporated under the Florida Business Corporation Act ("FBCA") (or prior law) and its status is active. *[See Section III.A. of the Report.]*

2. The Company was organized under the FBCA (or prior law, as applicable). *[See Section III.B. of the Report.]*

3. To our knowledge after limited investigation *[See Sections II.J. and III.C. of the Report[5]]*, the Company is required to be qualified as a foreign corporation in the States of ______________, ______________ and ______________. Based on the Certificates of Good Standing *[or appropriate names of certificates]* issued by the States of ______________, ______________ and

3. The attorney-client privilege and the potential waiver thereof by disclosure of factual certificates to the addressee should be considered by opining counsel and the client. *See* Sections I.F. and II.I. of the Report.

4. Each opinion should be prefaced to identify the level of factual inquiry (or limitation of factual inquiry) intended by opining counsel. *See* Section II.J. of the Report.

5. The "to our knowledge after limited investigation" standard may not be the appropriate level of inquiry for the foreign qualification opinion in every instance.

_______________, the Company is qualified as a foreign corporation to conduct business in these States.

4. The Company has the corporate power to conduct its business and to execute and deliver the Agreement and to perform its obligations under the Agreement. *[See Section III.D. of the Report.]*

5. The Company has authorized the execution, delivery and performance of the Agreement by all necessary corporate action. *[See Section III.E. of the Report. If counsel has relied on the presumption of regularity in rendering this opinion, counsel should add: "In rendering this opinion, we have relied on the presumption of regularity as to the minutes of the board of directors of the Company from __________ to __________ because, after diligent search, these minutes could not be located (or other reason)."]*

6. *[Include this paragraph only if opining counsel witnesses execution of the Agreements or relies on a factual certificate as to execution and delivery. See Section III.F. of the Report. If execution and delivery have not been witnessed, it may be appropriate to list execution and delivery of the Agreement as an assumption counsel is making in rendering the opinions.]* The Agreement has been executed and delivered by the Company.

7. The execution and delivery of the Agreement, performance by the Company of its obligations under the Agreement and the exercise by the Company of the rights created by the Agreement do not (i) violate the Company's Articles of Incorporation or bylaws; (ii) to our knowledge *[See Section II.J. of the Report for a definition of this limitation and other appropriate knowledge limitations]* constitute a breach of or a default under any agreement or instrument to which the Company is a party or by which it or its assets are bound, or result in the creation of a mortgage, security interest or other encumbrance upon the assets of the Company (except as set forth in the Agreement); (iii) to our knowledge *[See Section II.J. of the Report]*, violate a judgment, decree or order of any court or administrative tribunal, which judgment, decree or order is binding on the Company or its assets; or (iv) violate any Federal or Florida law, rule or regulation. *[If the "no conflict" opinion is to be qualified or limited by exclusion of the laws, rules or regulations of any particular governmental, regulatory or administrative entity, the following sentence should be added:]* We have not expressed an opinion as to matters of _______________ law. *[If an opinion of local/specialist counsel is being rendered, include a paragraph referring to the local/specialist law opinion.]*

8. Except for the consent and approval of _______________, no notice, report or other filing or registration with, and no consent, approval or authorization of,

any Federal, Florida or local governmental authority is required to be submitted, made or obtained in connection with the execution, delivery and performance of the Agreement, which, if not obtained, could have a materially adverse impact on the transaction contemplated by the Agreement.

9. Subject to the limitations contained in the next paragraph, the Agreement is a valid and binding obligation of the Company enforceable against the Company under the law of Florida and the Federal law of the United States.

Our opinion concerning the validity, binding effect and enforceability of the Agreement means that (i) the Agreement constitutes an effective contract under applicable law, (ii) the Agreement is not invalid in its entirety because of a specific statutory prohibition or public policy and is not subject in its entirety to a contractual defense, and (iii) subject to the last sentence of this paragraph, some remedy is available if the Company is in material default under the Agreement. This opinion does not mean that (i) any particular remedy is available upon a material default, or (ii) every provision of the Agreement will be upheld or enforced in any or each circumstance by a court. Furthermore, the validity, binding effect and enforceability of the Agreement may be limited or otherwise affected by (i) bankruptcy, insolvency, reorganization, moratorium, fraudulent conveyance or other similar statutes, rules, regulations or other laws affecting the enforcement of creditors' rights and remedies generally and (ii) the unavailability of, or limitation on the availability of, a particular right or remedy (whether in a proceeding in equity or at law) because of an equitable principle or a requirement as to commercial reasonableness, conscionability or good faith.

[If the addressee is receiving an additional or supplemental opinion from one or more local/specialist counsel, the following paragraph should be included. See Section II.H. of the Report.]

In rendering the foregoing opinion, we have not expressed an opinion on matters of *[state or specialized area]* law. These matters are covered by the opinion of *[name of local/specialist counsel]* addressed to you and dated ________________.

This opinion is furnished to you by us as counsel for *[client]*, is solely for your benefit [and the benefit of *named persons*], and is rendered solely in connection with the transaction to which this opinion relates. This opinion may be relied upon only in connection with this transaction and may not be relied upon by any other person[s] without our prior written consent [except that a copy of this opinion may be delivered by you to *[insert name(s) of persons to which a copy of this opinion may be delivered]* in connection with *[describe, with specificity, the circumstances in which this opinion may be delivered]* and these persons may rely on this opinion as if it were addressed to them].

Very truly yours,

____

(Law Firm Name) *[See Section II.N. of the Report]*

APPENDIX B

Federal Bar Association's Model Rules of Professional Conduct for Federal Lawyers

PREFACE

The Federal Bar Association (FBA) has adopted the Federal Bar Association's Model Rules of Professional Conduct for Federal Lawyers (Rules) to serve as a guide for all lawyers involved in Federal practice, both Government lawyers and Non-Government lawyers. These Rules recognize many of the special aspects of the practice of law with the Federal Government.

The FBA is not empowered to discipline members or enforce these Rules. However, the FBA encourages Federal Agencies to adopt rules of professional responsibility based on these Rules to govern the conduct of lawyers employed by the Federal Agency and lawyers who practice before the Federal Agency and its tribunals.

The FBA's Professional Ethics Committee gratefully acknowledges the important contributions of the American Bar Association: the American Bar Association (ABA) Model Rules of Professional Responsibility (ABA Model Rules); the Judge Advocates Generals of the Armed Forces and the Army's Rules of Professional Conduct for Lawyers, the Navy's Rules of Professional Conduct for Judge Advocates, the Air Force Rules of Professional Responsibility, the Coast Guard's draft Rules of Professional Responsibility, and the 1984 Interservice Working Group's Proposed Rules of Professional Conduct; the District of Columbia Bar's Special Committee on Government Lawyers Report and the Model Rules of Professional Conduct; Michael E. Robinson, Esq., of the Department of Justice, in his capacity as a Committee Member of the District of Columbia Bar Special Committee on the Application of the Model Rules of Conduct to Government Lawyers; Robert D. Poling, Specialist in American Public Law, Congressional Research Service, Library of Congress; and the pre-existing work product of the Federal Bar Association Ethics Committee, in particular the Canons of Ethics, Federal Ethical Considerations, and Ethics Opinion 73-1.

While the ABA Model Rules were the basis of these Rules, changes were required to ensure that these Rules met the needs of the Federal lawyer. Reasons for the changes include but are not limited to — an ABA Rule's inapplicability to practice within or before a Federal Agency; the need for guidance tailored to Federal government practice; differences in approach to the resolution of specific ethical issues for Federal lawyers; and editorial and stylist changes. Some ABA Rules that do not pertain to the practice of law within the Federal Government were omitted. In these cases the Non-Government lawyer should consult the applicable rules of the various states in which the Non-Government lawyer practicing before Federal agencies and courts is licensed. In particular, deference has been given to state rules involving the setting of fees, advertising, and the organization of private law firms.

The Rules contain Comment sections, designed to explain or amplify the Rules, place them in context, or provide additional guidance. The Comments are interpretive tools, not binding upon Federal lawyers, but helpful in understanding and using the Rules. In doing so, Federal lawyers must be aware that these Rules were specifically adapted to the unique needs and demands of the Federal lawyer. Federal lawyers should carefully consider these Rules as guidance in specific situations.

Federal lawyers shall be thoroughly acquainted with and shall adhere at all times to the rules of professional responsibility adopted by the Federal Agency that employs them or before which they practice. In the absence of Federal Agency rules, they should comply with the rules of the state bars in which they are licensed to practice.

These Rules supersede existing FBA Canons of Ethics and Federal Ethical Considerations (F.E.C.s). Applicable portions of the FBA's Canons of Ethics and F.E.C.s have been added to the Rules and commentary, where applicable.

The Rules seek to balance the Federal Agency's needs with the needs of the Federal lawyers, who are members, and often leaders, in the mainstream of the legal profession. It is an appropriate balance, but one that carries heavy obligations to the service and the profession.

STATUTES, REGULATIONS, AND GUIDANCE:

The Federal lawyer, particularly Government and former-Government lawyers, may be bound by statutory provisions contained in Titles 2, 5, 18, and 28 App. of the U.S. Code; the Ethics in Government Act; relevant Executive Orders; Federal Agency rules and directives including, but not limited to, Federal Agency Standards of Conduct regulations and 5 C.F.R. 735-738; Office of Government Ethics Regulations and Formal Advisory Opinions; Memoranda of Attorney General; and state Rules of Professional Conduct. Federal lawyers admitted to practice in more than one jurisdiction should exercise caution in ascertaining the content of ethical requirements in each state and the application of such requirements to their practice.

One of the most difficult issues Government lawyers may confront is the identity of the client and where counsel's loyalties belong. Rule 1.13 addresses this question at length and cautions that under some circumstances, a Government lawyer may encounter a conflict between his or her obligation to the Federal Agency as the client, and the needs and interests of individual officials, employees, and agents of the Federal Agency. Another difficult area, addressed in Rule 1.6, is the question of client confidentiality. The Comments to both of these Rules are extensive and intended to offer additional guidance.

Another area in which a Government lawyer's actions may be regulated by law involves the release of information, which is also regulated by the Freedom of Information Act, 5 U.S.C. § 552, the Privacy Act, 5 U.S.C. § 552a, and the laws governing the protection of national security and defense information.

Federal Bar Association

TABLE OF CONTENTS

PREAMBLE: A FEDERAL LAWYER'S RESPONSIBILITIES

A Federal lawyer is a representative of clients, an officer of the legal system, and a public citizen having special responsibility for the quality of justice. The Federal lawyer should demonstrate the highest standards of ethical conduct, personal dignity, truthfulness, honesty, fortitude, and professional integrity. The Federal lawyer should also promote public service.

As a representative of clients, a Federal lawyer performs various functions. As an advisor, a Federal lawyer provides a client with informed understanding of the client's rights and obligations and explains their practical implications. As an advocate, a Federal lawyer zealously asserts the client's position under the law and the ethical rules of the adversary system. As negotiator, a Federal lawyer seeks results advantageous to the client, but consistent with the requirement of honest dealing with others. As a mediator between clients, a Federal lawyer seeks to reconcile their divergent interests as an advisor and, to a limited extent, as a spokesperson for each client. A Federal lawyer acts as evaluator by examining client's legal affairs and reporting about them to the client or to others.

In all professional functions a Federal lawyer should be competent, prompt, diligent, and honest. A Federal lawyer should maintain communication with a client concerning the representation. A Federal lawyer should keep in confidence information relating to representation of a client, except insofar as disclosure is required or permitted by these Rules or other law.

A Federal lawyer's conduct should conform to the requirements of the law, both in professional service to clients and in the Federal lawyer's personal affairs. A Federal lawyer should use legal procedures only for their lawfully intended purposes and not to harass or intimidate others. A Federal lawyer should demonstrate respect for the legal system and for those who serve it, including judges, other Federal lawyers, and public officials. To the Federal Agency, the Federal lawyer owes the duties of professional dignity and integrity. While it is a Federal lawyer's duty, when necessary, to challenge the rectitude of official action, it is also a Federal lawyer's duty to uphold legal process.

As a public citizen, a Federal lawyer should seek improvement of the law, the administration of justice, and the quality of service rendered by the legal profession. Federal lawyers should strive at all times to uphold the honor and dignity of the Federal legal profession and to improve the administration of justice. As a member of a learned profession, a Federal lawyer should cultivate knowledge of the law beyond its use for clients, employ that knowledge in reform of the law where needed, and work to strengthen legal education.

Many of a Federal lawyer's professional responsibilities are prescribed in these Rules, as well as in substantive and procedural law. However, a Federal lawyer is also guided by personal conscience and the approbation of professional peers. A Federal lawyer should strive to attain the highest level of skill, to improve the law and the legal profession, to exemplify the legal profession's ideals of public service, and to respect the truth finding role of the courts.

A Federal lawyer's responsibilities as a representative of clients, an officer of the legal system, and a public citizen are usually harmonious. Thus, when an opposing party is well represented, a Federal lawyer can be zealous in advocating the interests of a client and justice will be served. A Federal lawyer also can be sure that preserving client confidence ordinarily serves the public interest because people are more likely to ask legal advice, and thereby heed their legal obligations, when they know their communications will be private.

A Federal lawyer should always uphold and promote the highest standards for the practice of law within the Federal sector. A Federal lawyer should seek to advance the development of sound Federal laws and the establishment and maintenance of an efficient Federal legal and judicial system. A Federal lawyer should promote the public's confidence in the Federal legal system. A Federal lawyer also should promote the highest professional standards for and the professional well being of all Federal lawyers. A Federal lawyer should seek to encourage outstanding lawyers to enter the Federal service.

In addition to the high standards of conduct expected of all Federal lawyers, the Government lawyer has a specific responsibility to strive to promote the public interest. The Government lawyer should not realize personal gain from the performance of official duties and should avoid any interest or activity that is in conflict with the Government lawyer's official duties. The Government lawyer should strive for personal professional excellence and encourage the professional development of other staff members and those seeking to enter the field of Government law practice.

Due to the nature of legal practice, however, Federal lawyers encounter conflicting responsibilities. Virtually all difficult ethical problems arise from conflicts between a Federal lawyer's responsibilities to clients, to the legal system, and to the Federal lawyer's own interest in remaining an upright person. These Rules prescribe terms for resolving such conflicts. Within the framework of these Rules many difficult issues of professional discretion can arise. Such issues must be resolved through the exercise of sensitive professional and moral judgment guided by the basic principles underlying these Rules.

SCOPE

These Rules, in conjunction with laws and regulations that control the practice of Federal lawyers, are intended to govern the ethical conduct of Federal lawyers.

They have been adopted by the National Council of the Federal Bar Association. The Federal Bar Association is not empowered to discipline members or enforce these Rules. As such, these Rules regulate professional conduct of Federal lawyers and impose certain duties only to the extent to which they are adopted by a Federal Agency. The Federal Bar Association encourages Federal agencies to adopt rules of professional responsibility based, in whole or in part, on these Rules. If so adopted, failure to comply with an obligation or prohibition imposed by a Rule may be the basis for invoking administrative or disciplinary action. The Rules presuppose that disciplinary assessment of a Federal lawyer's conduct will be made on the basis of the facts and circumstances as they existed at the time of the conduct in question and in recognition of the fact that a Federal lawyer often has to act upon uncertain or incomplete evidence of the situation. Moreover, these Rules presuppose that whether or not discipline should be imposed for a violation, and severity of a sanction, depend on all of the circumstances, such as the willfulness and seriousness of the violation, extenuating factors, and whether there have been previous violations. Violations of a Rule should not give rise to a cause of action nor should they create a presumption that a legal duty has been breached. These Rules are designed to provide guidance to Federal lawyers and to provide a structure for regulating conduct. They are not designed to be a basis for civil liability.

Furthermore, the purpose of these Rules can be subverted when they are invoked by opposing parties as procedural weapons. The fact that a Rule is a just basis for a Federal lawyer's self-assessment, or for sanctioning a Federal lawyer under the administration of a disciplinary authority, does not imply that an antagonist in a collateral proceeding or transaction has standing to seek enforcement of the Rule. Accordingly, nothing in these Rules should be deemed to augment any substantive legal duty of Federal lawyers or the extra-disciplinary consequences of violating such duty.

They are to be used in conjunction with laws and regulation that control the practice of Federal lawyers. Although not punitive in nature, the Rules establish the minimum standards of ethical conduct demanded of Federal lawyers.

The ethical conduct of lawyers specially retained by the Government is also intended to be governed by these Rules of Professional Conduct.

These Rules presuppose a larger legal context shaping the Federal lawyer's role. That context includes statutes and court rules relating to matters of licensing, laws defining specific obligations of Federal lawyers, and substantive and procedural law in general. Compliance with these Rules, as with all laws in an open society, depends primarily upon understanding and voluntary compliance, secondarily upon reinforcement by peer and public opinion, and finally, when applicable and necessary, upon enforcement through disciplinary proceedings. These Rules do not, however, exhaust the moral and ethical considerations that should inform a Federal lawyer, for no worthwhile human activity can be completely defined by legal rules. These Rules simply provide a framework for the ethical practice of law.

Furthermore, for purposes of determining the Federal lawyer's authority and responsibility, principles of substantive law external to these Rules determine whether a client-lawyer relationship exists. Whether a client-lawyer relationship exists for any specific purpose can depend on the circumstances and may be a question of fact.

Moreover, these Rules are not intended to govern or affect judicial application of either the attorney-client or work product privilege. Those privileges were developed to promote compliance with law and fairness in litigation. In reliance on the attorney-client privilege, clients are entitled to expect that communications within the scope of the privilege will be protected against compelled disclosure. The attorney-client privilege is that of the client and not of the Federal lawyer. The fact that in exceptional situations the Federal lawyer under these Rules is required or permitted to disclose client confidence does not vitiate the proposition that, as a general matter, the client has a reasonable expectation that information relating to the client will not be voluntarily disclosed and that disclosure of such information may be compelled only in accordance with recognized exceptions to the attorney-client and work product privileges.

The Federal lawyer's exercise of discretion not to disclose information under Rule 1.6(c) should not be subject to reexamination. Permitting such reexamination would be incompatible with the general policy of promoting compliance with law through assurances that communications will be protected against disclosure.

These Rules of Professional Conduct are rules of reason. They should be interpreted with reference to the purposes of legal representation and of the law itself. Some of these Rules are imperative, cast in the terms "shall" or "shall not." These define proper conduct for purposes of professional discipline. Others, generally cast in the term "may" are permissive and define areas under these Rules in which the Federal lawyer has professional discretion. No disciplinary action should be taken when the Federal lawyer chooses not to act or acts within the bounds of such discretion. Other Rules define the nature of relationships between the Federal lawyer and others. These Rules are thus partly obligatory and partly descriptive in that they define a Federal lawyer's professional role. Many of the comments use the term "should". Comments do not add obligations to these Rules, but provide guidance for practicing in compliance with these Rules. The comments are interpretative, while the text of each Rule is authoritative.

The Preamble and this note on Scope provide general orientation.

DEFINITIONS

Within the scope of these Rules:

"Attorney-client" is the term used to describe the evidentiary privilege against disclosure of communications between a Federal lawyer's client and the Federal lawyer. It is not used to describe the relationship between a Federal lawyer and the lawyer's client.

"Belief" or "believes" mean that the individual involved actually concludes the fact in question to be true. A individual's belief may be inferred from circumstances.
"Client-lawyer" is used to express the professional relationship between a Federal lawyer and the lawyer's client. The term is not used to reference any evidentiary privileges, such as the "attorney-client" privilege.

"Consult" or "consultation" means communication of information reasonably sufficient to permit the client to appreciate the significance of the matter in question.

"Federal Agency" means: (1) An Executive agency, including an Executive department, military department, Government corporation, Government controlled corporation, and an independent establishment; (2) The Congress, committees of Congress, members of Congress who employ lawyers, and Congressional agencies; (3) The courts of the United States and agencies of the Judiciary; (4) The Governments of the territories and possessions of the United States; or (5) The Government of the District of Columbia.

"Federal lawyer" means a Government lawyer or a Non-Government lawyer, as hereinafter defined.

"Firm" means the organizational entity through which Non-Government lawyers transact business. The term includes private law firms, the legal departments of corporations and other business entities that hire lawyers as employees, and legal service organizations. The term does not include a Federal Agency.

"Government employee" means an officer or employee of a Federal Agency. The term includes members of the Armed Forces.

"Government lawyer" means a Government employee who holds a position as an attorney with a Federal Agency or serves as a judge advocate in one of the Armed Forces, but only while performing official duties. The term includes a lawyer in private practice who has contracted with or been specially retained by a Federal Agency to represent the Agency or another person while engaged in the performance of the contractual obligation.

"Fraud" or "fraudulent" means conduct having deceit as its purpose and does not encompass merely negligent misrepresentation or failure to apprise another of relevant information.

"Individual" is used to describe a single human being.

"Knowingly," "known," or "knows" means actual knowledge of the fact in question. A person's knowledge may be inferred from circumstances.

"Law" as used in these Rules includes statutes, treaties and international agreements, legal precedents, Federal Agency regulations, directives, and orders.

"Non-Government lawyer" means an individual who is a member of the bar of a Federal court or the highest court of a State or Territory, who represents persons before a Federal Agency. When a Government lawyer is engaged in the private practice of law or pro bono representation not related to the Government lawyer's official duties, the lawyer is considered a Non-Government lawyer.

"Person" means an individual, a corporation, a company, an association, a firm, a partnership, a society, a joint stock company, or any other legal entity.

"Reasonable" or "reasonably" when used in relation to conduct by Federal lawyer means the conduct of a reasonably prudent and competent lawyer.

"Reasonable belief" or "reasonably believes" when used in reference to a Federal lawyer means that the lawyer believes the matter in question and that the circumstances are such that the belief is reasonable.
"Reasonably should know" when used in reference to a Federal lawyer means that a lawyer of reasonable prudence and competence would ascertain the matter in question.

"Substantial" when used in reference to degree or extent means a material matter of clear and weighty importance.

"Supervisory lawyer" means a Federal lawyer within an office or organization with authority over or responsibility for the direction, coordination, evaluation, or assignment of responsibilities and work of subordinate lawyers, contract legal representation, nonlawyer assistants (e.g., paralegals), and clerical personnel.

"Tribunal" means a court, board, hearing officer, investigating officer, judge, jury, panel, or other body or official that receives evidence and makes a ruling or determination.

Federal Bar Association

CLIENT-LAWYER RELATIONSHIP

RULE 1.1 Competence

A Federal lawyer shall provide competent representation to a client. Competent representation requires the legal knowledge, skill, thoroughness, and preparation reasonably necessary for the representation.

COMMENT:

Legal Knowledge and Skill

In determining whether a Federal lawyer employs the requisite knowledge and skill in a particular matter, relevant factors include the relative complexity and specialized nature of the matter, the lawyer's general experience, the lawyer's training and experience in the field in question, the preparation and study the lawyer is able to give the matter, and whether it is feasible to refer the matter to, or consult with, a lawyer of established competence in the field in question. In most instances, the required proficiency is that generally afforded to clients by other lawyers in similar matters. Expertise in a particular field of law may be required in some circumstances.

Initial determinations as to the competence of a Government lawyer for a particular assignment will be made by a supervisory lawyer prior to case or issue assignments. However, once assigned, a Government lawyer may consult with the supervisory lawyer concerning competence to continue handling a particular case or issue. See Rules 5.1 and 5.2.

A Federal lawyer need not necessarily have special training or prior experience to handle legal problems of a type with which the Federal lawyer is unfamiliar. A newly admitted Federal lawyer can be as competent as a practitioner with long experience. Some important legal skills, such as the analysis of precedent, the evaluation of evidence, and legal drafting, are required in all legal problems. Perhaps the most fundamental legal skill consists of determining what kind of legal problems a situation may involve, a skill that necessarily transcends any particular specialized knowledge. A Federal lawyer can provide adequate representation in a wholly novel field through necessary study or consultation with a Federal lawyer of established competence in the field in question.

A Federal lawyer may become involved in representing a client whose needs exceed either the lawyer's competence or authority to act in the client's behalf. In such a situation, the Federal lawyer should refer the matter to another Federal lawyer who has the requisite competence or authority to meet the client's needs. For Non-Government lawyers practicing before Federal agencies, competent representation may also be provided through the association of a Non-government lawyer of established competence in the field in question.

A Federal lawyer may give advice or assistance in a matter in which the Federal lawyer does not have the skill ordinarily required where referral to or consultation with another Federal lawyer would be impractical. However, assistance should be limited to that reasonably necessary in the circumstances, for ill-considered action can jeopardize the client's interest.

Thoroughness and Preparation

Competent handling of a particular matter includes inquiry into and analysis of the factual and legal elements of the problem, and use of methods and procedures meeting the standards of competent practitioners. It also includes adequate preparation. The attention and preparation required are determined in part by what is at stake; major litigation and complex transactions ordinarily require more elaborate treatment than matters of lesser consequence.

Maintaining Competence

To maintain the requisite knowledge and skill, a Federal lawyer should engage in continuing study and education.

CROSS REFERENCES:

Rule 1.2 Scope of Representation
Rule 1.3 Diligence
Rule 1.13 The Federal Agency as the Client
Rule 1.16 Declining or Terminating Representation
Rule 2.1 Advisor
Rule 3.1 Meritorious Claims and Contentions
Rule 3.4 Fairness to Opposing Party and Counsel
Rule 5.1 Responsibilities of a Supervisory Lawyer
Rule 5.2 Responsibilities of a Subordinate Lawyer

RULE 1.2 Scope of Representation

(a) A Federal lawyer shall abide by a client's decisions concerning the objectives of representation, subject to paragraphs (c), (d), (e), and (f), and shall consult with the client as to the means by which these decisions are to be pursued. A Federal lawyer shall abide by a client's decision whether to accept an offer of settlement of a matter. In a criminal case, and to the extent applicable in civil cases and administrative hearings, the Federal lawyer shall abide by the client's decision, after consultation with the Federal lawyer, as to choice of counsel (as provided by law), a plea to be entered, selection of trial forum, whether to enter into a pretrial agreement, and whether the client will testify.

(b) A Federal lawyer's representation of a client, including representation by appointment, does not constitute an endorsement of the client's political, economic, social, or moral views or activities.

(c) A Federal lawyer may limit the objectives of the representation if the client consents after consultation or as required by law and communicated to the client.

(d) A Federal lawyer shall not counsel a client to engage, or assist a client, in conduct that the lawyer knows is criminal or fraudulent, but a Federal lawyer may discuss the legal and moral consequences of any proposed course of conduct with a client and may counsel or assist a client to make a good faith effort to determine the validity, scope, meaning, or application of the law.

(e) When a Federal lawyer knows that a client expects assistance not permitted by these Rules of Professional Conduct or other law, the lawyer shall advise the client of the relevant limitations on the lawyer's conduct.

(f) A Government lawyer's authority and control over decisions concerning the representation may, by law, be expanded beyond the limits imposed by paragraphs (a) and (c).

COMMENT:

General
In many cases, straightforward application of Rule 1.2 is possible. However, in other cases, primarily in the litigation context, the scope of representation is necessarily altered and set out by law. For example, a Government lawyer representing an individual may have significant control over the litigation decisions. Similarly, except as otherwise provided by law, the Department of Justice, under 28 U.S.C. § 516, is given the authority to represent certain Federal agencies in litigation. Procedures for resolving inter-agency disputes should be followed in cases of conflict between a position recommended by the litigating attorney and the Federal Agency being represented.

Scope of Representation

Both Federal lawyer and client have authority and responsibility in the objectives and means of representation. The client has ultimate authority to determine the purposes to be served by legal representation, within the limits imposed by law and the Federal lawyer's professional obligations. Within those limits, a client also has a right to consult with the Federal lawyer about the means to be used in pursuing those objectives. At the same time, a Federal lawyer is not required to pursue objectives or employ means simply because a client may wish that the Federal lawyer do so. A clear distinction between objectives and means sometimes cannot be drawn, and in many cases the client-lawyer relationship becomes a joint undertaking. In questions of means, the Federal lawyer should assume responsibility for technical and legal tactical issues, such as what witnesses to call, whether and how to conduct cross-examination, what court members to challenge, and what options to make. Except where precluded by Rule 4.4, the Federal lawyer should defer to the client regarding such questions as expenses to be incurred and concern for third persons who might be affected adversely.

When the client appears to be suffering mental disability, the Federal lawyer's duty to abide by the client's decisions is to be guided by Rule 1.14.

Service Limited in Objectives or Means

The objectives or scope of services provided by a Federal lawyer may be limited by agreement with the client or by the law governing the conditions under which the Federal lawyer's services are made available to the client. Formation of client-lawyer relationships and representation of clients by a Government lawyer is permissible only when authorized by competent authority. When the objectives or scope of services provided by a Federal lawyer are limited by law, the Federal lawyer should inform the client of such limitations at the earliest opportunity.

If a Government lawyer is uncertain of the scope of services permitted by the law governing the conditions under which the Federal lawyer's services are made available to a client, the Government lawyer should consult with the Government lawyer's supervisory lawyer concerning the matter. See Rule 5.2.

An agreement concerning the scope of representation must accord with these Rules of Professional Conduct and other law. Thus, the client shall not be asked to agree to representation so limited in scope as to violate Rule 1.1, to surrender the right to terminate the Federal lawyer's services, or to conclude a matter that the Federal lawyer might wish to continue.

Rules 1.2 & 1.3

Criminal, Fraudulent, and Prohibited Transactions

A Federal lawyer is required to give an honest opinion about the consequences likely to result from a client's conduct. Simply because a client uses advice in a course of action that is criminal or fraudulent does not, of itself, make a Federal lawyer a party to the course of action. However, a Federal lawyer shall not knowingly assist a client in criminal or fraudulent conduct. A critical distinction exists between presenting an analysis of legal aspects of questionable conduct and recommending the means by which a crime or fraud might be committed with impunity.

When the client's course of action has already begun and is continuing, the Federal lawyer's responsibility is especially delicate. The Federal lawyer is not permitted to reveal the client's wrongdoing, except where required or permitted by Rule 1.6 or Rule 3.3. However, the Federal lawyer is required to avoid furthering an illegal purpose, for example, by suggesting how it might be concealed. A Federal lawyer shall not continue assisting a client in conduct that the Federal lawyer originally supposes is legally proper but then discovers is criminal or fraudulent. Seeking to withdraw from the representation, therefore, may be appropriate.

Paragraph (d) applies whether or not the defrauded party is a party to the transaction. Hence, a Federal lawyer should not participate in a sham transaction; for example, a transaction to effectuate criminal or fraudulent escape of tax liability. The last clause of paragraph (d) recognizes that determining the validity or interpretation of a statute or regulation may include a course of action contrary to the terms of the statute or regulation or of the interpretation placed upon it by governmental authorities.

CROSS REFERENCES:

Rule 1.1 Competence
Rule 1.6 Confidentiality of Information
Rule 1.13 The Federal Agency as the Client
Rule 1.14 Client Under a Disability
Rule 2.1 Advisor
Rule 2.3 Evaluation for use by Third Person
Rule 3.3 Candor Toward the Tribunal
Rule 4.4 Respect for Rights of Third Persons
Rule 5.1 Responsibilities of a Supervisory Lawyer
Rule 5.2 Responsibilities of a Subordinate Lawyer

RULE 1.3 Diligence

A Federal lawyer shall act with reasonable diligence and promptness in representing a client.

COMMENT:

A Federal lawyer should pursue a matter on behalf of a client despite opposition, obstruction, or personal inconvenience to the Federal lawyer, and may take whatever lawful and ethical measures are required to vindicate a client's cause or endeavor. A Federal lawyer should act with commitment and dedication to the interests of the client and with morality in advocating the client's position. However, a Federal lawyer is not bound to press for every advantage that might be realized for a client. Although a Federal lawyer may be bound by court precedent to pursue certain matters on behalf of a client, a Federal lawyer has professional discretion in determining the means by which a matter should be pursued. See Rules 1.2 and 1.4(b). A Federal lawyer's work load should be managed by both the Federal lawyer and a supervisory lawyer so that each matter can be handled adequately. See Rule 5.1.

Perhaps no professional shortcoming is more widely resented than procrastination. A client's interest often can be adversely affected by the passage of time or the chance of condition; in extreme instances, as when a Federal lawyer overlooks a statute of limitation, the client's legal position may be destroyed. Even when the client's interests are not affected in substance, however, unreasonable delay can cause a client needless anxiety and undermine confidence in the Federal lawyer's trustworthiness.

Unless the relationship is terminated as provided in Rule 1.16, and to the extent permitted by law, a Federal lawyer should carry through to conclusion all matters undertaken for a client. If a Federal lawyer's representation is limited to a specific matter, the relationship terminates when the matter has been resolved. Doubt about whether a client-lawyer relationship exists should be clarified by the Federal lawyer, preferably in writing, so that the client will not mistakenly suppose the Federal lawyer is looking after the client's affairs when the Federal lawyer has ceased to do so. For example, a Federal lawyer who has handled a judicial or administrative proceeding that produced a result adverse to the client should advise the client of the possibility of appeal before relinquishing responsibility for the matter.

CROSS REFERENCES:

Rule 1.1 Competence
Rule 1.4 Communication
Rule 1.2 Scope of Representation
Rule 1.16 Declining or Terminating Representation
Rule 3.1 Meritorious Claims and Contentions
Rule 3.2 Expediting Litigation
Rule 4.1 Truthfulness of Statements to Others
Rule 5.1 Responsibilities of a Supervisory Lawyer

RULE 1.4 Communication

(a) A Federal lawyer shall keep a client reasonably informed about the status of a matter and promptly comply with reasonable requests for information.

(b) A Federal lawyer shall explain a matter to the extent reasonably necessary to permit the client to make informed decisions regarding the representation.

COMMENT:

A client should have sufficient information to participate intelligently in decisions concerning the objectives of the representation and the means by which they are to be pursued, to the extent a client is willing and able to do so. For example, a Federal lawyer negotiating a pretrial agreement on behalf of a client should provide the client with facts relevant to the matter, inform the client of communications from the Government, and take other reasonable steps that permit the client to make a decision regarding the feasibility of further negotiation with the Government. A Federal lawyer representing the Government who receives from the defendant an offer for a pretrial agreement must communicate that offer, and should provide advice as to that offer, to the appropriate authority.

Adequacy of communications depends in part on the kind of advice or assistance involved. For example, in negotiations where there is time to explain a proposal, a Federal lawyer should review all important provisions with the client before proceeding to an agreement. In litigation, a Federal lawyer should explain the general strategy and prospects of success and ordinarily should consult the client on tactics that might injure or coerce another. On the other hand, a Federal lawyer ordinarily cannot be expected to describe trial or negotiation strategy in detail. The guiding principle is that a Federal lawyer should fulfill reasonable client expectations for information consistent with the duty to act in the client's best interests, taking into account client's overall requirements as to the character of representation.

When the client is the Federal Agency, it is often impossible or inappropriate to inform all of its members about its legal affairs. Ordinarily, a Government lawyer should address communications to the appropriate officials of the Federal Agency. See Rule 1.13.

When the representation involves many routine matters, a system of limited or occasional reporting may be arranged with the client. Practical exigencies may limit the opportunity for consultation and also require a Federal lawyer to act for a client without prior consultation.

In some circumstances, a Federal lawyer may be required to withhold information from a client. For example, classified information shall not be disclosed without proper authority. In other circumstances, a Federal lawyer maybe justified in delaying transmission of information when the client would be likely to react imprudently to an immediate communication. Thus, a Federal lawyer might withhold a psychiatric diagnosis of a client when the examining psychiatrist indicates that disclosure would harm the client. A Federal lawyer shall not withhold information to serve the Federal lawyer's own interest or convenience, or where disclosure would be favorable to the defense of a criminal defendant. Rules or court orders governing litigation may provide that information supplied to a Federal lawyer shall not be disclosed to the client. Rule 3.4(c) directs compliance with such rules or orders.

CROSS REFERENCES:

Rule 1.1 Competence
Rule 1.2 Scope of Representation
Rule 1.3 Diligence
Rule 1.6 Confidentiality of Information
Rule 1.7 Conflict of Interest: General Rule
Rule 1.13 The Federal Agency as the Client
Rule 2.1 Advisor
Rule 2.2 Mediator
Rule 3.2 Expediting Litigation
Rule 3.4 Fairness to Opposing Party and Counsel
Rule 3.8 Special Responsibilities of a Prosecutor
Rule 4.1 Truthfulness of Statements to Others

RULE 1.5 Fees

(a) A Federal lawyer shall be regulated by the Rules of Professional Conduct or other applicable rules of the jurisdictions in which the Federal lawyer is licensed or is practicing law, and otherwise by law in regard to matters concerning fees.

(b) A Government lawyer, in connection with the Government lawyer's official duties, may not request or accept any compensation from a client other than that provided by the United States for the performance of duties.

COMMENT:

Non-Government Lawyers

Rather than adopting a rule based on Rule 1.5 of the ABA Model Rule of Professional Conduct that would apply only to Non-Government lawyers practicing before Federal agencies, the Federal Agency defers on this matter to the rules of the jurisdictions in which these Non-Government lawyers are licensed, and otherwise by law.

Government Lawyers

Government lawyers are prohibited by statute from accepting, as compensation for services as a Government employee any salary or contribution to or supplementation of salary from any source other than the Government of the United States. See, for example, 18 U.S.C. § 203 and § 209.

A Government lawyer shall not request or accept any gratuity, salary, or other compensation from a client, other than the Federal Agency that employs the Government lawyer, incident to the performance of duties as a Government employee.
However, to the extent permitted by applicable laws, a Government lawyer who is active in a non-Government organization or who delivers a speech to an organization may accept reimbursement from the organization for the Government lawyer's costs incurred as a result of the Government lawyer's participation, on the Government lawyer's own time, in that organizations activities.

While a Government lawyer may be able to represent clients in a private or pro bono capacity, the Rule prohibits the Government lawyer from using the Government lawyer's official position to solicit or obtain clients for the Government lawyer's private practice.

CROSS REFERENCES:

Rule 1.2 Scope of Representation
Rule 1.7 Conflict of Interest: General Rule
Rule 1.8 Conflict of Interest: Prohibited Transactions
Rule 1.16 Declining or Terminating Representation

RULE 1.6 Confidentiality of Information

(a) A Federal lawyer shall not reveal information relating to the representation of a client unless the client consents after consultation, except for disclosures that are impliedly authorized in order to carry out the representation, and except as stated in paragraphs (b), (c), and (d).

(b) A Federal lawyer shall reveal such information to the extent the Federal lawyer reasonably believes necessary to prevent the client from committing a criminal act that the Federal lawyer believes is likely to result in imminent death or substantial bodily harm, or imminent and significant impairment of national security or defense.

(c) A Federal lawyer may reveal such information to the extent the Federal lawyer reasonably believes necessary to establish a claim or defense on behalf of the Federal lawyer in a controversy between the Federal lawyer and the client, to establish a defense to a criminal charge or civil claim against the Federal lawyer based upon conduct in which the client was involved, or to respond to allegations in any proceeding concerning the Federal lawyer's representation of the client.

(d) A Government lawyer may reveal such information when required or authorized by law.

COMMENT:

The Federal lawyer is part of a judicial system charged with upholding the law. One of the Federal lawyer's functions is to advise clients so that they avoid any violation of the law in the proper exercise of their rights.

The observance of the ethical obligation of a Federal lawyer to hold inviolate confidential information of the client not only facilitates the full development of facts essential to proper representation of the client but also encourages people to seek early legal assistance.

Almost without exception, clients come to Federal lawyers in order to determine what their rights are and what, in the maze of laws and regulations, is deemed to be legal and correct. The common law recognize that the client's confidences must be protected from disclosure. Based upon experience, Federal lawyers know that most clients follow the advice given, and the law is upheld.

A fundamental principle in the client-lawyer relationship is that the Federal lawyer maintains confidentiality of information relating to the representation. The client is thereby encouraged to communicate fully and frankly with the Federal lawyer even as to embarrassing or legally damaging matters.

The principle of confidentiality is given effect in two related bodies of law — the attorney-client privilege (which includes the work product doctrine) in the law of evidence and the rule of confidentiality established in professional ethics. The attorney-client privilege applies in judicial and other proceedings in which a Federal lawyer may be called as a witness or otherwise required to produce evidence concerning a client. The rule of client-lawyer confidentiality applies in situations other than those where evidence is sought from the Federal lawyer through compulsion of law. The confidentiality rule applies not merely to matters communicated in confidence by the client but also to all information relating to the representation, whatever its source. A Federal lawyer shall not disclose such information except as authorized or required by these Rules of Professional Conduct or other lawful order, directive, regulation, or statute. See also Scope.

The requirement of maintaining confidentiality of information relating to representation applies to Government lawyers, even those who may disagree with the policy goals that their representation is designed to advance.

Authorized Disclosure

A Federal lawyer is impliedly authorized to make disclosures about a client when appropriate in carrying out the representation, except to the extent that the client's instructions or special circumstances limit that authority. For example, a Federal lawyer may disclose information in litigation by admitting a fact that cannot properly be disputed, or in negotiation by making a disclosure that facilitates a satisfactory conclusion.

Federal lawyers may disclose to supervisory lawyers within the office and to nonlawyer assistants subject to the direction and control of the lawyer or the lawyer's supervisory lawyer information relating to a client, unless the client has instructed that particular information be confined to specified lawyers, or unless otherwise prohibited by these Rules of Professional Conduct or by law.

Disclosure Adverse to Client.

The confidentiality rule is subject to limited exceptions. In becoming privy to information about a client, a Federal lawyer may foresee that the client intends serious harm to another person. However, to the extent a Federal lawyer is required or permitted to disclose a client's purposes, the client will be inhibited from revealing facts which would enable the Federal lawyer to counsel against a wrongful course of action. The public is better protected if full and open communication by the client is encouraged than if it is inhibited.

Several situations must be distinguished.

First, the Federal lawyer shall not counsel or assist a client in conduct that is criminal or fraudulent. See Rule 1.2(d). Similarly, a Federal lawyer owes a duty of candor to the court and has a duty under Rule 3.3(a)(3) not to use false evidence. These duties are essentially special instances of the duty prescribed in Rule 1.2(d) to avoid assisting a client in criminal or fraudulent conduct.

Second, the Federal lawyer may have been innocently involved in past conduct by the client that was criminal or fraudulent. In such a situation the Federal lawyer has not violated Rule 1.2(d), because to "counsel or assist" criminal or fraudulent conduct requires knowing that the conduct is of that character.

Third, the Federal lawyer may learn that a client intends prospective conduct that is criminal and likely to result in imminent death or substantial bodily harm, or imminent and significant impairment of national security or defense. As stated in paragraph (b), the Federal lawyer has a professional obligation to reveal the information to the extent that Federal lawyer reasonably believes necessary to prevent such consequences.

In any case, a disclosure adverse to the client's interest should be no greater than the Federal lawyer reasonably believes necessary to the purpose giving rise to the disclosure.

Withdrawal

If a Federal lawyer's services will be used by a client in materially furthering a course of criminal or fraudulent conduct, the Federal lawyer must seek to withdraw, as stated in Rule 1.16(a)(1).

After withdrawal the Federal lawyer is required to refrain from making disclosure of the client's confidence, except as otherwise provided in this Rule. Nothing in this Rule, Rule 1.8(b), or Rule 1.16(d) prevents the Federal lawyer from giving notice of the fact of withdrawal, and the Federal lawyer may also withdraw or disaffirm any opinion, document, affirmation, or the like.

Rule 1.6

When the client is a Federal Agency, the Federal lawyer may doubt whether contemplated conduct will actually be carried out. When necessary to guide conduct in connection with the Rule, the Federal lawyer may make inquiry within the Federal Agency as indicated in Rule 1.13(b).

Dispute Concerning a Federal Lawyer's Conduct

When a legal claim or disciplinary charge alleges complicity of the Federal lawyer in a client's conduct, or other misconduct of the Federal lawyer involving representation of the client, the Federal lawyer may respond to the extent the Federal lawyer reasonably believes necessary to establish a defense. The same is true with respect to a claim involving the conduct or representation of a former client. The Federal lawyer's right to respond arises when an assertion of such complicity has been made. Paragraph (c) does not require the Federal lawyer to await the commencement of an action or proceeding that charges such complicity. The defense may be established by responding directly to a third party who has made such an assertion. The right to defend, of course, applies where a proceeding has been commenced. Where practicable and not prejudicial to the Federal lawyer's ability to establish the defense, the Federal lawyer should advise the client of the third party's assertion and request that the client respond appropriately. In any event, disclosure should be no greater than the Federal lawyer reasonably believes is necessary to vindicate innocence; the disclosure should be made in a manner which limits access to the information to the tribunal or other persons having a need to know it; and appropriate protective orders or other arrangements should be sought by the Federal lawyer to the fullest extent practicable.

If a Federal lawyer is charged with wrongdoing in which the client's conduct is implicated, the rule of confidentiality should not prevent the Federal lawyer from defending against the charge. Such a charge can arise in a civil, criminal, or professional disciplinary proceeding, and can be based on a wrong allegedly committed by the Federal lawyer against the client, or a wrong alleged by a third person; for example, a person claiming to have been defrauded by the Federal lawyer and client acting together. A Non-Government lawyer entitled to a fee is permitted by paragraph (c) to prove the services rendered in an action to collect it. This aspect of the Rule expresses the principle that the beneficiary of a fiduciary relationship shall not exploit it to the detriment of the fiduciary. As stated above, the Federal lawyer must make every effort practicable to avoid unnecessary disclosure of information relating to a representation, to limit disclosure to those having the need to know it, and to obtain protective orders or make other arrangements to minimize the risk of disclosure.

Disclosure Otherwise Required or Authorized

If a Federal lawyer is called as a witness to give testimony concerning a client, absent waiver by the client, paragraph (a) requires the Federal lawyer to invoke the attorney-client privilege when it is applicable. The Federal lawyer must comply with the final orders of a court or other tribunal of competent jurisdiction requiring the Federal lawyer to give information about the client.

These Rules of Professional Conduct in various circumstances permit or require a Federal lawyer to disclose information relating to the representation. See Rules 2.2, 2.3, 3.3, and 4.1. In addition to these provisions, a Federal lawyer may be obligated or permitted by other provision of law to give information about a client. Whether another provision of law supersedes Rule 1.6 is a matter of interpretation beyond the scope of these Rules, but a presumption should exist against such a supersession.

Former Client

The duty of confidentiality continues after the client-lawyer relationship has terminated.

Government Lawyers

The identification of the client, for purposes of the Government lawyer, is critical to the application of this Rule. Generally, a Federal Agency is the Government lawyer's client for the purposes of this Rule. Communications by the Government lawyer, both outside and within the Federal Agency, may or may not be considered breaches of this Rule. There are numerous statutes, regulations, and directives that may affect the Government lawyer's obligations under this Rule. A secondary issue concerns statutory protections against reprisal for Government employees who disclose violations or abuses - - the "whistleblower statutes." However, in such situations there may be a conflict with attorney-client privileges.

Government lawyers are often formally employed by a Federal Agency but assigned to an organizational element within the Federal Agency. Unless otherwise specifically provided, the Federal Agency, not the organizational element, is ordinarily considered the client.

Paragraph (d) permits disclosures that the Government authorizes its lawyers to make in connection with their professional services to the Government. Such disclosures may be authorized or required by statute, Executive Order, regulation, or directive, depending on the constitutional or statutory powers of the authorizing entity. This paragraph also clarifies that, under 28 U.S.C. § 516, Government lawyers may disclose all information relevant to representation by the Department of Justice to the Department's assigned attorney, and authorizes such information to be further disclosed by the assigned attorney to other Department of Justice lawyers concerned with the representation.

There are circumstances in which a Government lawyer may be assigned to provide an individual with counsel or representation in which it is clear that an obligation of confidentiality runs directly to that individual and not to the Federal Agency. Examples of such representation include a Government lawyer representing a defendant sued for damages arising out of the performance of the defendant's Government employment, a judge advocate representing an accused in a court-martial, or representation by a public defender.

The relevant circumstances may indicate the extent to which the individual client will be deemed to have granted or denied consent to disclosures by the Government lawyer to the Government lawyer's employing Agency under paragraph (d).

While the general thrust of this Rule may serve as guidance for the Government attorney, the Government lawyer's actions are defined and circumscribed by various Federal laws and these Rules. As a practical matter, in addition to determining the extent to which Rule 1.6 applies to a given situation, it is always advisable for Government lawyers to review the applicable Federal law that may govern their conduct under the circumstances, and to consult with their supervisors.

For example, Government employees are prohibited from using, for financial gain or other improper purposes, non-public information obtained by reason of their status as an employee. See 5 CFR 735.206. See also 28 CFR Part 17, which sets out regulations protecting confidential information relating to national security; 28 CFR 50.2, which establishes policy regarding the release of information relating to criminal and civil proceedings; 28 CFR 50.15(a)(3), which regulates the treatment of confidential attorney-client information in the context of Department of Justice representation of individual Government employees. The Privacy Act and other laws also prohibit the disclosure of certain types of confidential Government information. See 5 U.S.C. § 552a (personal information), 18 U.S.C. § 1905 (trade secrets), 18 U.S.C. § 798 (classified information), and 50 U.S.C. § 783(b) (classified information). Unique Government privileges also play a role in shaping a Government lawyer's duties and responsibilities regarding confidential Government information. Thus, for example, the law recognizes a deliberative process privilege, which protects from public disclosure predecisional communications that are part of the decision making processes of government agencies. See NLRB v. Sears, Roebuck & Co., 421 U.S. 132, 149, 150-51 (1975). See also 5 U.S.C. § 552(b)(5).

CROSS REFERENCES:
Rule 1.1 Competence
Rule 1.2 Scope of Representation
Rule 1.8 Conflict of Interest: Prohibited Transactions
Rule 1.13 The Federal Agency as the Client
Rule 1.16 Declining and Terminating Representation
Rule 2.1 Advisor
Rule 2.2 Mediator
Rule 2.3 Evaluation for Use by Third Persons
Rule 3.3 Candor toward the Tribunal
Rule 4.1 Truthfulness of Statements to Others
Rule 5.4 Professional Independence of a Federal Lawyer

RULE 1.7 Conflict of Interest: General Rule

(a) A Federal lawyer shall not represent a client if the representation of that client will be directly adverse to another client, unless:

(1) The Federal lawyer reasonably believes the representation will not adversely affect the relationship with the other client; and

(2) Each client consents after consultation.

(b) A Federal lawyer shall not represent a client if the representation of that client may be materially limited by the lawyer's responsibilities to another client or to a third person, or by the Federal lawyer's own interests, unless:

(1) The Federal lawyer reasonably believes the representation will not be adversely affected; and

(2) The client consents after consultation. When representation of multiple clients in a single matter is undertaken, the consultation shall include explanation of the implications of the common representation and the advantages and risks involved.

COMMENT:

Loyalty is an essential element in the Federal lawyer's relationship to a client. If an impermissible conflict of interest exists before representation, the Federal lawyer should decline to represent the client. If such a conflict arises after representation has been undertaken, the Federal lawyer should seek to withdraw from representation of the subsequent client. See Rule 1.16. When more than one client is involved and the Federal lawyer is permitted to withdraw because a conflict arises after the representation has begun, the Federal lawyer's ethical ability to continue to represent any of the clients is determined by Rule 1.9. See also Rule 2.2(c). As to whether a client-lawyer relationship exits or, having once been established, is continuing, see Comment to Rule 1.3.

As a general proposition, loyalty to a client prohibits undertaking representation directly adverse to that client without that client's consent. Paragraph (a) expresses that general rule. Thus, a Federal lawyer ordinarily shall not act as advocate against a person the Federal lawyer represents in some other matter, even if it is wholly unrelated. On the other hand, simultaneous representation in unrelated matters of clients whose interests are only generally adverse, does not require consent of either client. Paragraph (a) applies only when the representation of one client would be directly adverse to the other.

Rule 1.7

Loyalty to a client is also impaired when a Federal lawyer cannot consider, recommend, or carry out an appropriate course of action for the client because of the Federal lawyer's other responsibilities or interests. This type of conflict effectively forecloses alternatives that would otherwise be available to the client. Paragraph (b) addresses such situations. A possible conflict does not itself preclude the representation. The critical questions are — the likelihood that a conflict will eventuate and, if it does, whether it will materially interfere with the Federal lawyer's independent professional judgment in considering alternatives or foreclose courses of action that reasonably should be pursued on behalf of the client. Consideration should be given to whether the client wishes to accommodate the other interest involved.

Consultation and Consent

A client, including an organization (see Rule 1.13(b), may consent to representation notwithstanding a conflict. However, as indicated in paragraph (a)(1) with respect to representation directly adverse to a client, and paragraph (b)(1) with respect to material limitations on representation of a client, when a disinterested Federal lawyer would conclude that the client should not agree to the representation under the circumstances, the Federal lawyer involved cannot properly ask for such agreement to provide representation on the basis of the client's consent. When more than one client is involved, the question of conflict must be resolved as to each client. Moreover, there may be circumstances where it is impossible to make the disclosure necessary to obtain consent.

Federal Lawyer's Interests

The Federal lawyer's own interests should not be permitted to have an adverse effect on representation of a client. (See, e.g., 18 U.S.C. 208.) If the probity of a Federal lawyer's own conduct in a transaction is in serious question, it may be difficult or impossible for the Federal lawyer to give a client detached advice. A Federal lawyer shall not allow related business interests to affect representation, for example, by referring clients to an enterprise in which the Federal lawyer has an undisclosed interest.

Conflict of Litigation

Paragraph (a) prohibits representation of opposing parties in litigation. Simultaneous representation of parties whose interest in litigation may conflict, such a co-plaintiffs or co-defendants, is governed by paragraph (b). An impermissible conflict may exist by reason of substantial discrepancy in the parties testimony, incompatibility in position in relation to an opposing party, or the fact that there are substantially different possibilities of settlement of the claims or liabilities in question. Such conflicts can arise in criminal cases, as well as, civil matters. The potential for a conflict of interest in representing multiple defendant in a criminal case is so grave that ordinarily a Federal lawyer should not represent more than one co-defendant. On the other hand, common representation of persons having similar interests is proper if the risk of adverse effect is minimal and the requirements of paragraph (b) are met. Compare Rule 2.2 involving intermediation between clients.

Ordinarily, a Federal lawyer shall not act as advocate against a client the Federal lawyer represents in some other matter, even if the other matter is wholly unrelated. However, there are circumstances in which a Government lawyer may act as advocate against the Government lawyer's Federal Agency. For example, Government lawyers in some circumstances may represent another Government employee in proceedings (e.g., courts-martial or adverse personnel action proceedings) in which a Federal Agency is the opposing party. The propriety of concurrent representation can depend on the nature of the litigation. For example, a suit charging fraud entails conflict to a degree not involved in a suit for declaratory judgment concerning statutory interpretation.

A Federal lawyer may represent parties having antagonistic positions on a legal question that has arisen in different cases, unless representation of either client would be adversely affected. Thus, it is ordinarily proper to assert such positions in cases pending in different trial courts, but it may be improper to do so in cases pending in an appellate court.

Interest of a Person Paying for a Federal Lawyer's Service

A Non-Government lawyer may be paid from a source other than the client, if the client is informed of that fact, consents, and the arrangement does not compromise the Federal lawyer's duty of loyalty to the client. See Rule 1.8(f). For example, an defendant's family may pay a Non-Government lawyer to represent a defendant at trial.

Other Conflict Situations

Conflicts of interest in contexts other than litigation sometimes may be difficult to assess. Relevant factors in determining whether there is potential for adverse effect include the duration and intimacy of the Federal lawyer's relationship with the client or clients involved, the functions being performed by the Federal lawyer, the likelihood that actual conflict will arise and the likely prejudice to the client from the conflict if it does arise. The question is often one of the proximity and degree.

Although the Federal lawyer must be careful to avoid conflict of interest situations, resolving questions of conflict of interest is primarily the responsibility of the supervisory lawyer or the judge. See also Rule 5.1.

Conflict Charged by an Opposing Party

In litigation, courts raise conflict of interest issues when reason exists to believe that a Federal lawyer may have neglected his or her responsibilities. In a criminal case, inquiry by the court is generally required when a Federal lawyer represents multiple defendants. When an apparent conflict calls into question the fair or efficient administration of justice, opposing counsel may properly raise the issue. Such objections should be viewed with caution, however, for they can be misused as a technique of harassment. See Scope.

Government Lawyers

This Rule is not intended to apply to conflicts between Federal agencies or components of government (Federal, State or local), where the resolution of such conflicts has been entrusted by law to a specific individual or entity. Thus, for example, 28 U.S.C. § 516, authorizes the Attorney General and the Government lawyers of the Justice Department to resolve conflicts between certain Government agencies for purposes of litigation and even to assert positions in litigation that might be adverse to positions urged upon the Department of Justice by a client Agency. (See also Executive Order 12146, sections 1 - 4, which directs Executive agencies that are unable to resolve a legal dispute to submit the dispute to the Attorney General). Moreover, this rule is not intended to supersede Government regulations, such as 28 CFR 50.15, et seq., governing the resolution of conflicts in the context of representation of Government employees sued in their individual or personal capacities.

CROSS REFERENCES:

Rule 1.1 Competence
Rule 1.2 Scope of Representation
Rule 1.3 Diligence
Rule 1.4 Communication
Rule 1.8 Conflict of Interest: Prohibited Transactions
Rule 1.9 Conflict of Interest: Former Client
Rule 1.12 Former Judge or Arbitrator
Rule 1.13 The Federal Agency as the Client Rule 1.16 Declining or Terminating Representation
Rule 2.2 Mediator
Rule 2.3 Evaluation for Use by Third Person
Rule 5.1 Responsibilities of a Supervisory Lawyer
Rule 5.4 Professional Independence of a Federal Lawyer

RULE 1.8 Conflict of Interest: Prohibited Transactions

(a) A Federal lawyer shall not enter into a business transaction with a client or knowingly acquire an ownership, possessory, security, or other pecuniary interest adverse to a client unless:

(1) The transaction and terms on which the Federal lawyer requires the interest are fair and reasonable to the client and are fully disclosed and transmitted in writing to the client in a manner which can be reasonably understood by the client;

(2) The client is given a reasonable opportunity to seek the advice of independent counsel in the transaction; and

(3) The client consents in writing thereto.

(b) A Federal lawyer shall not use information relating to representation of a client to the disadvantage of the client unless the client consents after consultation.

(c) A Federal lawyer shall not prepare an instrument giving the lawyer or an individual related to the lawyer as parent, child, sibling, or spouse any substantial gift from a client, including a testamentary gift, except where the client is related to the donee.

(d) While representing a client, a Federal lawyer shall not make or negotiate an agreement giving the lawyer literary or edit rights to a portrayal or account based in substantial part on information relating to the representation.

(e) A Federal lawyer shall not provide financial assistance to a client in connection with pending or contemplated litigation, except that:

(1) A Non-Government lawyer practicing before a Federal Agency may advance court costs and expenses of litigation, the repayment of which may be contingent on the outcome of the matter; and

(2) A Non-Government lawyer practicing before a Federal Agency representing an indigent client may pay court costs and expenses of litigation on behalf of the client.

(f) A Federal lawyer shall not accept compensation for representing a client from one other than the client unless:

Rule 1.8

(1) The client consents after consultation;

(2) There is no interference with the Federal lawyer's independence of professional judgment or with the Federal lawyer-client relationship; and

(3) Information relative to representation of a client is protected as required by Rule 1.6.

(g) A Federal lawyer who represents two or more clients shall not participate in making an aggregate settlement of the claims of or against the clients, or in a criminal case an aggregate agreement as to guilty pleas or nolo contendere pleas, unless each client consents after consultation, including disclosure of the existence and nature of all the claims or pleas involved and of the participation of each person in the settlement.

(h) A Federal lawyer shall not:

(1) Make an agreement prospectively limiting the lawyer's liability to a client for malpractice unless permitted by law and the client is independently represented in making the agreement.

(2) Settle a claim for liability due to allegations of malpractice with an unrepresented client or former client without first advising that person in writing that independent representation is appropriate in connection therewith.

(i) A Federal lawyer related to another lawyer as parent, child, sibling, or spouse shall not represent a client if the client's interest is directly adverse to a person who the Federal lawyer knows is represented by the other lawyer, except with the consent of the client after consultation regarding the relationship.

(j) A Non-Government lawyer shall not acquire a proprietary interest in the cause of action or subject matter of litigation the lawyer is conducting for a client, except that the lawyer may:

(1) Acquire a lien granted by law to secure the Non-Government lawyer's fee or expenses; and

(2) Contract with a client for a reasonable contingent fee in a civil case.

COMMENT:

Government Lawyers

Government lawyers shall strictly adhere to Federal Agency standards of conduct regulations and applicable laws in all dealings with individual clients. (See generally 18 U.S.C. § 202 -211.) Such laws generally prohibit entering into business transactions with clients, deriving financial benefit from representations of client, and accepting gifts from clients or other entities for the performance of official duties. This Rule does not authorize conduct otherwise prohibited by such regulations. A Government lawyer shall not refer legal or other business to any private Non-Government lawyer or enterprise with whom the Government lawyer has any present or expected direct or indirect personal interest. Special care will be taken to avoid giving preferential treatment to other Government lawyers in their private capacities.

A Government lawyer shall not request or accept any gratuity, salary, or other compensation from a client incident to the performance of duties as a Government employee.

Transactions Between Client and Federal Lawyer

As a general principle, all business transactions between client and Federal lawyer should be fair and reasonable to the client. In such transactions, a review by independent counsel on behalf of the client is often advisable. Furthermore, a Federal lawyer shall not exploit information relating to the representation to the clients disadvantage. For example, a Federal lawyer who has learned that the client is investing in specific real estate shall not, without the client's consent, seek to acquire nearby property where doing so would adversely affect the client's plan for investment. Paragraph (a) does not apply to standard commercial transactions between the Federal lawyer and the client for products or services that the client generally markets to others, for example, banking or brokerage services, medical services, products manufactured or distributed by the client, and utility services. In such transactions, the lawyer has no advantage in dealing with the client, and the restrictions in paragraph (a) are unnecessary and impracticable. All transactions must comply with promulgated standards of conduct and other laws. See also Rule 1.5.

Literary Rights

An agreement by which a Federal lawyer acquires literary or media rights concerning the conduct of the representation creates a conflict between the interests of the client and the personal interests of the Federal lawyer. Measures suitable in the representation of the client may detract from the publication value of an account of that representation.

Person Paying for a Federal Lawyer's Services

Paragraph (f) requires the Federal lawyer to disclose the fact that the Federal lawyer's services are being paid for by a third party. Such an arrangement must also conform to the requirements of Rule 1.6 concerning confidentiality and Rule 1.7 concerning conflict of interest.

Family Relationships Between Federal Lawyers

Paragraph (i) applies to related Federal lawyers who are in the same or different Federal Agency. Related Federal lawyers in the same office also are governed by Rules 1.7, 1.9, and 1.10. The disqualification stated in paragraph (i) is personal and is not imputed to other Federal lawyers in the offices with whom the Federal lawyer performs duty.

Acquisition of Interest in Litigation

Paragraph (j) states the traditional general rule that Federal lawyers are prohibited from acquiring a proprietary interest in litigation. This general rule, which has its basis in common law champerty and maintenance, is subject to specific exceptions developed in decisional law and continued in these Rules, such as the exception for reasonable contingent fees set forth in Rule 1.5 of the ABA Model Rules of Professional Conduct and the exception for certain advances of the costs of litigation set forth in paragraph (e).

The Rule is not intended to apply to customary qualifications and limitations in legal opinions and memoranda.

CROSS REFERENCES:

Rule 1.1 Competence
Rule 1.2 Scope of Representation
Rule 1.5 Fees
Rule 1.7 Conflict of Interest: General Rule
Rule 1.9 Conflict of Interest: Former Client
Rule 1.10 Imputed Disqualification: General Rule
Rule 1.16 Declining or Terminating Representation

RULE 1.9 Conflict of Interest: Former Client

(a) A Federal lawyer who has formerly represented a client in a matter shall not thereafter represent another person in the same or a substantially related matter in which the person's interests are materially adverse to the interests of the client unless the former client consents after consultation.

(b) A Federal lawyer shall not knowingly represent a person in the same or a substantially related matter in which a firm with which the lawyer formerly was associated had previously represented a client:

(1) Whose interests are materially adverse to that person; and

(2) About whom the lawyer had acquired information protected by Rules 1.6 and 1.9(c) that is material to the matter;

unless the former client consents after consultation.

(c) A Federal lawyer who has formerly represented a client in a matter or whose present or former firm has formerly represented a client in a matter shall not thereafter:

(1) Use information relating to the representation to the disadvantage of the former client except as Rule 1.6 would permit with respect to a client or when the information has become generally known.

(2) Reveal information relating to the representation except as Rule 1.6 or Rule 3.3. would permit or require with respect to a client.

COMMENT:

After termination of a client-lawyer relationship, a Federal lawyer shall not represent another client except in conformity with this Rule. The principles in Rule 1.7 determine whether the interests of the present and former client are adverse. The principles in Rule 1.11 govern successive Government and private employment.

The scope of a "matter" for purposes of paragraph (a) may depend on the facts of a particular situation or transaction. The Federal lawyer's involvement in a matter can also be a question of degree. When a Federal lawyer has been directly involved in a specific transaction, subsequent representation of other clients with materially adverse interest clearly is prohibited. On the other hand, a Federal lawyer who recurrently handled a type of problem for a former client is not precluded from later representing another client in a wholly distinct problem of that type, even though the subsequent representation involves a position adverse to the prior client. Thus, the reassignment of judge

Rule 1.9

advocates between defense, prosecution, review, claim, and legal assistance functions within the same legal office is not precluded by this Rule.

Lawyers Moving Between Firms

When Non-Government lawyers have been associated within a firm, but then end their association, the question of whether the Non-Government lawyer should undertake representation is more complicated. There are several competing considerations. First, the client previously represented by the former firm must be reasonably assured that the principle of loyalty to the client is not compromised. Second, the rule should not be so broadly cast as to preclude other persons from having reasonable choice of legal counsel. Third, the rule should not unreasonably hamper lawyers from forming new associations and taking on new clients after having left a previous association. In this connection, it should be recognized that today many lawyers practice in firms, that many lawyers to some degree limit their practice to one field or another, and that many move from one association to another several times in their careers. If the concept of imputation were applied with unqualified rigor, the result would be radical curtailment of the opportunity of lawyers to move from one practice setting to another and of the opportunity of clients to change counsel.

Reconciliation of these competing principles in the past has been attempted under two rubrics. One approach has been to seek per se rules of disqualification. For example, it has been held that a partner in a law firm is conclusively presumed to have access to all confidences concerning all clients of the firm. Under this analysis, if a lawyer has been a partner in one law firm and then becomes a partner in another law firm, there may be a presumption that all confidences known by the partner in the first firm are known to all partners in the second firm. This presumption might properly be applied in some circumstances, especially where the client has been extensively represented, but may be unrealistic where the client was represented only for limited purposes. Furthermore, such a rigid rule exaggerates the difference between a partner and an associate in modern law firms.
The other rubric formerly used for dealing with disqualification is the appearance of impropriety proscribed in Canon 9 of the ABA Model Code of Professional Responsibility. This rubric has a twofold problem. First, the appearance of impropriety can be taken to include any new client-lawyer relationship that might make a former client feel anxious. If that meaning were adopted, disqualification would become little more than a question of subjective judgment by the former client. Second, since "impropriety" is undefined, the term "appearance of impropriety" is question-begging. It therefore has to be recognized that the problem of disqualification cannot be properly resolved either by simple analogy to a lawyer practicing alone or by the very general concept of appearance of impropriety.

Confidentiality

Preserving confidentiality is a question of access to information. Access to information, in turn, is essentially a question of fact in particular circumstances, aided by inferences, deductions, or working presumptions that reasonably may be made about the way in which lawyers work together. A lawyer may have general access to files of all clients of a law firm and may regularly participate in discussions of their affairs; it should be inferred that such a lawyer in fact is privy to all information about all of the firm's clients. In contrast, another lawyer may have access to the files of only a limited number of clients and participate in discussions of the affairs of no other clients; in the absence of information to the contrary, it should be inferred that such a lawyer in fact is privy to information about the clients actually served but not those of other clients.

Application of paragraph (b) depends on a situation's particular facts. In such an inquiry, the burden of proof should rest upon the lawyer whose disqualification is sought.

Paragraph (b) operates to disqualify the lawyer only when the lawyer involved has actual knowledge of information protected by Rules 1.6 and 1.9(c). Thus, if a lawyer while with one firm acquired no knowledge or information relating to a particular client of the firm, and that lawyer later joins another firm, neither the lawyer individually nor the second firm is disqualified from representing another client in the same or a related matter even though the interests of the two clients conflict. See Rule 1.10(b) for the restrictions on a firm once a lawyer has terminated association the firm.

Independent of the question of disqualification of a firm, a lawyer changing professional association has a continuing duty to preserve confidentiality of information about a client formerly represented. See Rules 1.6 and 1.9.

Adverse Positions

The underlying question is whether the Federal lawyer was so involved in a particular matter that the subsequent representation can be justly regarded as a changing of sides in the matter in question.

Information acquired by the Federal lawyer in the course of representing a client shall not later be used by the Federal lawyer to the disadvantage of the client. However, just because a Federal lawyer once represented a client does not preclude the Federal lawyer from using generally known information about that client when later representing another client.

Disqualification from subsequent representation is for the protection of clients and can be waived by them. A waiver is effective only if it is preceded by full disclosure of the circumstances, including the Federal lawyer's role in behalf of the new client.

With regard to an opposing party's raising a question of conflict of interest, see Comment to Rule 1.7.

CROSS REFERENCES:

Rule 1.1 Competence
Rule 1.2 Scope of Representation
Rule 1.6 Confidentiality
Rule 1.7 Conflict of Interest: General Rule
Rule 1.11 Successive Government and Private Employment
Rule 1.16 Declining or Terminating Representation
Rule 2.2 Mediator

RULE 1.10 Imputed Disqualification: General Rule

(a) Government lawyers working in the same Federal Agency are not automatically disqualified from representing a client because any of them practicing alone would be prohibited from doing so by Rules 1.7, 1.8(c), 1.9, or 2.2.

(b) When a Federal lawyer has terminated an association with a firm, the firm is not prohibited from thereafter representing a person with interests materially adverse to those of a client represented by the formerly associated lawyer and not currently represented by the firm, unless:

(1) The matter is the same or substantially related to that in which the formerly associated lawyer represented the client; and

(2) Any Federal lawyer remaining in the firm has information protected by Rules 1.6 and 1.9(c) that is material to the matter.

(c) A disqualification under this Rule may be waived by the affected client under the conditions stated in Rule 1.7.

COMMENT:

Government Federal Agency Practice

The circumstances of Government service may require representation of opposing sides by Government lawyers working in the same Federal Agency. Such representation is permissible so long as conflicts of interest are avoided and independent judgment, zealous representation, and protection of confidences are not compromised. Thus, the principle of imputed disqualification is not automatically controlling for Government lawyers. The knowledge, action, and conflicts of interest of one Government lawyer are not to be imputed to another simply because they operate from the same office. For example, a number of military defense counsels or public defenders operating from one office under a common supervisory lawyer and sharing clerical assistance are not prohibited from representing co-defendants at trial.

While it is permissible under this rule for a Government lawyer to represent an individual client in a military justice or an administrative proceeding that is under the control of a superior of the Government lawyer, particular care and attention is required when potential conflicts of interest exist between the organizational client of a supervisory lawyer and the individual clients of the Government lawyer being supervised.

Preserving confidentiality is a question of access to information. Access to information, in turn, is essentially a question of fact in particular circumstance, aided by inferences, deductions, or working presumptions that reasonably may be made about the way in which Government lawyers work together. A Government lawyer may have general access to files of all clients of a Federal Agency legal staff and may regularly participate in discussions of their affairs. It may be inferred that such a Government lawyer in fact is privy to all information about all the office's clients. In contrast, another Government lawyer may have access only to the files of his or her clients and does not participate in discussion of the affairs of other clients. In the absence of information to the contrary, it should be inferred that such a Government lawyer in fact is privy to information about the clients actually served, but not to information of other clients.

General

Whether a Federal lawyer is disqualified requires a functional analysis of the facts in a specific situation. The analysis should include consideration of whether the following will be compromised: preserving attorney-client confidentiality; maintaining independence of judgment; and avoiding positions adverse to a client.

Additionally, a Federal lawyer changing jobs has a continuing duty to preserve confidentiality of information about a client formerly represented. See Rules 1.6 and 1.9.

Maintaining independent judgment allows a Federal lawyer to consider, recommend, and carry out any appropriate course of action for a client without regard to the Federal lawyer's personal interests or the interests of another. When such independence is lacking or unlikely, representation cannot be zealous.

Rules 1.10 & 1.11

Another aspect of loyalty to a client is the Federal lawyer's obligation to decline subsequent representation involving positions adverse to a former client in substantially related matters. This obligation requires abstention from adverse representation by the individual Federal lawyer involved, but does not properly entail abstention of other Federal lawyers through imputed disqualification. Hence this aspect of the problem is governed by Rule 1.9(a).

CROSS REFERENCES:

Rule 1.6 Confidentiality
Rule 1.7 Conflict of Interest: General Rule
Rule 1.8 Conflict of Interest: Prohibited Transactions
Rule 1.9 Conflict of Interest: Former Client
Rule 2.2 Mediator

RULE 1.11 Successive Government and Private Employment

(a) Except as law may otherwise expressly permit, a Federal lawyer shall not represent a private client in connection with a matter in which the Federal lawyer participated personally and substantially as a Government employee unless the appropriate Government Agency consents after consultation. No lawyer in a firm with which that lawyer is associated may knowingly undertake or continue representation in such matter unless:

(1) The disqualified Federal lawyer is screened from any participation in the matter and is apportioned no part of the fee therefrom; and

(2) Written notice is promptly given to the appropriate government Agency to enable it to ascertain compliance with the provisions of this Rule.

(b) Except as law may otherwise expressly permit, a Federal lawyer having information that the lawyer knows is confidential Government information about a person acquired when the lawyer was a Government employee shall not represent a private client whose interests are adverse to that person in a matter in which the information could be used to the material disadvantage of that person. A firm with which that lawyer is associated may undertake or continue representation in the matter only if the disqualified lawyer is screened from any participation in the matter and is apportioned no part of the fee therefrom.

(c) Except as law may otherwise expressly permit, a Federal lawyer serving as a Government employee shall not:

(1) Participate in a matter in which the Federal lawyer participated personally and substantially while in private practice or nongovernmental employment, unless under applicable law no one is, or by lawful delegation may be, authorized to act in the lawyer's stead in the matter.

(2) Negotiate for private employment with any person who is involved as a party or as attorney for a party in a matter in which the Federal lawyer is participating personally and substantially.

(d) As used in this Rule, the term "matter" includes:

(1) Any judicial or other proceeding, application, request for a ruling or other determination, contract, claim, controversy, investigation, charge, accusation, arrest, or other particular matter involving a specific party or parties.

(2) Any other matter covered by the conflict of interest rules of the appropriate Federal Agency.

(e) As used in this Rule, the term "confidential Governmental information" means information which has been obtained under Governmental authority and that, at the time this Rule is applied, the Government is prohibited by law from disclosing to the public or has a legal privilege not to disclose, and which is not otherwise available to the public.

COMMENT:

This Rule prevents a Federal lawyer from exploiting public office for the advantage of a private client.

A Government lawyer representing a Federal Agency is subject to these Rules of Professional Conduct, including the prohibition against representing adverse interests stated in Rule 1.7 and the protections afforded former clients in Rule 1.9. In addition, such a Government lawyer is subject to Rule 1.11 and to laws regarding conflicts of interest, including 18 U.S.C. § 205 (prohibits Government employees from representing parties in actions against the United States), § 207 (restrictions on successive Government and private employment), § 208 (financial conflict of interest restrictions), and § 281 (restrictions on retired military officers); 5 CFR Part 2637 (regulations concerning post Government employment); and any Federal Agency regulations or directives. Such statutes and regulations may circumscribe the extent to which the Federal Agency may give consent under this Rule. If a Federal Agency has adopted rules governing practice before the agency by former federal lawyers, such issues (e.g., notice requirements) are governed by the Federal Agency rules and this Rule is not intended to displace such Agency requirements.

Where the successive clients are a Federal Agency and a private client, the risk exists that power or discretion vested in public authority might be used for the special benefit of a private client. A Federal lawyer should not be in a position in which benefit to a private client might affect performance of the Federal lawyer's professional functions on behalf of public authority. Also, unfair advantage could accrue to the private client by reason of access to confidential Government information about the client or by reason of access to confidential Government information about the client's adversary obtainable only through the Federal lawyer's government service. The rules governing Federal lawyers presently or formerly employed by a Federal Agency, however, should not be so restrictive as to inhibit transfer of employment to and from the Government. The Government has a legitimate need to attract qualified Federal lawyers as well as to maintain high ethical standards. The provisions for screening and waiver are necessary to prevent the disqualification rule from imposing too severe a deterrent against entering public service.

When the client is an agency of one government, that agency should be treated as a private client for purposes of this Rule if the Federal lawyer thereafter represents an agency of another government: as when a Federal lawyer represents a city and subsequently is employed by a Federal Agency.

Paragraphs (a)(1) and (b) do not prohibit a Federal lawyer from receiving salary or partnership income where established by prior independent agreement. They prohibit directly relating the Federal lawyer's compensation to the fee in the matter in which the Federal lawyer is disqualified.

Paragraph (a)(2) does not require that a Federal lawyer give notice to the Federal Agency at a time when premature disclosure would injure the client; a requirement for premature disclosure might preclude engagement of the Federal lawyer. Such notice is, however, required to be given as soon as practicable to give the Federal Agency a reasonable opportunity to determine if the Federal lawyer is complying with Rule 1.11 and to take appropriate action if it believes the Federal lawyer is not complying.

Paragraph (b) operates only when the Federal lawyer in question has knowledge of the information. This means actual knowledge. Paragraph (b) does not operate with respect to information that merely could be imputed to the Federal lawyer.

CROSS REFERENCES:

Rule 1.6 Fees
Rule 1.7 Conflict of Interest: General Rule
Rule 1.8 Conflict of Interest: Prohibited Transactions
Rule 1.9 Conflict of Interest: Former Client

RULE 1.12 Former Judge or Arbitrator

(a) Except as stated in paragraph (d), a Federal lawyer shall not represent anyone in connection with a matter in which the lawyer participated personally and substantially as a judge or other adjudicative officer, arbitrator, or law clerk to such a person, unless all parties to the proceeding consent after disclosure.

(b) A Federal lawyer shall not negotiate for employment with any person who is involved as a party or as attorney for a party in a matter in which the lawyer is participating personally and substantially as a judge or other adjudicative officer, or arbitrator.

(c) If a Federal lawyer is disqualified by paragraph (a), no Federal lawyer in a firm with which the lawyer is associated may knowingly undertake or continue representation in the matter unless:

(1) The disqualified Federal lawyer is screened from any participation in the matter and is apportioned no part of the fee therefrom.

(2) Written notice is promptly given to the appropriate tribunal to enable it to ascertain compliance with the provisions of this Rule.

(d) An arbitrator selected as a partisan of a party in a multi-member arbitration panel is not prohibited from subsequently representing that party.

COMMENT:

This Rule generally parallels Rule 1.11. The term "personally and substantially" means that a judge who was a member of a multi-member court, and thereafter left judicial office, is not prohibited from representing a client in a matter pending in the court, so long as it is a matter in which the former judge did not participate. Likewise, a former judge's exercise of administrative responsibility in a court or judiciary office does not prevent the former judge from acting as a Federal lawyer in a matter in which the judge had previously exercised remote or incidental administrative responsibility that did not affect the merits. Compare the Comment to Rule 1.11. The term "adjudicative officer" includes such officials as hearing officers, legal advisors to administrative boards, and investigating officers.

CROSS REFERENCES:

Rule 1.7 Conflict of Interest: General Rule
Rule 1.8 Conflict of Interest: Prohibited Transactions
Rule 1.11 Successive Government and Private Employment

RULE 1.13 The Federal Agency as the Client

(a) Except when representing another client pursuant to paragraphs (e), (f) and (g), a Government lawyer represents the Federal Agency that employs the Government lawyer. Government lawyers are often formally employed by a Federal Agency but assigned to an organizational element within the Federal Agency. Unless otherwise specifically provided, the Federal Agency, not the organizational element, is ordinarily considered the client. The Federal Agency acts through its authorized officials. These officials include the heads of organizational elements within the Federal Agency. When a Government lawyer is assigned to an organizational element and designated to provide legal services and advice to the head of that organization, the client-lawyer relationship exists between the Government lawyer and the Federal agency, as represented by the head of the organization, as to matters within the scope of the official business of the organization. The head of the organization may only invoke the attorney-client privilege or the rule of confidentiality for the benefit of the Federal Agency. In so invoking, either the attorney-client privilege or attorney-client confidentiality on behalf of the Federal Agency, the head of the organization is subject to being overruled by higher agency authority.

(b) If a Government lawyer knows that a Government employee is acting, intending to act, or refusing to act in a matter related to the representation in a manner such that either a violation of a legal obligation to the Federal Agency or a violation of law reasonably might be imputed to the Federal Agency, the Government lawyer shall proceed as is reasonably necessary in the best interest of the Federal Agency. In determining how to proceed, the Government lawyer shall give due consideration to the seriousness of the violation and its consequences, the scope and nature of the Government lawyer's representation, the responsibility in the Federal Agency, the apparent motivation of the person involved, the policies of the Federal Agency concerning such matters, and any other relevant considerations. Any measures taken shall be designed to minimize disruption of the Federal Agency and the risk of revealing information relating to the representation to persons outside the Federal Agency. Such measures may include, among others:

(1) Advising the person that, in the Government lawyer's opinion, the action, planned action, or refusal to act is contrary to law; advising the person of the Federal Agency's policy on the matter concerned; advising the person that his or her personal legal interests are at risk and that he or she should consult independent counsel, because their may be a conflict of interest with the Government lawyer's responsibility to the organization; and asking the person to reconsider the matter.

(2) Advising the person that a separate legal opinion on the matter be sought for presentation to appropriate authority in Federal Agency.

(3) Advising the person that the lawyer is ethically obligated to preserve the interests of the Federal Agency and, as a result, must consider discussing the matter with supervisory lawyers within the Government lawyer's office or at a higher level within the Federal Agency.

(4) Referring the matter to or seeking guidance from higher authority in the Federal Agency, including, if warranted by the seriousness of the matter, referral to the highest authority that can act on behalf of the Federal Agency.

(c) If, despite the Government lawyer's efforts in accordance with paragraph (b), the highest authority that can act concerning the matter insists upon action, or refusal to act, that is clearly a violation of law, the Government lawyer shall terminate representation with respect to the matter in question. In no event may the Government lawyer participate or assist in the illegal activity.

(d) In dealing with the Government employee, a Government lawyer shall explain the identity of the client when it is apparent that the Federal Agency's interests are adverse to those of the Government employee.

(e) A Government lawyer shall not form a client-lawyer relationship or represent a client other than the Federal Agency unless specifically assigned or authorized by competent authority.

(f) A Government lawyer representing the Federal Agency may also represent any of its Government employees subject to the provisions of paragraph (f), Rule 1.7, and other applicable authority. If the Federal Agency's consent to dual representation is required by Rule 1.7, the consent shall be given by an appropriate official of the Federal Agency, other than the individual to be represented.

(g) A Government lawyer who has been duly assigned or authorized to represent an individual who is subject to disciplinary action or administrative proceedings, or to provide civil legal assistance to an individual, has, for those purposes, a lawyer-client relationship with that individual.

COMMENT:

The Comment to the ABA Model Rule acknowledges the applicability of this Rule to governmental organizations: the balance between maintaining confidentiality and assuring that wrongful official acts are prevented or rectified; and the difficulty in defining precisely the identity of the client (and prescribing the resulting obligations of such lawyers) in the government context.

Model Rules of Professional Conduct

Rule 1.13

Except when a Government lawyer is assigned to represent the interest of another client, the Federal Agency that employs the Government lawyer is the client. This principle is critical to the application of these Rules, since the identity of the client affects significant confidentiality and conflict issues.

Because the Federal Agency is the Government lawyer's client, the Government lawyer represents the Federal Agency acting through its duly authorized constituents. Any application of Rule 1.13 to Government lawyers must, however, take into account the differences between Federal agencies and other organizations. These exceptions include, but are not limited to, Government lawyers assigned to represent individuals under subsection (g); prosecutors who represent the Government of the United States; Government lawyers authorized to represent several Federal agencies in intragovernmental legal controversies; and counsel assigned to perform special duties, such as assignment to other Federal agencies or subagencies.

In most cases, the Federal Agency will be a discrete entity with identifiable lines of authority. Federal Agency regulations and directives provide clear benchmarks for assessing conduct. In some situations, the Government lawyer may represent a branch of Government rather than a Federal Agency. Although arguments have been made that the Government lawyer's ultimate obligation is to serve the public interest or the "government as a whole", for practical purposes, these may be unworkable ethical guidelines, particularly with regard to client control and confidentiality.

A Federal Agency may, of course, establish different client-lawyer obligations by Executive or court order, regulation, or statute. See e.g., 5 U.S.C. 2302.

Nevertheless, the conclusion that the government lawyer's client is the lawyer's employing agency does not answer every ethical question. There are special considerations that affect the ethical responsibilities of the Government lawyer. For example, the Government lawyer has a responsibility to question the conduct of agency officials more extensively than a lawyer for a private organization would in similar circumstances. Government lawyers, in many situations, are asked to represent diverse client interests. For example, Government lawyers in the Executive branch also represent other branches of Government in a number of different situations. Here it becomes especially clear that the Government attorney's responsibilities are affected by the attorney's more general obligations to the United States, as for example, when it is necessary to refuse to defend an unconstitutional statute or regulation or to resist the encroachment by one branch on another's sphere of power. The client-lawyer obligations of Government lawyers in other branches of Government raise still different considerations. For example, lawyers engaged by the Senate or the House of Representatives, by Congressional committees, or on the staffs of individual members of Congress may develop client-lawyer relationships with those bodies, committees or individuals. Yet these relationships must themselves be viewed in the context of the Government lawyer's broader obligations to the Congress as a whole and ultimately to the United States.

Relation to Other Rules

The authority and responsibility provided in paragraph (b) are concurrent with the authority and responsibility provided in other Rules. In particular, this Rule does not limit or expand the Government lawyer's responsibility under Rules 1.6, 1.8, 1.16, 3.3, or 4.1. If the Government lawyer's services are being used by an organization to further a crime or fraud by the organization, Rule 1.2(d) may be applicable.

Termination of Representation

Paragraph (c) recognizes that the Government lawyer is not always free to withdraw from representation. Specific facts will govern each case.

Clarifying the Government Lawyer's Role

When the Federal Agency's interests are adverse to those of one or more of its Government employees, the Government lawyer should advise the Government employee that the Government lawyer cannot continue to advise that person and that person may wish to obtain independent representation. Care must be taken to ensure that the individual understands that, when there is such adversity of interest, the Government lawyer can no longer provide legal advice to that person on those matters in which the person's interests are adverse, and that discussions between the Government lawyer and the individual are not confidential or privileged.

Whether such a warning should be given by the Government lawyer to any Government employee may turn on the facts of each case.

Dual Representation

Paragraph (e) recognizes that a Government lawyer may only enter into a client-lawyer relationship and represent persons when specifically authorized by a Federal Agency directive or an authorized superior. Unless authorized and assigned to represent a specific person or class of persons, the Government lawyer shall not establish a client-lawyer relationship. If a Government lawyer is uncertain as to the scope of representation authorized, the Government lawyer shall consult the supervisory lawyer. Recognition is given to the Government lawyer representing a Government employee of the Federal Agency.

Paragraph (f) recognizes that a Government lawyer may also represent a Government employee of the Federal Agency.

Paragraph (g) recognizes that the Government lawyer who is designated to represent another individual in Federal Government service against whom disciplinary or administrative proceedings have been brought, establishes a client-lawyer relationship with its privilege and professional responsibility to protect and defend the interest of the individual represented. This is also true for Federal lawyers providing legal assistance. But See Rule 1.2. Representation of members of the Federal Agency, other Government employees, and other individuals in accordance with paragraph (g) and the assumption of the traditional client-lawyer relationship with such individuals is not inconsistent with the Government lawyer's duties to the Federal Agency.

CROSS REFERENCES:

Rule 1.2 Scope of Representation
Rule 1.6 Confidentiality of Information
Rule 1.7 Conflict of Interest: General Rule
Rule 1.8 Conflict of Interest: Prohibited Transactions
Rule 1.16 Declining or Terminating Representation
Rule 2.1 Advisor
Rule 3.3 Candor Toward the Tribunal
Rule 3.8 Special Responsibilities of a Prosecutor
Rule 4.1 Truthfulness in Statements to Others
Rule 5.1 Responsibilities of a Supervisory Lawyer
Rule 5.2 Responsibilities of a Subordinate Lawyer
Rule 5.4 Professional Independence of a Federal Lawyer

RULE 1.14 Client Under a Disability

(a) When a client's ability to make adequately considered decisions in connection with the representation is impaired, whether because of minority, mental disability, or for some other reason, the Federal lawyer shall, as far as reasonably possible, maintain a normal client-lawyer relationship with the client.

(b) A Federal lawyer may seek the appointment of a guardian or take other protective action with respect to a client, only when the Federal lawyer reasonably believes the client cannot adequately act in the client's own interest.

COMMENT:

The normal client-lawyer relationship is based on the assumption that the client, when properly advised and assisted, is capable of making decisions about important matters. When the client is a minor or suffers from a mental disorder or disability, however, maintaining the ordinary client-lawyer relationship shall not be possible in all respects. In particular, an incapacitated person may have no power to make legally binding decisions. Nevertheless, a client lacking legal competence often has the ability to understand, deliberate upon, and reach conclusions about the matters affecting the client's own well-being. Furthermore, to an increasing extent, the law recognizes intermediate degrees of competence. For example, children as young as five or six years of age, and certainly those of ten or twelve, are regarded as having opinions that are entitled to weight in legal proceedings concerning their custody. Also, some persons of advanced age can be quite capable of handling routine financial matters while needing special legal protection concerning major transactions.

Simply because a client is under a disability does not diminish the Federal lawyer's obligation to treat the client with attention and respect. If the person has no guardian or legal representative, the Federal lawyer should take action so that procedures are initiated for the appointment of a guardian by the person's relatives, civil authorities, or the Veterans Administration. Even if the person does have a legal representative, the Federal lawyer should as far as possible accord the represented person the status of client, particularly in maintaining communication.

If a legal representative already has been appointed for the client, the Federal lawyer ordinarily should look to the representative for decisions on behalf of the client. If a legal representative has not been appointed, the Federal lawyer should consider recommending such an appointment when it would serve the client's best interests.

Disclosure of the Client's Conditions

Rules of procedure in civil litigation generally provide that minors or persons suffering mental disability shall be represented by a guardian or next friend if they do not have a general guardian. Disclosure of the client's disability, however, can adversely affect the client's interests. For example, raising the question of disability could, in some circumstances, lead to proceedings for involuntary commitment or to disclosure of information that would be detrimental to a client. The Federal lawyer's position in such cases is an unavoidably difficult one. The Federal lawyer may seek guidance from an appropriate diagnostician but military law does not recognize a physician-patient privilege.

CROSS REFERENCES:

Rule 1.2 Scope of Representation
Rule 1.3 Diligence
Rule 1.6 Confidentiality of Information

RULE 1.15 Safekeeping Property

(a) A Federal lawyer shall hold property of clients or third persons that is in the lawyer's possession in connection with a representation separate from the lawyer's own property. Funds shall be kept in a separate account maintained in the state in which the Federal lawyer's office is situated, or elsewhere with the consent of the client or third person. Other property shall be identified as belonging to the client and safeguarded appropriately. Complete records of such account funds and other property shall be kept by the lawyer and shall be preserved for a period of five years after termination of the representation.

(b) Upon receiving funds or other property in which a client or third person has an interest, a Federal lawyer shall promptly notify the client or the third person. Except as stated in this Rule or as otherwise permitted by law or by agreement with the client, the lawyer shall promptly deliver to the client or third person any funds or other property that the client or third person is entitled to receive and, upon request by the client or third person, shall promptly render full accounting regarding such property.

(c) When in the course of representation a Federal lawyer is in possession of property in which both the lawyer and another person claim interests, the property shall be kept separate by the lawyer until an accounting is made and their respective interests are severed. If a dispute arises concerning their respective interests, the portion in dispute shall be kept separate by the lawyer until the dispute is resolved.

(d) When property of a client or third party is admitted into evidence or otherwise included in the record of a proceeding, the Federal lawyer should take reasonable action to ensure its prompt return.

COMMENT:

Government lawyers normally will not hold property of clients or third persons. Should a Government lawyer find it necessary to hold such property, care must be taken to ensure the United States Government does not become responsible for any claims for the property. This rule does not authorize a Government lawyer to hold property of clients or third persons when otherwise prohibited from doing so.

A Federal lawyer should hold property of others with the care required of a professional fiduciary. Securities should be kept in safe deposit boxes, except when some other form of safekeeping is warranted by special circumstances. All property that belongs to clients or third persons should be kept separate from the Federal lawyer's business and personal property and, if money, in one or more trust accounts. Separate trust accounts may be warranted when administering estate monies or acting in a similar fiduciary capacity.

When it is necessary to use a client's property as evidence, a Federal lawyer should seek to obtain court permission to withdraw the property as an exhibit and to substitute a description or photograph after trial. If a Federal lawyer is offered contraband property, the Federal lawyer should refer to Rule 3.4 and its accompanying Comment for guidance.

Federal lawyers often receive funds from third parties from which the Federal lawyer's fee will be paid. If a risk exists that the client may divert the funds without paying the fee, the Federal lawyer is not required to remit the portion from which the fee is to be paid. A Federal lawyer shall not hold funds to coerce a client into accepting the Federal lawyer's contention, however. The disputed portion of the funds should be kept in trust and the Federal lawyer should suggest means such as arbitration for prompt resolution of the dispute. The undisputed portion of the funds shall be distributed promptly.

Third parties, such as a client's creditors, may have just claims against funds or other property in a Federal lawyer's custody. A Federal lawyer may have a duty under applicable law to protect such third-party claims against wrongful interference by the client, and accordingly may refuse to surrender the property to the client. A Federal lawyer should not unilaterally assume to arbitrate a dispute between the client and the third party, however.

The obligations of a Federal lawyer under this Rule are independent of those arising from activity other than rendering legal services. For example, a Federal lawyer who serves as an escrow agent is governed by the applicable law relating to fiduciaries even though the Federal lawyer does not render legal services in the transaction.

A Federal attorney who holds the property of others that was admitted into evidence or otherwise included in the record of a proceeding should take reasonable steps to secure the return of the property to its rightful owner or proper custodian. Where possible copies, descriptions, or photographs should be substituted for the original item in the record.

CROSS REFERENCES:

Rule 3.4 Fairness to Opposing Party and Counsel

RULE 1.16 Declining or Terminating Representation

(a) Except as stated in paragraph (c), a Federal lawyer shall not represent a client, or, once representation has commenced, shall seek to withdraw from the representation of a client, if:

(1) The representation will result in violation of these Rules of Professional Conduct or law.

(2) The Federal lawyer's physical or mental condition materially impairs the lawyer's ability to represent the client.

(3) The Federal lawyer is dismissed by the client.

(b) Except as stated in paragraph (c), a Federal lawyer may seek to withdraw from representing a client if withdrawal can be accomplished without material adverse effect on the interests of the client, or if:

(1) The client persists in a course of action involving the Federal lawyer's services that the lawyer reasonably believes is criminal or fraudulent.

(2) The client has used the Federal lawyer's services to perpetrate a crime or fraud.

(3) A client insists upon pursuing an objective that the Federal lawyer considers repugnant or imprudent.

(4) The client fails substantially to fulfill an obligation to the Federal lawyer regarding the lawyer's services and has been given reasonable warning that the Federal lawyer will seek to withdraw unless the obligation is fulfilled.

(5) The representation will result in an unreasonable financial burden on the Federal lawyer or has been rendered unreasonable by the client.
(6) Other good cause for withdrawal exists.

(c) When properly ordered to do so by a tribunal or other competent authority, a Federal lawyer shall continue representation notwithstanding good cause for terminating the representation.

(d) Upon termination of representation, a Federal lawyer shall take steps to the extent reasonably practicable to protect a client's interests, such as giving reasonable notice to the client, allowing time for employment of other counsel, surrendering papers and property to which the client is entitled, and refunding any advance payment of fees that has not been earned. The Federal lawyer may retain papers relating to the client to the extent permitted by law.

COMMENT:

A Federal lawyer should not represent a client in a matter unless it can be performed competently, promptly, without improper conflict of interest, and to completion.

Mandatory Withdrawal

A Federal lawyer ordinarily must seek to withdraw from representation if the client demands that the Federal lawyer engage in conduct that is illegal or violates these Rules of Professional Conduct or other law. The Federal lawyer is not obliged to seek to withdraw simply because the client suggests such a course of conduct; a client may make such a suggestion in the hope that a Federal lawyer will not be constrained by a professional obligation.

Continued Representation Notwithstanding Good Cause

Notwithstanding the existence of good cause for terminating representation, a Federal lawyer appointed to represent a client shall continue such representation until relieved by competent authority. Who is competent authority will differ with the circumstances. A Government lawyer representing the Federal Agency may be authorized to withdraw from the representation by the Federal Agency's chief legal official or the Federal lawyer's supervisory lawyer. Difficulty may be encountered where competent authority requires an explanation for the termination and such explanation would necessitate the revelation of confidential facts. When necessary and practicable, a Federal lawyer should seek the advice of a supervisory lawyer. The decision by one authority to continue representation does not prevent the Federal lawyer from seeking withdrawal from other competent authority.

Discharge by the Client

A client has a right to discharge a Federal lawyer with or without cause. Where future disputes about the withdrawal are anticipated, it may be advisable to prepare a written statement reciting the circumstances leading to withdrawal.

Whether a client can release appointed counsel may depend on applicable law. A client seeking to release appointed counsel must be given a full explanation of the consequences. Those consequences may include a decision by the appointing authority that appointment of successor counsel is unjustified, thus requiring the client to represent him or herself.

If the client is mentally incompetent, the client may lack the legal capacity to discharge the Federal lawyer, and in any event, the discharge may be seriously adverse to the client's interests. See Rule 1.14.

Optional Withdrawal

A Federal lawyer may seek to withdraw from representation in some circumstances. The Federal lawyer has the option of seeking to withdraw if it can be accomplished without material adverse effect to the client's interests. Seeking to withdraw is also justified if the client persists in a course of action that the Federal lawyer reasonably believes is criminal or fraudulent, for a Federal lawyer is not required to be associated with such conduct even if the Federal lawyer does not further it. Seeking to withdraw also is permitted if the Federal lawyer's services were misused in the past, even if that would materially prejudice the client. The Federal lawyer also may seek to withdraw when the client insists on a repugnant or imprudent objective.

As the scope of a Federal lawyer's representation may be limited by the law under which the Federal lawyer's services are made available to the client, see Comment to Rule 1.2, good cause to seek withdrawal may exist when a Federal lawyer changes duty stations or duties within an office. For example, a legal assistance Federal lawyer has good cause to seek withdrawal when the Federal lawyer is reassigned within the office to duties as prosecutor. In such a circumstance, the legal assistance Federal lawyer has been granted permission to withdraw from representation of legal assistance clients by virtue of the reassignment to prosecutor duties. If a question arises as to whether a Federal lawyer has permission to withdraw from a particular representation, the Federal lawyer should consult with the supervisory lawyer who has the authority to grant permission to withdraw from the representation.

Assisting the Client upon Withdrawal

A Federal lawyer who has withdrawn from representation must take all reasonable steps to mitigate adverse consequences to the client. Such steps may include referring of the client to another Federal lawyer who is able to represent the client further. A Federal lawyer making such a referral should ensure that these Rules and any agency policy governing referral of clients is followed. If a Federal lawyer must refer a client to another Federal lawyer due to a conflict of interest, the referring Federal lawyer should be careful not to disclose confidential information relating to representation of another client.

Government Lawyers

Paragraph (c) recognizes that the Government lawyer is not always free to withdraw from representation. Competent authority may be the Government lawyer's supervisory lawyers or, in some cases, other Federal Agency officials in the Government lawyer's chain of command. Specific facts will govern each case.

Whether a Government lawyer may, under certain unusual circumstances, have a legal obligation to the Federal Agency after withdrawing or being released by the Federal Agency's highest authority is beyond the scope of these Rules.

CROSS REFERENCES:

Rule 1.2 Scope of Representation
Rule 1.6 Confidentiality of Information
Rule 1.7 Conflict of Interest: General Rule
Rule 1.13 The Federal Agency as the Client
Rule 1.14 Client Under A Disability
Rule 3.1 Meritorious Claims and Contentions
Rule 3.3 Candor Toward the Tribunal
Rule 3.8 Special Responsibilities of a Prosecutor

COUNSELOR

RULE 2.1 Advisor

In representing a client, a Federal lawyer shall exercise independent professional judgment and render candid advise. In rendering advice, a Federal lawyer may refer not only to law but to other considerations, such as moral, social, and political factors, that may be relevant to the client's situation, but not in conflict with the law.

Rules 2.1 & 2.2

COMMENT:

Scope of Advice

A client is entitled to straightforward advice expressing the Federal lawyer's honest assessment. Legal advice often involves unpleasant facts and alternatives that a client may be reluctant to confront. In presenting advice, a Federal lawyer endeavors to sustain the client's morale and may put advice in as acceptable a form as honesty permits. Nevertheless, a Federal lawyer should not be deterred from giving candid advice by the prospect that the advice will be unpalatable to the client.

Advice couched in narrowly legal terms may be of little value to a client, especially where practical considerations, such as cost or effects on other people, are predominant. Purely technical legal advice, therefore, can sometimes be inadequate. It is proper for a Federal lawyer to refer to other relevant considerations in giving advice. Such considerations impinge upon most legal questions and may decisively influence how the law will be applied.

A client may expressly or impliedly ask the Federal lawyer for purely technical advice. When such a request is made by a client experienced in legal matters, the Federal lawyer may accept it at face value. When such a request is made by client inexperienced in legal matters, however, the Federal lawyer's responsibility as advisor may include indicating more may be involved than strictly legal considerations.

Matters that go beyond strictly legal questions may also be in the domain of another profession. Family matters can involve problems within the professional competence of psychiatry, clinical psychology, or social work; business matters can involve problems within the competence of the accounting profession or of financial specialists. When consultation with a professional in another field is itself something a competent Federal lawyer would recommend, the Federal lawyer should make such a recommendation. At the same time, a Federal lawyer's best advice often consists of recommending a course of action in the face of conflicting recommendations of experts.

Offering Advice

When a Non-Government lawyer knows that a client proposes a course of action that is likely to result in substantial adverse legal consequences to the client, however, duty to the client under Rule 1.4 may require that the Non-Government lawyer act if the client's course of action is related to the representation. A Non-Government lawyer ordinarily has no duty to initiate investigation of a client's affairs or to give advice the client has indicated is unwanted, but a Non-Government lawyer should initiate advice to a client when doing so appears to be in the client's interest.

A Government lawyer has an affirmative duty to offer advice to a Government employee of the Federal Agency that employs the Government lawyer, if the Government lawyer knows that the Government employee is engaging in or about to engage in a course of conduct that would be a violation of law or that may result in substantial adverse legal consequences to the Federal Agency. A Government lawyer has the duty to provide the advice, even if the advice is unwanted.

CROSS REFERENCES:

Rule 1.1 Competence
Rule 1.4 Communication
Rule 1.6 Confidentiality of Information Rule 1.13 Federal Agency a Client
Rule 3.1 Meritorious Claims and Contentions
Rule 5.4 Professional Independence of a Federal lawyer

RULE 2.2 Intermediary

(a) A Federal lawyer may act as an intermediary between individuals if:

(1) The Federal lawyer consults with each client concerning the implications of common representation, including the advantages and risks involved and the effect on the attorney-client confidentiality, and obtains each client's consent to the common representation;

(2) The Federal lawyer reasonably believes that the matter can be resolved on terms compatible with each client's best interest, that each client will be able to make adequately informed decisions in the matter, and that there is little risk of material prejudice to the interests of any of the clients if the contemplated resolution is unsuccessful; and

(3) The Federal lawyer reasonably believes that the common representation can be undertaken impartially and without improper effect on other responsibilities the lawyer has to any of the clients.

(b) While acting as an intermediary, the Federal lawyer shall consult with each client concerning the decisions to be made and the considerations relevant in making them, so each client can make adequately informed decisions.

(c) A Federal lawyer shall withdraw as an intermediary if any of the clients so requests or if any of the conditions stated in paragraph (a) is no longer satisfied. Upon withdrawal, the lawyer shall not represent any of the clients in the matter that was the subject of the common representation unless each client consents.

COMMENT:

A Federal lawyer acts as an intermediary under this Rule when the Federal lawyer represents two or more clients with potentially conflicting interests. Because confusion can arise as to the Federal lawyer's role when each client is not separately represented, it is important that the Federal lawyer make clear the relationship.

A Federal lawyer acts as an intermediary in seeking to establish or adjust a relationship between clients on an amicable and mutually advantageous basis. The Federal lawyer seeks to resolve potentially conflicting interests by developing the clients' mutual interests. The alternative can be that each client may have to obtain separate representation, with the possibility in some situations of incurring additional cost, complications, or even litigation. Given these and other relevant factors, all the clients may prefer the Federal lawyer to act as intermediary.

In considering whether to act as an intermediary, a Federal lawyer should remember that if the common representation fails the result can be additional cost, embarrassment, and recrimination. In some situations the risk of failure is so great that common representation is plainly impossible. For example, a Federal lawyer cannot undertake mediation among clients when contentious litigation is imminent or when contentious negotiations are contemplated. More generally, if the relationship between the clients has already assumed definite antagonism, the possibility that the clients' interests can be adjusted by common representation ordinarily is not very good.

The appropriateness of intermediation can depend on its form. One form may be appropriate in circumstances in which another would not. Other relevant factors include whether the Federal lawyer subsequently will represent either client on a continuing basis and whether the situation involves creating or terminating a relationship between the clients.

Confidentiality and Privilege

A particularly important factor in determining the appropriateness of common representation is the effect on attorney-client confidentiality of information relating to the common representation. See Rules 1.4 and 1.6. As the Federal lawyer represents neither individual in the intermediation there is neither attorney-client privilege nor attorney-client confidentiality.

Since the Federal lawyer is required to be impartial between commonly represented clients, intermediation is improper when that impartiality cannot be maintained. For example, a Federal lawyer who has represented one of the clients for a long period and in a variety of matters might have difficulty being impartial between that client and one to whom the Federal lawyer has only recently been introduced.

Consultation

In acting as a intermediary between clients, the Federal lawyer is required to consult with the clients on the implications of doing so, and proceed only upon consent based on such a consultation. The consultation should make clear that the Federal lawyer's role is not that of partisanship normally expected in other circumstances.

Where the Federal lawyer is an intermediary, the clients ordinarily must assume greater responsibility for decisions than when each client is represented by a Federal lawyer.

Withdrawal

Common representation does not diminish the rights of each client in the client-lawyer relationship. Each client has the right to loyal and diligent representation. Any of the clients may discharge the Federal lawyer as stated in Rule 1.16 and gain the protection of Rule 1.9 concerning obligations to former clients.

CROSS REFERENCES:

Rule 1.4 Communication
Rule 1.6 Confidentiality of Information
Rule 1.7 Conflicts of Interest: General Rule
Rule 1.9 Conflicts of Interest: Former Client
Rule 1.13 The Federal Agency as the Client
Rule 1.16 Declining or Terminating Representation

Rules 2.3

RULE 2.3 Evaluation for Use by Third Persons

(a) A Federal lawyer may undertake an evaluation of a matter affecting a client for the use of someone other than the client if:

(1) The Federal lawyer reasonably believes that making the evaluation is compatible with other aspects of the lawyer's relationship with the client, and

(2) The client consents after sufficient consultation.

(b) Except a disclosure is required in connection with a report of an evaluation, information relating to the evaluation is otherwise protected by Rule 1.6.

COMMENT:

Definition
An evaluation may be performed at the client's direction but for the primary purpose of establishing information for the benefit of third parties; for example, a Government lawyer is asked to prepare a brief setting forth the Federal Agency's position on a situation for use by another Federal Agency or the Congress.

A Government lawyer may be called upon to give a formal opinion on the legality of action contemplated by the Federal Agency. In making such an evaluation, the Government lawyer acts at the behest of the Federal Agency as the client, but for the purpose of establishing the limits of the Federal Agency's authorized activity. Such an opinion may be confidential legal advice, depending on whether the Federal Agency intended it to be confidential.

If a Federal lawyer believes that making an evaluation is incompatible with other aspects of the Federal lawyer's relationship with the client, the Federal lawyer should consult with a supervisory lawyer for advice and guidance.

A legal evaluation should be distinguished from an investigation of a person with whom the Federal lawyer does not have a Federal lawyer-client relationship. For example, a Government lawyer assigned to conduct an investigation of a traffic accident between a private citizen and a Government employee in accordance with applicable Federal Agency regulations and directives does not have a client-lawyer relationship with the Government employee. So also, an investigation into a person's affairs by a Government lawyer is not an evaluation as that term is used in this rule.

The question is whether the Government lawyer represents the person whose affairs are being examined. When the Government lawyer does represent the person, the general rules concerning loyalty to client and preservation of confidences apply. For this reason, the client must be identified. The identity of the client should be made clear not only to the person under examination, but also to others to whom the results are to be made available.

Duty to Third Person

When the evaluation is intended for the information or use of a third person, a legal duty to that person may or shall not arise. That legal question is beyond the scope of this rule. However, since such an evaluation involves a departure from the normal client-lawyer relationship, careful analysis of the situation is required. The Federal lawyer must be satisfied as a matter of professional judgment that making the evaluation is compatible with other functions undertaken on behalf of the client. For example, if the Federal lawyer is acting as advocate in defending the client against charges of fraud, it would normally be incompatible with that responsibility for the Federal lawyer to perform an evaluation for others concerning the same or a related transaction. Assuming no such impediment is apparent, however, the Federal lawyer should advise the client of the implications of the evaluation, particularly the Federal lawyer's responsibilities to third persons and the duty to disseminate the findings.

CROSS REFERENCES:

Rule 1.2 Scope of Representation
Rule 1.6 Confidentiality of Information
Rule 1.7 Conflict of Interest: General Rule
Rule 1.9 Conflict of Interest: Former Client
Rule 1.13 The Federal Agency as the Client
Rule 1.16 Declining or Terminating Representation
Rule 4.1 Truthfulness in Statements to Others
Rule 4.2 Communication with Persons Represented by Counsel
Rule 4.3 Dealing with Unrepresented Persons
Rule 4.4 Respect for the Rights of Third Persons

ADVOCATE

RULE 3.1 Meritorious Claims and Contentions

A Federal lawyer shall not bring or defend a proceeding, or assert or controvert an issue therein, unless there is a basis for doing so that is not frivolous. This basis may include a good faith argument for an extending, modifying, or reversing existing law. A Federal lawyer for the defendant in a criminal proceeding, or the respondent in a proceeding that could result in incarceration or other adverse action, may nevertheless so defend the proceeding as to require that every element of the case be established.

COMMENT:

The advocate has a duty to use legal procedure for the fullest benefit of the client's cause, but also a duty not to abuse legal procedure. The law, both procedural and substantive, establishes the limits within which an advocate may proceed. Nevertheless, the law is not always clear and is never static. Accordingly, in determining the proper scope of advocacy, account must be taken of the law's ambiguities and potential for change.

The filing of a cause of action, defense, or similar act taken on behalf of a client is not frivolous merely because the facts have not first been fully substantiated or because the Federal lawyer expects vital evidence to develop only through discovery. Such action is not frivolous even though the Federal lawyer believes the client's position ultimately will not prevail. Merely because an issue has never been raised before, or because it may have been raised and resolved under different circumstances, does not make revisiting the issue frivolous. The action is frivolous, however, if the client desires to have the action taken solely for the purpose of harassing or maliciously injuring a person, or if the Federal lawyer is unable either to make a good faith argument on the merits of the action taken or to support the action taken by a good faith argument for an extending, modifying, or reversing of existing law.

A Federal lawyer does not violate this Rule by raising issues in good faith compliance with court precedent.

CROSS REFERENCES:

Rule 1.3 Diligence
Rule 1.4 Communication
Rule 1.6 Confidentiality of Information
Rule 3.2 Expediting Litigation
Rule 3.3 Candor Toward the Tribunal
Rule 3.4 Fairness to Opposing Party and Counsel
Rule 3.8 Special Responsibilities of a Prosecutor

RULE 3.2 Expediting Litigation

A Federal lawyer shall make reasonable efforts to expedite litigation and other proceedings consistent with the interests of the client and the lawyer's responsibilities to the tribunal to avoid unwarranted delay.

COMMENT:

Dilatory practices bring the administration of justice into disrepute. The legitimate interests of the client are rarely well-served by such tactics. Delay exacts a toll upon a litigant in uncertainty, frustration, and apprehension. Expediting litigation, in contrast, often can directly benefit the client's interest in obtaining bargaining concessions and in obtaining an early resolution of the matter. Delay should not be indulged merely for the convenience of the advocates, or for the purpose of frustrating an opposing party's attempt to obtain rightful redress or repose. It is not a justification that similar conduct is often tolerated by the bench and bar. The question is whether a competent Federal lawyer acting in good faith would regard the course of action as having some substantial purpose other than delay. Realizing financial or other benefit from otherwise improper delay in litigation is not a legitimate interest of the client.

CROSS REFERENCES:

Rule 1.4 Communication
Rule 3.1 Meritorious Claims and Contentions
Rule 3.3 Candor Toward the Tribunal

RULE 3.3 Candor Toward the Tribunal

(a) A Federal lawyer shall not knowingly:

(1) Make a false statement of material fact or law to a tribunal.

(2) Fail to disclose a material fact to a tribunal when disclosure is necessary to avoid assisting a criminal or fraudulent act by the client.

Rule 3.3

(3) Fail to disclose to the tribunal legal authority in the controlling jurisdiction known to the Federal lawyer to be directly adverse to the position of the client and not disclosed by opposing counsel.

(4) Offer evidence that the lawyer knows to be false. If a Federal lawyer has offered material evidence and comes to know of its falsity, the lawyer shall take reasonable remedial measures.

(5) Disobey an obligation or order imposed by a tribunal, unless done openly before the tribunal in a good faith assertion that no valid obligation or order should exist.

(b) The duties stated in paragraph (a) continue to the conclusion of the proceeding, and apply even if compliance requires disclosure of information otherwise protected by Rule 1.6.

(c) A Federal lawyer may refuse to offer evidence that the lawyer reasonably believes to be false.

(d) In an ex parte proceeding, a Federal lawyer shall disclose to the tribunal all material facts known to the lawyer that are reasonably necessary to enable the tribunal to make an informed decision, whether or not the facts are adverse.

COMMENT:

The advocate's task is to present the client's case with persuasive force. Performance of that duty while maintaining confidences of the client is qualified by the advocate's duty of candor to the tribunal. An advocate does not vouch for the evidence submitted in a cause, however. The tribunal is responsible for assessing its probative value.

Relationship with Rule 1.6

The conflicting duties to reveal fraud and to preserve confidences have existed side-by-side for some time. A Federal lawyer should not be confronted with the necessity of either breaching the client's privilege or breaching a disciplinary Rule. This Rule recognizes that the policies underlying Rule 1.6 take precedence over Rule 3.3 in all but the most serious cases. When Rule 1.6 either permits or mandates disclosure of otherwise confidential information, Rule 3.3 requires that the Federal lawyer reveal criminal or fraudulent acts by the client. When Rule 1.6 requires confidentiality of information, Rule 3.3 does not permit the Federal lawyer to disclose such information to a tribunal, even if the disclosure would be necessary to avoid assisting a criminal or fraudulent act by the client. A Federal lawyer who follows the guidance in the Perjury by a Criminal Client section of this comment is not assisting a criminal or fraudulent act by a client for purposes of these Rules. See Rule 1.2(d) and Comment.

Representations by a Federal lawyer

An advocate is responsible for pleadings and other documents prepared for litigation, but is usually not required to have personal knowledge of matters asserted therein, for litigation documents ordinarily present assertions by the client, or by someone on the client's behalf, not assertions by the Federal lawyer. Compare Rule 3.1. An assertion purporting to be on the Federal lawyer's own knowledge (as in an affidavit by the Federal lawyer or in a statement in open court), however, may properly be made only when the Federal lawyer knows the assertion is true or believes it to be true on the basis of a reasonably diligent inquiry. Circumstances can arise in which failure to make a disclosure is the equivalent of an affirmative misrepresentation. The obligation prescribed in Rule 1.2(d) not to counsel a client to commit or to assist the client in committing a fraud applies in litigation. Regarding compliance with this Rule, see Rule 11 of the Federal Rules of Civil Procedure. Regarding compliance with Rule 1.2(d), see the Comment to that Rule. See also the Comment to Rule 8.4(b).

Misleading Legal Argument

Legal argument based on a knowingly false representation of law constitutes dishonesty toward the tribunal. A Federal lawyer is not required to make a disinterested exposition of the law, but must recognize the existence of pertinent legal authorities. Furthermore, as stated in paragraph (a)(3), an advocate has a duty to disclose directly adverse authority in the controlling jurisdiction that has not been disclosed by the opposing party. The underlying concept is that legal argument is a discussion seeking to determine the legal premises properly applicable to the case. A Federal lawyer also should disclose to the tribunal legal authority from a non-controlling jurisdiction, directly adverse to the position of the client and not disclosed by opposing counsel, if the issue being litigated has not been decided by a controlling jurisdiction and the judge would reasonably consider it important to resolving the issue.

False Evidence

When evidence a Federal lawyer knows to be false is provided by a person who is not the client, the Federal lawyer must refuse to offer it regardless of the client's wishes.

When false evidence is offered by the client, however, a conflict may arise between the Federal lawyer's duty to keep revelations of the client confidential and the duty of candor to the tribunal. Upon discovering that material evidence is false, the Federal lawyer should try to persuade the client not to offer it. If the client has already offered the false evidence, the Federal lawyer should try to persuade the client to withdraw it.

If the client cannot be persuaded to withdraw the already offered false evidence, the Federal lawyer generally must disclose the client's deception to the tribunal or to the other party. This disclosure may result in grave consequences to the client, including not only a sense of betrayal, but also loss of the case and perhaps prosecution for perjury. The alternative, however, would be the Federal lawyer's participation in deceiving the tribunal, which would subvert the truth-finding process the adversary system is designed to implement. See Rule 1.2(d). Consequently, in seeking to persuade the client to withdraw false evidence, the Federal lawyer's intention to disclose the falsity if the client does not withdraw it must be made clear. Otherwise the client could simply reject the advice and insist upon the Federal lawyer's silence, thus effectively coercing the Federal lawyer into becoming a party to a fraud on the tribunal.

Perjury by a Criminal Defendant

A criminal case where the defendant insists on offering testimony the Federal lawyer knows is perjurious is the most difficult situation a Federal lawyer faces. The Federal lawyer's effort to rectify the situation can increase the likelihood of the client's being convicted, as well as, opening the possibility of a prosecution for perjury. On the other hand, if the Federal lawyer does not exercise control over the proof, the Federal lawyer participates, although passively, in deception of the tribunal.

If the defendant has admitted to the Federal lawyer facts that establish guilt and the Federal lawyer's independent investigation establishes the truth of the admissions, but the defendant insists on exercising the right to testify, the Federal lawyer must advise the client against taking the witness stand to testify falsely. If before trial the defendant insists on testifying falsely, the Federal lawyer shall seek to withdraw from representation. See Rule 1.16. If that is not permitted or if the situation arises during the trial or other proceedings and the defendant insists upon testifying falsely, it is unprofessional conduct for the Federal lawyer to lend aid to the client in presenting perjured testimony.

A criminal defendant has a right to the assistance of an advocate, a right to testify, and a right of communicate confidentially with counsel. A defendant does not have a right to the assistance of counsel in committing perjury, and an advocate has an obligation, not only in professional ethics but under the law, to avoid implication in the commission of perjury or other falsification of evidence. See Rule 1.2(d).

Remedial Measures

If perjured testimony or false evidence has been offered, the advocate's proper course ordinarily is to remonstrate with the client confidentially. If that effort fails, the advocate should seek to withdraw if that will remedy the situation. If withdrawal will not remedy the situation or is impossible, the advocate should make disclosure to the tribunal, subject to Rule 1.6.

Duration of Obligation

A practical time limit on the obligation to rectify the presentation of false evidence has to be established. The conclusion of the proceeding is a reasonably definite point for the termination of this obligation.

Refusing to Offer Proof Believed to be False

Generally speaking, a Federal lawyer has authority to refuse to offer testimony or other proof the Federal lawyer believes is untrustworthy. Offering such proof may reflect adversely on the Federal lawyer's ability to discriminate in the quality of evidence and thus impair the Federal lawyer's effectiveness as an advocate.

Ex Parte Proceedings

Ordinarily, an advocate has the limited responsibility of presenting one side of the matters that a tribunal should consider in reaching a decision; the conflicting position is expected to be presented by the opposing party. In an ex parte proceeding, however, such as in application for a temporary restraining order, there is no balance of presentation by opposing advocates. The object of an ex parte proceeding is, nevertheless, to yield a substantially just result. The judge, magistrate, or other official has an affirmative responsibility to accord the absent party just consideration. The Federal lawyer for the represented party has the correlative duty to disclose material facts known to the Federal lawyer and reasonably believed to be necessary to an informed decision.

CROSS REFERENCES:

Rule 1.2 Scope of Representation
Rule 1.6 Confidentiality of Information
Rule 3.1 Meritorious Claims and Contentions
Rule 3.4 Fairness to Opposing Party and Counsel
Rule 3.8 Special Responsibilities of a Prosecutor
Rule 4.1 Truthfulness in Statements to Others
Rule 8.4 Misconduct
Rule 8.5 Jurisdiction

RULE 3.4 Fairness to Opposing Party and Counsel

A Federal lawyer shall not:

(a) Unlawfully obstruct another party's access to evidence or unlawfully alter, destroy, or conceal a document or other material having potential evidentiary value. A Federal lawyer shall not counsel or assist another person to do any such act.

(b) Falsify evidence, counsel, or assist a witness to testify falsely, or offer an inducement to a witness that is prohibited by law.

(c) Knowingly disobey an obligation to an opposing party and counsel under the rules of a tribunal, except for an open refusal based on an assertion that no valid obligation exists.

(d) In pretrial procedure, make a frivolous discovery request or fail to make reasonably diligent efforts to comply with a legally proper discovery request by an opposing party.

(e) In trial, allude to any matter that the lawyer does not reasonably believe is relevant or that will not be supported by admissible evidence, assert personal knowledge of facts in issue except when testifying as a witness, or state a personal opinion as to the justness of a cause, the credibility of a witness, the culpability of a civil litigant, or the guilt or innocence of a defendant.

(f) Request a person other than a client to refrain from voluntarily giving relevant information to another party unless:

(1) The person is a relative or an employee or other agent of a client; and

(2) The Federal lawyer reasonably believes the person's interests will not be adversely affected by refraining from giving such information.

COMMENT:

The procedure of the adversary system contemplates that the evidence in a case is to be marshalled competitively by the contending parties. Fair competition in the adversary system is secured by prohibitions against destruction or concealment of evidence, improperly influencing witnesses, obstructive tactics in discovery procedure, and the like.

Documents and other items of evidence are often essential to establish a claim or defense. Subject to evidentiary privileges, the right of an opposing party, including the Government, to obtain evidence through discovery or subpoena is an important procedural right. The exercise of that right can be frustrated if relevant material is altered, concealed, or destroyed. Most criminal codes, including the Uniform Code of Military Justice, proscribe the destruction of material in an attempt to preclude its availability in a pending proceeding or reasonably foreseeable proceeding. Falsifying evidence is also a criminal offense. Paragraph (a) applies to evidentiary material generally, including computerized information.

A Federal lawyer who receives (i.e., has in the Federal lawyer's possession) an item of physical evidence implicating the client in criminal conduct shall disclose the location of or shall deliver that item to proper authorities when required by law or court order. Thus, if a Federal lawyer receives contraband, the Federal lawyer has no legal right to possess it and must always surrender it to lawful authorities. If a Federal lawyer receives stolen property, the Federal lawyer must surrender it to the owner or lawful authority to avoid violating the law. The appropriate disposition of such physical evidence is a proper subject to discuss confidentially with a supervisory lawyer. When a client informs the Federal lawyer about the existence of material having potential evidentiary value adverse to the client or when the client presents, but does not relinquish possession of such material to the Federal lawyer, the Federal lawyer should inform the client of the Federal lawyer's legal and ethical obligations regarding evidence. Frequently, the best course for the Federal lawyer is to refrain from either taking possession of such material or advising the client as to what course of action should be taken regarding it. See Rules 1.6 and 1.7. If a Federal lawyer discloses the location of or delivers an item of physical evidence to proper authorities, it should be done in the way best designed to protect the client's interest. The Federal lawyer should consider methods of return or disclosure that best protect (a) the client's identity; (b) the client's words concerning the item; (c) other confidential information; and (d) the client's privilege against self-incrimination.

Neither a Federal lawyer when interviewing victims or witnesses not represented by counsel nor another person appointed by a Federal lawyer to act in such capacity unlawfully obstructs another party's access to evidence or to material having potential evidentiary value by performing those duties in accordance with Federal Agency regulations or directives. For example, a Federal lawyer, upon the request of a victim or witness, may require prosecutor and defense counsel to coordinate with another person for interviews of a victim of or witness to the crime that forms the basis of a court-martial.

With regard to paragraph (b), it is not improper to pay a witness expenses or to compensate an expert witness on terms permitted by law. The common law rule in most jurisdictions is that it is improper to pay an occurrence witness any fee for testifying and that it is improper to pay an expert witness a contingent fee.

With regard to paragraph (c), a "rule of a tribunal" includes Rule 6(e) of the Federal Rules of Criminal Procedure governing discussion of grand jury testimony.

Paragraph (f) permits a Federal lawyer to advise relatives, employees, or other agents of a client to refrain from giving information to another party, because such persons may identify their interests with those of the client. See also Rule 4.2.

CROSS REFERENCES:

Rule 1.2 Scope of Representation
Rule 1.6 Confidentiality of Information
Rule 1.7 Conflict of Interest: General Rule
Rule 3.3 Candor Toward the Tribunal
Rule 4.1 Truthfulness in Statements To Others
Rule 4.2 Communication with Persons Represented by Counsel
Rule 4.4 Respecting Rights of Third Persons
Rule 5.2 Responsibilities of a Subordinate Federal lawyer
Rule 5.4 Professional Independence of a Federal lawyer

RULE 3.5 Impartiality and Decorum of the Tribunal

A Federal lawyer shall not:

(a) Seek to influence a tribunal, a member of a tribunal, a prospective member of a tribunal, or other official by means prohibited by law.

(b) Communicate ex parte with such a person about the matter except as permitted by law.

(c) Engage in conduct intended to disrupt a tribunal.

COMMENT:

Many forms of improper influence upon a tribunal are proscribed by law. The ABA Model Code of Judicial Conduct sets standards for the conduct of judges and other members of a tribunal. An advocate should be familiar with that Code, in order to avoid contributing to a violation by a tribunal.

The advocate's function is to present evidence and argument so that the cause may be decided according to law. Refraining from abusive or obstreperous conduct is a corollary of the advocate's right to speak on behalf of litigants. A Federal lawyer may stand firm against abuse by a judge but should avoid reciprocation; the judge's default is no justification for similar dereliction by an advocate. An advocate can present the cause, protect the record for subsequent review, and preserve professional integrity no less effectively by patient firmness than by belligerence or theatrics.

Because many tribunals are permanent or semi-permanent bodies, it may be impossible for Federal lawyers in the same community to avoid all communications with the members of a tribunal in the course of normal business, social, and professional activities. What is forbidden is any discussion with the individuals regarding a particular case or issue that has been or is likely to be referred to that tribunal for ultimate decision. Any Federal attorney who inadvertently engages in any conversations concerning a prohibitive subject should immediately report the incident to his supervisory lawyer, opposing counsel, and to the tribunal.

However, a Federal lawyer should always strive to avoid contact with a member of a tribunal when such contact could be perceived by an opposing party or member of the public to be an attempt to improperly influence the tribunal.

CROSS REFERENCES:

Rule 1.2 Scope of Representation
Rule 3.3 Candor Toward the Court
Rule 3.4 Fairness to Opposing Party and Counsel

RULE 3.6 Tribunal Publicity

(a) A Federal lawyer shall not make an extrajudicial statement that a reasonable person would expect to be disseminated by means of public communication if the lawyer knows or reasonably should know that it will have a substantial likelihood of materially prejudicing an adjudicative proceeding or an official review process thereof.

(b) A statement referred to in paragraph (a) ordinarily is likely to have such an effect when it refers to a civil matter triable to a jury, a criminal matter, any other proceeding that could result in incarceration, or other adverse action and that statement relates to:

(1) The character, credibility, reputation, or criminal record of a party, suspect in a criminal investigation, or witness, the identity of a witness, or the expected testimony of a party or witness.

Rule 3.6

(2) The possibility of a plea of guilty to the offense or the existence or contents of any confession, admission, or statement given by an defendant or suspect, or that person's refusal or failure to make a statement.

(3) The performance or results of any examination or test, the refusal or failure of a person to submit to an examination or test, or the identity or nature of physical evidence expected to be presented.
(4) Any opinion as to the guilt or innocence of a defendant or suspect in a original case or proceeding that could result in incarceration or other adverse action.

(5) Information the Federal lawyer knows or reasonably should know is likely to be inadmissible as evidence in a trial and that would, if disclosed, create a substantial risk of prejudicing an impartial trial.

(6) A defendant's having been charged with a crime, unless included therein is a statement explaining that the charge is merely an accusation and the defendant is presumed innocent until and unless proven guilty.

(c) Notwithstanding paragraphs (a) and (b)(1-5), a Federal lawyer involved in the investigation or litigation of a matter may state without elaboration:

(1) The general nature of the claim or defense.

(2) Information contained in a public record.

(3) That an investigation of the matter is in progress, including the general scope of the investigation, the offense or claim or defense involved and, except when prohibited by law, the identity of the persons involved.

(4) The scheduling or result of any step in litigation.

(5) A request for assistance in obtaining evidence and information necessary in litigation.

(6) A warning of danger concerning the behavior of the person involved, when there is reason to believe the likelihood of substantial harm to an individual or to the public interest exists.

(7) In a criminal case:

(i) The identity, place of business, occupation, and family status of the defendant.

(ii) If the defendant has not been apprehended, information necessary to aid in apprehension of that person.

(iii) The fact, time, and place of apprehension.

(iv) The identity of investigating and apprehending officers or agencies and the length of the investigation.

(d) The protection and release of information in matters pertaining to the Government shall be consistent with law.

COMMENT:

It is difficult to strike a balance between protecting the right to a fair trial and safeguarding the right of free expression. Preserving the right to a fair trial necessarily entails some curtailment of the information that may be disseminated about a party prior to trial, particularly when trial by jury or members is involved. If there were no such limits, the result would be the practical nullification of the protective effect of the rules of forensic decorum and the exclusionary rules of evidence. On the other hand, there are vital social interests served by the free dissemination of information about events having legal consequences and about legal proceedings themselves. The public has a right to know about threats to its safety and measures aimed at assuring its security. It also has a legitimate interest in the conduct of judicial proceedings, particularly in matters of general public concern. Furthermore, the subject matter of legal proceedings is often of direct significance in debate and deliberation over questions of public policy.
No body of rules can simultaneously satisfy all interests of fair trial and all those of free expression. Special rules of confidentiality may validly govern proceedings involving classified material, juveniles, domestic relations, and mental disability proceedings, and perhaps other types of proceedings. Rule 3.4(c) requires compliance with such Rules.

Special rules of confidentiality may validly govern proceedings involving classified material, juveniles, domestic relations and mental disability proceedings, and perhaps other ty;.:s of proceedings. Rule 3.4(c) requires compliance with such Rules.

Rule 3.6(d) acknowledges that a Government lawyer's release of information is governed not only by Rule 3.6 but also by law. Prior to releasing any information, a Government lawyer should consult the appropriate statute, directive, regulation, or policy guideline.

CROSS REFERENCES:

Rule 1.6 Confidentiality of Information
Rule 3.4 Fairness to Opposing Party and Counsel
Rule 3.5 Impartiality and Decorum of the Tribunal
Rule 3.8 Special Responsibilities of a Prosecutor

RULE 3.7 Federal Lawyer as Witness

(a) A Federal lawyer shall not act as advocate at a trial in which the lawyer is likely to be a necessary witness except when:

(1) The testimony relates to an uncontested issue.

(2) The testimony relates to the nature, value, and quality of legal services rendered in the case.

(3) Disqualification of the Federal lawyer would work substantial hardship on the client.

(b) A Federal lawyer may act as advocate in a matter in which another lawyer in the Federal lawyer's agency or firm is likely to be called as a witness unless precluded from doing so by Rule 1.7 or Rule 1.9.

COMMENT:

Combining the roles of advocate and witness can prejudice the opposing party and involve a conflict of interest between the Federal lawyer and client.

The opposing party has a proper objection when the combination of roles may prejudice that party's rights in the litigation. A witness is required to testify on the basis of personal knowledge, while an advocate is expected to explain and comment on evidence given by others. It shall not be clear whether a statement by an advocate-witness should be taken as proof or as an analysis of the proof.

Rule 3.7(a)(1) recognizes that if the testimony will be uncontested, the ambiguities in the dual role are purely theoretical. Rule 3.7(a)(2) recognizes that, if the testimony concerns the value and quality of legal services rendered in the action in which the testimony is offered, permitting the Federal lawyer to testify avoids the need for a second trial with new counsel to resolve that issue. Moreover, in such a situation the judge has firsthand knowledge of the matter in issue; hence, there is less dependence on the adversary process to test the credibility of the testimony.

Apart from these two exceptions, Rule 3.7(a)(3) recognizes that a balancing is required between the interests of the client and those of the opposing party. Whether the opposing party is likely to suffer prejudice depends on the nature of the case, the importance and probable tenor of the Federal lawyer's testimony, and the probability that the Federal lawyer's testimony will conflict with that of other witnesses. Even if there is risk of such prejudice, in determining whether the Federal lawyer should be disqualified, due regard must be given to the effect of disqualification on the Federal lawyer's client. That one or both parties could reasonably have foreseen the probability that the Federal lawyer would be a witness is relevant to this determination.

Whether the combination of roles involves an improper conflict of interest with respect to the client is determined by Rule 1.7 or 1.9. For example, if substantial conflict is likely between the testimony of the client and that of the Federal lawyer the representation is improper. The problem can arise whether the Federal lawyer is called as a witness on behalf of the client or is called by the opposing party. Determining whether such a conflict exists is primarily the responsibility of the Federal lawyer involved. See Comment to Rule 1.7.

CROSS REFERENCES:

Rule 1.6 Confidentiality of Information
Rule 1.7 Conflict of Interest: General Rule
Rule 1.9 Conflict of Interest: Former Client
Rule 3.4 Fairness to Opposing Party and Counsel

RULE 3.8 Special Responsibilities of a Prosecutor

A prosecutor shall:

(a) Refrain from prosecuting a charge that the prosecutor knows is not supported by probable cause, or if not authorized to decline the prosecution of a charge to recommend to the appropriate authority that any charge not warranted by the evidence be withdrawn;

(b) Make reasonable efforts to ensure that the defendant has been advised of the right to and the procedure for obtaining counsel and has been given reasonable opportunity to obtain counsel;

(c) Not seek to obtain from an unrepresented defendant a waiver of important pretrial rights;

(d) Make timely disclosure to the defense of all evidence or information known to the Federal lawyer that tends to negate the guilt of the defendant or mitigates the offense, and, in connection with sentencing, disclose to the defense all unprivileged mitigating information known to the Federal lawyer, except when the Federal lawyer is relieved of this responsibility by a protective order or regulation; and

(e) Exercise reasonable care to prevent investigators, law enforcement personnel, employees, or other persons assisting or associated with the Federal lawyer in a criminal case from making extrajudicial statements that the prosecutor would be prohibited from making under Rule 3.6.

(f) Respect the attorney-client privilege of defendants and not diminish the privilege through investigative or judicial processes.

COMMENT:

A prosecutor is not simply an advocate but is responsible for seeing that the defendant is accorded procedural justice and that guilt is decided upon the basis of sufficient evidence. See also Rule 3.3(d), governing ex parte proceedings. Applicable law may require other measures by the prosecutor and knowing disregard of those obligations or a systematic abuse of prosecutorial discretion could constitute a violation of Rule 8.4.

The exception in Rule 3.8 (d) recognizes that a prosecutor may seek an appropriate protective order from the tribunal if disclosures of information to the defense could result in substantial harm to an individual or organization or to the public interest. This exception also recognizes that applicable regulations may proscribe the disclosure of certain information without proper authorization.

A prosecutor may comply with Rule 3.8(e) in a number of ways. These include personally informing others of the Federal lawyer's obligations under Rule 3.6, promulgating guidelines, conducting training of law enforcement personnel, and appropriately supervising the activities of personnel assisting the prosecutor.

CROSS REFERENCES:

Rule 1.11 Successive Government and Private Employment
Rule 3.1 Meritorious Claims and Contentions
Rule 3.3 Candor Toward the Tribunal
Rule 3.4 Fairness To Opposing Party and Counsel
Rule 3.5 Impartiality and Decorum of the Tribunal
Rule 3.6 Trial Publicity
Rule 3.9 Advocate in Nonadjudicative Proceedings
Rule 4.4 Respect for the Rights of Third Persons
Rule 5.4 Professional Independence of a Federal lawyer

RULE 3.9 Advocate in Nonadjudicative Proceedings

A Federal lawyer representing a client before a legislative or administrative tribunal in a nonadjudicative proceeding shall disclose that the appearance is in a representative capacity and shall conform to the provisions of rules 3.3(a) - (c), 3.4(a) - (c), and 3.5.

COMMENT:

In representation before bodies such as legislatures, municipal councils, and executive and administrative agencies acting in a rulemaking or policy-making capacity, Federal lawyers present facts, formulate issues, and advance argument in the matters under consideration. The decision-making body, like a court, should be able to rely on the integrity of the submissions made it. A Federal lawyer appearing before such a body should deal with the tribunal honestly and in conformity with applicable rules of procedure.

Federal lawyers have no exclusive right to appear before nonadjudicative bodies. The requirements of this Rule, therefore, may subject Federal lawyers to regulations inapplicable to advocates who are not lawyers. Legislatures and administrative agencies, however, have a right to expect Federal lawyers to deal with them in the same manner as Federal lawyers deal with courts.

CROSS REFERENCES:

Rule 1.1 Competence
Rule 1.6 Confidentiality of Information
Rule 3.3 Candor Toward the Tribunal
Rule 3.4 Fairness to the Opposing Party or Counsel
Rule 3.5 Impartiality and Decorum of the Tribunal
Rule 4.1 Truthfulness in Statements to Others
Rule 5.4 Professional Independence of the Federal lawyer

TRANSACTIONS WITH PERSONS OTHER THAN CLIENTS

RULE 4.1 Truthfulness in Statements to Others

In the course of representing a client a Federal lawyer shall not knowingly:

(a) Make a false statement of material fact or law to a third person.

(b) Fail to disclose a material fact to a third person when disclosure is necessary to avoid assisting a criminal or fraudulent act by a client, unless disclosure is prohibited by Rule 1.6.

COMMENT:

Misrepresentation

A Federal lawyer is required to be truthful when dealing with others on a client's behalf, but generally has no affirmative duty to inform an opposing party of relevant facts. A misrepresentation can occur if the Federal lawyer incorporates or affirms statement of another person the Federal lawyer knows to be false. Misrepresentations also can occur by failing to act.

Statements of Fact

This Rule refers to statements of fact. Whether a particular statement should be regarded as one of fact depends on the circumstances. Under generally accepted conventions in negotiation, certain types of statements ordinarily are not taken as statements of material fact. Estimates of price or value are placed in this category.

Fraud by a Client

Paragraph (b) recognizes that substantive law may require a Federal lawyer to disclose certain information to avoid being deemed to have assisted the client's crime or fraud. The requirement of disclosure created by this paragraph, however, is subject to the obligations created by Rule 1.6.

CROSS REFERENCES:

Rule 1.6 Confidentiality of Information
Rule 3.3 Candor Toward the Tribunal
Rule 3.4 Fairness to Opposing Party and Counsel

RULE 4.2 Communication with Persons Represented by Counsel

(a) In representing a client, a Federal lawyer shall not communicate about the subject of the representation with a party the lawyer knows to be represented by another lawyer in the matter, unless the Federal lawyer has the consent of the other lawyer; in a criminal matter, the individual initiates the communication with the Government lawyer and voluntarily and knowingly waives the right to counsel for the purposes of that communication; or the Federal lawyer otherwise is authorized by law to do so.

(b) This Rule does not prohibit communications by a Non-Government lawyer with Federal Agency officials who have the authority to resolve a matter affecting the lawyer's client, whether or not the lawyer's communications relate to matters that are the subject of the representation, provided that the lawyer discloses the lawyer's identity; the fact that the lawyer represents a client in a matter involving the official's Federal Agency; and that the matter is being handled for the Federal Agency by a Government lawyer.

COMMENT:

This Rule does not prohibit communication with a party, or an employee or agent of a party, concerning matters outside the representation. For example, the existence of a controversy between a Federal Agency and private party does not prohibit a Federal lawyer from either from communicating with nonlawyer representatives of the other regarding a separate matter. Also, parties to a matter may communicate directly with each other and a Federal lawyer having independent justification for communicating with the other party is permitted to do so. Communications authorized by law include, for example, the right of a party to a controversy with a Federal Agency to speak with Federal Agency officials about the matter.

In the case of an organization, other than a Federal Agency, this Rule prohibits communications by a lawyer for one party concerning the matter in representation with individuals that having a managerial responsibility on behalf of the organization, and with any other person whose act or omission in connection with that matter may be imputed to the organization for purposes of civil or criminal liability or whose statement may constitute an admission on the part of the organization. If an agent or employee of the organization is represented in the matter by his or her own counsel, the consent by that counsel to a communication will be sufficient for purposes of this Rule. Compare Rule 3.4(f).

Federal Bar Association

Rules 4.2, 4.3 & 4.4

Paragraph (b) permits communications with those in government having the authority to resolve matters without the prior consent of the lawyer representing the government in such cases. A non-government lawyer making such a communication without the prior consent of the lawyer representing the government must make certain disclosures. If known, the lawyer should advise the Federal Agency official of the name of the Government lawyer handling the matter. This paragraph does not permit a lawyer to bypass counsel representing the Federal Agency on every issue which may arise in the course of disputes with the Federal Agency. It is intended to provide lawyers access to decisionmakers in government with respect to genuine grievances and not intended to provide direct access on routine disputes or routine aspects of the resolution of disputes.

This Rule also covers any person, even if not a party to a formal proceeding, who is represented by counsel concerning the matter in question.

In a criminal case there may be times when communications between a defendant and a Federal Agency without notice to defense counsel is in the interest of the defendant. Some communications will serve to protect the defendant and to identify sham representations. For example, in certain criminal enterprises, such as organized crime or drug rings, a defendant may wish to cooperate with a Federal Agency, but the counsel may also be the counsel of others involved in the enterprise. To ensure that in such instances there is no abuse, this rule would permit communications by the defendant with the Government lawyer, as long as the defendant voluntarily and knowingly waives the right to counsel.

CROSS REFERENCES:

Rule 3.8 Special Responsibilities of a Trial
Rule 4.1 Truthfulness in Statements to Others
Rule 4.4 Respect for Rights of Third Persons

RULE 4.3 Dealing with Unrepresented Persons

In dealing on behalf of a client with a person who is not represented by counsel, a Federal lawyer shall not state or imply that the lawyer is disinterested. When the Federal lawyer knows or reasonably should know that the unrepresented person misunderstands the lawyer's role in the matter, the lawyer shall make reasonable efforts to correct the misunderstanding.

COMMENT:

An unrepresented person, particularly one not experienced in dealing with legal matters, might assume a Federal lawyer is disinterested in loyalties or is a disinterested authority on the law even when the lawyer represents a client. During the course of a Federal lawyer's representation of a client, the lawyer should not give advice to an unrepresented person other than the advice to obtain counsel.

CROSS REFERENCES:

Rule 1.2 Scope of Representation
Rule 3.4 Fairness to Opposing Party and Counsel
Rule 4.1 Truthfulness in Statements to Others
Rule 4.4 Respect for Rights of Third Persons

RULE 4.4 Respect for Rights of Third Persons

In representing a client, a Federal lawyer shall not use means that have no substantial purpose other than to embarrass, delay, or burden a third person, or use methods of obtaining evidence that violate the legal rights of such a person.

COMMENT:

Responsibility to a client requires a Federal lawyer to subordinate the interests of others to those of the client. That responsibility does not imply that a Federal lawyer may disregard the rights of third persons. The duty of a Federal lawyer to represent the client with zeal does not mitigate against his concurrent obligation to treat with consideration all persons involved in the legal process and to avoid the infliction of needless harm. It is impractical to catalogue all such rights, but they include legal restrictions on methods of obtaining evidence from third persons.

CROSS REFERENCES:

Rule 3.2 Expediting Litigation
Rule 3.8 Special Responsibilities of a Prosecutor
Rule 4.1 Truthfulness in Statements to Others
Rule 4.2 Communication with Persons Represented by Counsel
Rule 4.3 Dealing with Unrepresented Persons

LEGAL OFFICES

RULE 5.1 Responsibilities of a Supervisory Lawyer

(a) A supervisory lawyer shall make reasonable efforts to ensure that all Federal lawyers conform to these Rules of Professional Conduct.

(b) A Federal lawyer shall be responsible for another Federal lawyer's violation of these Rules of Professional Conduct if:

(1) The Federal lawyer orders or, with knowledge of the specific conduct, ratifies the conduct involved; or

(2) The Federal lawyer has direct supervisory authority over the other Federal lawyer and knows of the conduct at a time when its consequences can be avoided or mitigated, but fails to take reasonable remedial action.
(c) A Federal lawyer, who is a supervisory lawyer, is responsible for ensuring that the subordinate lawyer is properly trained and is competent to perform the duties to which the subordinate lawyer is assigned.

(d) A Government lawyer, who is a supervisory lawyer, should encourage subordinate lawyers to participate in pro bono publico service activities and the activities of bar associations and law reform organizations.

COMMENT:

Paragraph 5.1(a) recognizes the responsibilities of the supervisory lawyers to effect and ultimately to enforce these Rules. The measures required to fulfill the responsibility prescribed in Rule 5.1(a) can depend on the office's structure and the nature of its practice. In a small office, informal supervision and occasional admonition ordinarily might be sufficient. In a large office, or in practice situations in which intensely difficult ethical problems frequently arise, more elaborate procedures may be necessary. In some offices, for example, junior lawyers can make confidential referral of ethical problems directly to a senior lawyer. See Rules 1.13 and 5.2. Offices may also rely on continuing legal education in professional ethics. In any event, the ethical atmosphere of an office can influence the conduct of all its members and a Federal lawyer having authority over the work of another shall not assume the subordinate lawyer will inevitably conform to these Rules.

Supervisory lawyers must be careful to avoid conflicts of interest in providing advice to subordinate lawyers. Depending on the circumstances, the supervisory lawyer may advise one subordinate Federal lawyer and refer the other subordinate Federal lawyer to another supervisory lawyer in a different office. Alternatively, the supervisory lawyer may refer both subordinate Federal lawyers to separate supervisory lawyers in the same or another office.

Paragraph 5.1(b)(1) expresses a general principle of supervisory responsibility for acts of another. See also Rule 8.4(a). Ratification as used in paragraph 5.1(b)(1) means approval of or consent to another Federal lawyer's conduct.

Paragraph 5.1(b)(2) defines the duty of a Federal lawyer having direct supervisory authority over the performance of specific legal work by another Federal lawyer. Whether a Federal lawyer has such supervisory authority in particular circumstances is a question of fact. Appropriate remedial action would depend on the immediacy of the supervisor's involvement and the seriousness of the misconduct. Apart from the responsibility that may be incurred for ordering or ratifying another Federal lawyer's conduct under paragraph 5.1(b)(1), the supervisor is required to intervene to prevent avoidable consequences of misconduct if the supervisor knows the misconduct occurred. Thus, if a supervisory lawyer knows that a subordinate misrepresented a matter to an opposing party in negotiation, the supervisor, as well as the subordinate, has a duty to correct the resulting misapprehension.

Professional misconduct by a Federal lawyer under supervision could reveal a violation paragraph 5.1(a) on the part of the supervisory lawyer even though it does not entail a violation of paragraph 5.1(b) because there was no direction, ratification, or knowledge of the violation.

Apart from this Rule and Rule 8.4(a), a Federal lawyer does not have disciplinary liability for the conduct of subordinate Federal lawyers. Whether a Federal lawyer may be liable civilly or criminally for another Federal lawyer's conduct is a question of law beyond the scope of these Rules.

CROSS REFERENCES:

Rule 1.13 The Federal Agency as the Client
Rule 5.2 Responsibilities of a Subordinate Lawyer
Rule 5.3 Responsibilities Regarding Nonlawyer Assistants Rule 5.4 Professional Independence of a Federal Lawyer
Rule 8.3 Reporting Professional Misconduct
Rule 8.4 Misconduct

RULE 5.2 Responsibilities of a Subordinate Federal Lawyer

(a) A Federal lawyer is bound by these Rules of Professional Conduct notwithstanding the Federal lawyer's acting at the direction of another person.

(b) A subordinate Federal lawyer does not violate these Rules of Professional Conduct if that lawyer acts in accordance with a supervisory lawyer's reasonable resolution of an arguable question of professional duty.

COMMENT:

Although a Federal lawyer is not relieved of responsibility for a violation by the fact that the Federal lawyer acted at the direction of a supervisor, that fact may be relevant in determining whether a Federal lawyer had the knowledge required to render conduct a violation of these Rules. For example, if a subordinate filed a frivolous motion at the direction of a supervisor, the subordinate would not be guilty of a professional violation, unless the subordinate knew of the document's frivolous character.

When Federal lawyers in a supervisor-subordinate relationship encounter a matter involving professional judgment as to ethical duty, the supervisor may assume responsibility for making the judgment. Otherwise a consistent course of action or position could not be taken. If the question can reasonably be answered only one way, the duty of both Federal lawyers is clear and they are equally responsible for fulfilling it. If the question is reasonably arguable, however, someone has to decide upon the course of action. That authority and responsibility ordinarily reposes in the supervisor, and a subordinate may be guided accordingly. For example, if a question arises whether the interests of two clients conflict under Rule 1.7, the supervisor's reasonable resolution of the question should protect the subordinate professionally if the resolution is subsequently challenged.

CROSS REFERENCES:

Rule 5.1 Responsibilities of the Supervisory Lawyers
Rule 5.4 Professional Independence of the Federal Lawyer
Rule 8.4 Misconduct

RULE 5.3 Responsibilities Regarding Nonlawyer Assistants

With respect to a nonlawyer under the authority, supervision, or direction of a Federal lawyer:

(a) A supervisory lawyer shall make reasonable efforts to ensure that the office has in effect measures giving reasonable assurance that the person's conduct is compatible with the professional obligations of the Federal lawyer.

(b) A Federal lawyer having direct supervisory authority over the nonlawyer shall make reasonable efforts to ensure that the nonlawyer's conduct is compatible with the professional obligations of the Federal lawyer.

(c) A Federal lawyer shall be responsible for conduct of the nonlawyer that would be a violation these Rules if engaged in by the Federal lawyer if:
(1) The Federal lawyer orders or, with the knowledge of the specific conduct, ratifies the conduct involved; or

(2) The Federal lawyer has direct supervisory authority over the nonlawyer, and knows of the conduct at a time when its consequences can be avoided or mitigated but fails to take reasonable remedial action.

COMMENT:

Various nonlawyer assistants are employed by federal lawyers in their practices, including paralegals, legal technicians, secretaries, clerks, investigators, law student interns, and others. Such assistants act for the Federal lawyer in rendition of the Federal lawyer's professional services. A Federal lawyer should give such assistants appropriate instruction and supervision concerning the ethical aspects of their performance, particularly regarding the obligation not to disclose information relating to representation of the client, and should be responsible for their work product. The measures employed in supervising nonlawyers should take account of their lack of legal training and their not being subject to professional discipline.

CROSS REFERENCES:

Rule 1.6 Confidentiality of Information
Rule 3.8 Special Responsibilities of a Prosecutor
Rule 4.1 Truthfulness in Statements to Others
Rule 4.4 Respect for Rights of Third Persons
Rule 5.5 Unauthorized Practice of Law

RULE 5.4 Professional Independence of a Federal Lawyer

(a) A Federal lawyer is expected to exercise professional independence of judgment during the representation of a client, consistent with these Rules.

(b) Notwithstanding a Government lawyer's status as a Government employee, a Government lawyer detailed or assigned to represent an individual Government employee or another person as the client is expected to exercise loyalty and professional independence during the representation, consistent with these Rules and to the same extent as required by a Non-Government lawyer in private practice.

(c) A Supervisory Government lawyer may not base an adverse evaluation or other prejudicial action against a Subordinate Government lawyer on the Subordinate Government lawyer's exercise of professional independence under (b) above.

(d) A Government lawyer shall obey the lawful orders of superiors when representing the United States and individual clients, but a Government lawyer shall not permit a nonlawyer to direct or regulate the Government lawyer's professional judgment in rendering legal services.

(e) A Non-Government lawyer shall not permit a nonlawyer who recommends, employs, or pays the Non-Government lawyer to render legal services for another to direct or regulate the Non-Government lawyer's professional judgment in rendering legal services.

(f) A Non-Government lawyer shall comply with the Rules of Professional Conduct or other applicable laws of the jurisdiction in which the Non-Government lawyer is licensed or is practicing law concerning the limitations on sharing fees and the organizational form of their practice.

COMMENT:

Federal lawyers

A Federal lawyer subjected to outside pressures that might impair or give the appearance of impairing the effectiveness of the representation should make full disclosure of the pressures to the client. If the Federal lawyer or the client believes the effectiveness of the representation has been or will be impaired thereby, the lawyer should take proper steps to withdraw from representation of the client.

Government Lawyers

This Rule recognizes that a Government lawyer is a Government employee required by law to obey the lawful orders of superiors. Nevertheless, the practice of law requires the exercise of judgment solely for the benefit of the client and free of compromising influences and loyalties. Thus, when a Government lawyer is assigned to represent an individual client, neither the lawyer's personal interests, the interests of other clients, nor the interests of third persons should affect loyalty to the individual client.

Non-Government Lawyers

Rather than adopting specific rules on the sharing of fees or the organizational makeup of law practices that would apply only to Non-government lawyers practicing before the Federal Agency, the Federal Agency defers on this matter to the rules and applicable laws of the jurisdictions in which these Non-Government lawyers are licensed.

CROSS REFERENCES:

Preamble
Rule 1.1 Competence
Rule 1.2 Scope of Representation
Rule 1.3 Diligence
Rule 1.7 Conflicts of Interest: General Rule
Rule 1.13 The Federal Agency as the Client
Rule 5.1 Responsibilities of a Supervisory Lawyer
Rule 5.2 Responsibilities of a Subordinate Lawyer

RULE 5.5 Unauthorized Practice of Law

A Federal lawyer shall not:

(a) Except as authorized by law, practice law in a jurisdiction where doing so violates the regulation of the legal profession in that jurisdiction; or

(b) Assist a person who is not a member of the bar in the performance of activity that constitutes the unauthorized practice of law.

COMMENT:

Limiting the practice of law to members of the bar protects the public against rendition of legal services by unqualified persons. A Government lawyer's performance of legal duties for a Federal Agency, however, is considered a Federal function and not subject to regulation by the states. Paragraph (b) does not prohibit a Federal lawyer from employing the services of nonlawyers and delegating functions to them, so long as the Federal lawyer supervises the delegated work and retains responsibility for their work. See Rule 5.3. Likewise, it does not prohibit Federal lawyers from providing professional advice and instruction to nonlawyers whose employment requires knowledge of law; for example, claims adjusters, social workers, accountants, and persons employed in Government agencies. In addition, a Federal lawyer may counsel nonlawyers who wish to proceed pro se, or nonlawyers authorized by law to practice in military proceedings.

The sole admission to practice requirement is applicable to Government lawyers. As such, admission in any of the several states should preclude the imposition of additional requirements on behalf of the U.S. Government.

CROSS REFERENCES:

Rule 1.2 Scope of Representation
Rule 5.3 Responsibilities Regarding Nonlawyer Assistants
Rule 8.5 Jurisdiction

PUBLIC SERVICE

RULE 6.1 Pro Bono Publico Service

(a) A Federal lawyer should render public interest legal service. A Federal lawyer may discharge this responsibility by providing professional services at no fee or a reduced fee to persons of limited means or to public service or charitable groups or organizations, by service in activities for improving the law, the legal system or the legal profession, and by financial support for organizations that provide legal service to persons of limited means.

(b) A Government lawyer should provide pro bono legal services consistent with applicable law.

COMMENT:

Each Federal lawyer has a basic responsibility to provide public interest legal services without fee, or at a substantially reduced fee, in one or more of the following areas: poverty law, civil rights law, public rights law, charitable organization representation, and the administration of justice. This Rule expresses that policy but is not intended to be enforced through disciplinary process.

The rights and responsibilities of individuals and organizations in the United States are increasingly defined in legal terms As a consequence, legal assistance in coping with the web of laws is imperative for persons of modest and limited means, as well as for the relatively well-to-do.

The basic responsibility for providing legal services for those unable to pay ultimately rests upon the individual lawyer, and personal involvement in the problems of the disadvantaged can be one of the most rewarding experiences in the life of a Federal lawyer. Every Federal lawyer, regardless of professional prominence or professional work load, should find time to participate in or otherwise support the provision of legal services to the disadvantaged. The provision of free legal services to those unable to pay reasonable fees continues to be an obligation of each Federal lawyer as well as the profession generally, but the efforts of individual Federal lawyers are often not enough to meet the need. Thus, it has been necessary for the profession and government to institute additional programs to provide legal services. Accordingly, legal aid offices, lawyer referral services, and other related programs have been developed, and others will be developed by the profession and government. Every Federal lawyer should support all proper efforts to meet this need for legal services.
18 U.S.C. § 205 and § 209 and other laws, including those governing off-duty employment by members of the Armed Forces, may regulate a Government lawyer's ability to provide legal services on a pro bono basis outside the scope of the Government lawyer's official duties.

RULE 6.2 Accepting Appointments

A Federal lawyer shall not seek to avoid appointment by a tribunal to represent a person except for good cause, such as:

(a) Representing the client is contrary to law or in violation of these Rules.

(b) Representing the client is likely to result in an unreasonable financial burden on the Federal lawyer.

(c) The client or the cause is so repugnant to the lawyer as to be likely to impair the client-lawyer relationship or the lawyer's ability to represent the client.

COMMENT:

A Federal lawyer ordinarily is not obliged to accept a client whose character or cause the Federal lawyer regards as repugnant. The Federal lawyer's freedom to select clients is, however, qualified. All lawyers have a responsibility to assist in providing pro bono publico service. See Rule 6.1. An individual Federal lawyer fulfills this responsibility by accepting a fair share of unpopular matters or indigent or unpopular clients. A Federal lawyer may also be subject to appointment by a court to serve unpopular clients or persons unable to afford legal services.

Appointed Counsel

For good cause a Federal lawyer may seek to decline an appointment to represent a person who cannot afford to retain counsel or whose cause is unpopular. Good cause exists if the Federal lawyer could not handle the matter competently, see Rule 1.1, or if undertaking the representation would result in an improper conflict of interest, for example, when the client or the cause is so repugnant to the Federal lawyer as to be likely to impair the client-lawyer relationship or the Federal lawyer's ability to represent the client. A Federal lawyer may also seek to decline an appointment if acceptance would be unreasonable burdensome, for example, when it would impose a financial sacrifice so great as to be unjust.

An appointed Federal lawyer has the same obligations to the client as retained counsel, including the obligations of loyalty and confidentiality, and is subject to the same limitations on the client-lawyer relationship, such as the obligation to refrain from assisting the client in violation of the Rules.

18 U.S.C. § 205 and other laws, including those governing off-duty employment, may prevent or restrict the types of cases that a Government lawyer may accept appointment to by a tribunal outside the scope of the Government lawyer's official duties.

RULE 6.3 Membership in Legal Services Organization

A Federal lawyer may serve as a director, officer, or member of a legal services organization, apart from the law firm or Federal Agency in which the lawyer practices, notwithstanding that the organization serves persons having interests adverse to a client of the Federal lawyer. The Federal lawyer shall not knowingly participate in a decision or action of the organization:

(a) If participating in the decision or action would be incompatible with the Federal lawyer's obligations to a client under Rule 1.7; or

(b) Where the decision or action could have a material adverse effect on the representation of a client of the organization whose interests are adverse to a client of the Federal lawyer.

COMMENT:

Federal lawyers should be encouraged to support and participate in legal service organizations. A Federal lawyer who is an officer or a member of such an organization does not thereby have a client-lawyer relationship with persons served by the organization. However, there is potential conflict between the interests of such persons and the interests of the Federal lawyer's clients. If the possibility of such conflict disqualified a Federal lawyer from serving on the board of a legal services organization, the profession's involvement in such organizations would be severely curtailed.

It may be necessary in appropriate cases to reassure a client of the organization that the representation will not be affected by conflicting loyalties of a member of the board. Established written policies in this respect can enhance the credibility of such assurances.

18 U.S.C. § 205 and § 208 and other laws may prevent or restrict a Government lawyer's participation in a legal services organization.

RULE 6.4 Membership in Bar Associations and Law Reform Activities Affecting Client Interests

A Federal lawyer may serve as a member, director, or officer of a bar association or an organization involved in reform of the law or its administration, notwithstanding that the reform may affect the interests of a client. The Federal lawyer shall not knowingly participate in a decision or action of the organization if participating in the decision would be incompatible with the Federal lawyer's obligations to the client under Rule 1.7. When the Federal lawyer knows the interests of the client may be materially benefitted by a decision in which the Federal lawyer participates, the Federal lawyer shall disclose that fact, but need not identify the client.

COMMENT:

Federal lawyers involved in organizations seeking law reform generally do not have a client-lawyer relationship with the organization. Otherwise, it might follow that a Government lawyer could not be involved in a bar association law reform program that might indirectly affect the United States. See also Rule 1.2(b). For example, a Government lawyer might be disqualified from participating in drafting proposed regulations. In determining the nature and scope of participation in such activities, a Federal lawyer should be mindful of obligations to clients under other Rules, particularly Rule 1.7. A Federal lawyer is professionally obligated to protect the integrity of the program by making an appropriate disclosure within the organization when the Federal lawyer knows that a client might be materially benefitted.

Federal Bar Association

Rules 6.4, 7.1 & 8.1

A Government lawyer who is active in bar association activities or who makes a presentation to a bar association in the lawyer's personal capacity, and not as a representative of the Government lawyer's Federal Agency, may accept reimbursement, subject to the provisions of applicable laws, for the Government lawyer's expenses in attending a meeting of the bar association on the Government lawyer's own time.

INFORMATION ABOUT LEGAL SERVICES

RULE 7.1 Communications Concerning a Federal Agency's Legal Services

A Government lawyer may advertise the Federal Agency's legal services through the public media, such as a telephone directory, newspaper, or other periodicals, outdoor sign, radio, television, or through written communications.

COMMENT:

To assist members of the public, Government employees, and dependents of Government employees, a Government lawyer may advertise or otherwise conduct information campaigns regarding the legal services that a Federal Agency makes available to the public, Government employees, and dependents of Government employees.

MAINTAINING THE INTEGRITY OF THE PROFESSION

RULE 8.1 Bar Admission and Disciplinary Matters

An applicant for admission to a bar or employment as a lawyer with a Federal Agency, a Federal lawyer seeking the right to practice before a Federal Agency, or a Federal lawyer in connection with a disciplinary matter, shall not:

(a) Knowingly make a false statement of material fact.

(b) Fail to disclose a fact necessary to correct a misapprehension known by the person to have arisen in the matter, or knowingly fail to respond to a lawful demand for information from an admission or disciplinary authority, except that the Rule does not require disclosure of information otherwise protected by Rule 1.6.

COMMENT:

The duty imposed by this Rule extends to applicants seeking admission to the bar or employment with a Federal Agency as well as to Federal lawyers. Hence, if a person makes a material false statement in connection with an application for admission, employment, or certification, it may form the basis for subsequent disciplinary action if the person is admitted or employed, and in any event may be relevant in a subsequent admission application. The duty imposed by this Rule applies to a Federal lawyer's own admission or discipline, as well as to that of others. Thus, it is a separate professional offense for a Federal lawyer to knowingly make a misrepresentation or omission in connection with a disciplinary investigation of the Federal lawyer's own conduct. This Rule also requires affirmative clarification of any misunderstanding on the part of the admission or disciplinary authority of which the person involved becomes aware.

A Federal lawyer representing an applicant for admission to the bar, or representing a Federal lawyer who is the subject of a disciplinary inquiry or proceeding, is governed by the Rules applicable to the client-lawyer relationship.

CROSS REFERENCES:

Rule 8.3 Reporting Professional Misconduct
Rule 8.4 Misconduct
Rule 8.5 Jurisdiction
Rule 6.3; Comment; last paragraph:

RULE 8.2 Judicial and Legal Officials

A Federal lawyer shall not make a statement the lawyer knows to be false or with reckless disregard as to its truth or falsity concerning the qualifications or integrity of a tribunal or of a candidate for election or appointment to judicial or legal office.

COMMENT:

Assessments by Federal lawyers are relied on in evaluating the professional or personal fitness of persons performing legal duties. Expressing honest and candid opinions on such matters contributes to improving the administration of justice. Conversely, false statements by a Federal lawyer can unfairly undermine confidence in the administration of justice.

To maintain the fair and independent administration of justice, Federal lawyers are encouraged to continue traditional efforts to defend judges and courts criticized unjustly.

RULE 8.3 Reporting Professional Misconduct

(a) A Federal lawyer having knowledge that another Federal lawyer has committed a violation of these Rules of Professional Conduct that raises a substantial question as to that lawyer's honesty, trustworthiness, or fitness as a Federal lawyer in other respects, shall report such a violation to the appropriate official as provided by law.

(b) A Federal lawyer having knowledge that a judge has committed a violation of applicable rules of judicial conduct that raises a substantial question as to the judge's fitness for office shall report such a violation to the appropriate official as provided by law.

(c) This Rule does not require disclosure of information otherwise protected by Rule 1.6.

COMMENT:

Self-regulation of the legal profession requires members of the profession to initiate disciplinary investigations when they know of violations of these Rules of Professional Conduct or other such rules. Federal lawyers have a similar obligation with respect to judicial misconduct. An apparently isolated violation may indicate a pattern of misconduct that only a disciplinary investigation can uncover. Reporting a violation is especially important if the victim is unlikely to discover the offense.

A report about misconduct is not required if it would involve violation of Rule 1.6. A Federal lawyer should, however, encourage a client to consent to disclosure when prosecution would not substantially prejudice the client's interests.

This Rule limits the reporting obligation to those offenses that a self-regulating profession must vigorously endeavor to prevent. A measure of judgment, therefore, is required in complying with this Rule. The term "substantial" refers to the seriousness of the possible offense and not the quantum of evidence of which the Federal lawyer is aware. Any report should be made to the appropriate official under the applicable law.

CROSS REFERENCES:

Rule 5.1 Responsibilities of the Supervisory Federal lawyers
Rule 8.4 Misconduct
Rule 8.5 Jurisdiction

RULE 8.4 Misconduct

It is professional misconduct for a Federal lawyer to:

(a) Violate or attempt to violate these Rules of Professional Conduct, knowingly assist or induce another to do so, or do so through the acts of another.

(b) Commit a criminal act that reflects adversely on the Federal lawyer's honesty, trustworthiness, or fitness as a Federal lawyer in other respects.

(c) Engage in conduct involving dishonesty, fraud, deceit, or misrepresentation.

(d) Engage in conduct prejudicial to the administration of justice.

(e) State or imply an ability to influence improperly a government Federal Agency or official.

(f) Knowingly assist a judge or judicial officer in conduct that violates applicable rules of judicial conduct or other law.

COMMENT:

Many kinds of illegal conduct reflect adversely on fitness to practice law, such as offenses involving fraud and the offense of willful failure to file an income tax return. However, some kinds of offenses carry no such implication. Traditionally, the distinction was drawn in terms of offenses involving "moral turpitude." That concept can be construed to include offense concerning some matters of personal morality, such as adultery and comparable offenses, which have no specific connection to fitness for the practice of law. Although a Federal lawyer is personally answerable under law, a Federal lawyer should be professionally answerable only for offenses that indicate lack of those characteristics relevant to law practice. Offenses involving violence, dishonesty, breach of truth, or serious interference with the administration of justice are in that category. One example of such conduct is the unlawful, unauthorized, or nonconsensual obtaining of confidential files, including confidential working paper files, of Federal lawyers who are known or reasonably should be known to be representing a client. Such conduct includes the solicitation or prompting of another person, not bound by these Rules, to engage in such activities. A pattern of repeated offenses, even ones of minor significance when considered separately, can indicate indifference to ethical obligations.

A Federal lawyer may refuse to comply with an obligation imposed by law upon a good faith belief that no valid obligation exists. The provision of Rule 1.2(d) concerning a good faith challenge to the validity, scope, meaning or application of the law applies to challenges of legal regulation of the practice of law.

A Government lawyer assumes legal responsibilities beyond those of other citizens. A Government lawyer's abuse of such status can suggest an inability to fulfill the professional role of Government lawyer and Federal lawyer.

CROSS REFERENCES:

Rule 8.3 Reporting Misconduct

RULE 8.5 Jurisdiction

(a) A Federal lawyer shall comply with the rules of professional conduct applicable to the Federal Agency that employs the Government lawyer or the Federal Agency before which the Federal lawyer practices.

(b) If the Federal Agency has not adopted or promulgated rules of professional conduct, the Federal lawyer shall comply with the rules of professional conduct of the state bars in which the Federal lawyer is admitted to practice.

COMMENT:

Many Federal lawyers practicing before Federal Agency tribunals practice outside the territorial limits of the jurisdiction in which they are licensed.

While the Federal lawyer may remain subject to the governing authority of their licensing jurisdiction, the Federal lawyer is also subject to these Rules. However, when a Government lawyer is engaged in the conduct of Federal Agency legal functions, whether servicing the Federal Agency as a client or serving an individual client in the course of official duties, these Rules are regarded as superseding any conflicting rules applicable in the jurisdictions in which the Government lawyer may be licensed.

When a Government lawyer is practicing before a Federal Agency whose rules conflict with these Rules, the Government lawyer shall comply with the rules of that Federal Agency.

A Non-Government lawyer practicing before a Federal Agency tribunal who violates these Rules may be suspended from practice before such tribunals.

CROSS REFERENCES:

Rule 5.1 Responsibilities of a Supervisory Lawyer
Rule 8.3 Reporting Professional Misconduct

Chapter 3

Judges

Judges and other judicial officers have also been victims of malpractice action. In *Pulliam v. Allen*,[1] for example, the U.S. Supreme Court ruled that judges can be personally liable for fees of civil rights attorneys. The Alabama Supreme Court in *In Re Burns*[2] ruled that the court was not precluded from censuring a judge for proposing an action of prostitution to a woman in violation of Canon 2, even though this conduct had already been the basis of the judge being found guilty of the criminal charge of disorderly conduct. Generally, judicial liability for criminal activity is treated quite differently than judicial liability for tortious or civil conduct. With one minor exception for malfeasance or misfeasance in office, judges possess no immunity for their criminal behavior. Whatever threat criminal liability might pose to judicial independence, it is not strong enough to override the importance of enforcing the criminal law, even against judges.[3]

In the civil law field, judicial immunity does not always ring true,[4] although judges do enjoy a substantial degree of immunity from civil liability. Judicial immunity stops short of shielding nonjudicial actions or actions taken in the clear absence of all jurisdiction, but these limits on the doctrine of judicial immunity are applied sparingly, if not reluctantly. And within these limits, even intentional and malicious civil wrongs of judges are frequently cloaked with absolute immunity. On occasions judges are sued for making remarks or written statements that allegedly are defamatory. The rule of absolute judicial immunity shields judges from civil liability for defamatory remarks or statements that they may make.[5] But a judge will not be granted immunity for statements made when the judge was acting in clear absence of jurisdiction or when the judge was acting in a nonjudicial capacity.[6] Statements made by the judge outside the courtroom as well as in the courtroom are immune if made as part of the judicial function.[7] But in *Murray v. Brancato*,[8] it was held that it was not part of a judge's function to send his opinion to an unofficial reporter, and therefore defamatory statements in the opinion were not cloaked with immunity!

There are cases in which judges have been found civilly liable for misappropriation of funds entrusted to their care.[9] Misappropriation of funds entrusted to the care of a judge is beyond the scope of immunity on the ground that it is not a judicial act. But judges do possess immunity for honest mistakes in the administration of funds or estates.[10] Ministerial acts of judges are usually regarded as nonjudicial in character and hence not within the gambit of immunity.[11] In June 1992, after nearly three years of study, an ad hoc committee of the Seventh U.S. Court of Appeals recommended the widespread adoption of "Standards for Professional Conduct of Litigation" for the federal courts. But these standards, according to the preamble, "shall not be used as a basis for litigation or for sanctions or penalties," and therefore the standards are truly a code of civility for lawyers and for judges.

Judges, like other public officials, have been named as defendants in numerous civil rights suits alleging violations of Section 1983 of the Civil Rights Act.[12] This fact appears to be anomalous in light of pronouncements of the U.S. Supreme Court that established absolute judicial immunity from civil liability as long as the judge was acting within his or her jurisdiction.[13] Where there is a "clear absence of jurisdiction," as delineated in *Stump v. Sparkman*,[14] judicial immunity will not preclude liability for official acts. In 1980 in the *Supreme Court of Virginia v. Consumers' Union of the United States*,[15] the highest court echoed the sentiment that there are situations where a judge may act in a nonjudicial capacity, and judicial immunity will not be accepted.[16] Judicial immunity, it would appear, has two foci, one of jurisdiction and the other of function. In the *Stump* case[17] it was held that long as an action is judicial and not taken in clear absence of jurisdiction, judicial immunity from liability is absolute: "[I]f a probate judge, with jurisdiction over only wills and estates, should try a criminal case, he would be acting in the clear absence of jurisdiction and would not be immune from liability for his action; on the other hand, if a judge of a criminal court should convict a defendant of a non-existence [*sic*] crime, he would merely be acting in excess of his jurisdiction and would be immune."

The second focus is function—that is, did the judge act in an official capacity? When a judge acts in an unofficial capacity, he does not act as a judicial officer and is not entitled to judicial immunity.[18] In the *Supreme Court of Virginia* case,[19] a consumer group was unable to prepare a legal directory of attorneys because of the Virginia Bar code's prohibition of attorney advertising.[20] In the suit of the federal court against the Virginia Supreme Court, promulgator of the code, the court was enjoined from enforcing the prohibition, and attorneys' fees were awarded since the court had refused to amend the code. The U.S. Supreme Court held that the doctrine of judicial immunity was not applicable because the case did not involve "judicial action." There is no judicial immunity when a judge acts negligently or maliciously in the performance of ministerial or executive acts. Prosecutorial activities, according to the highest court, occur primarily when a judge participates in decisions involving the initiation of disciplinary proceedings; such activity might include deciding whether to bring a criminal charge against a defendant or deciding which offense to charge.[21] While prosecutors generally enjoy absolute immunity from damages liability, judges who participate in prosecutorial activity do not.[22]

Judges are subject to various codes of judicial conduct, as evident in the ABA Model Code of Judicial Conduct of 1972, the ABA Model Code of Judicial Conduct of 1990, and the Guidelines for Cases Involving Judicial Disability.[23] Yet in *In. Re. XYP*[24] the Pennsylvania Supreme Court applied the principles of immunity to limit the authority possessed by the State Judicial Inquiry and Review Board to regulate judges. Here the board had admonished a judge for statements he had made in a written opinion that the board considered to be in violation of Canon 3(A) of the Code of Judicial Conduct. The board's action was taken without giving the judge prior notice or the right to a hearing!

The most important purpose behind judicial immunity is the protection of judicial independence.[25] Judicial independence is needed because judges, who often are called upon to decide controversial, difficult, and emotion-laden cases, should not have to fear that disgruntled litigants will hound them with litigation charging improper judicial behavior.[26] But there are aberrations as seen in *Stump v. Sparkman*,[27] where the U.S. Supreme Court reviewed a state court order authorizing the sterilization of a 15-year-old girl on the petition of her mother. The petition stated that the girl was somewhat retarded and had begun dating men, which made sterilization necessary to prevent pregnancy. In fact, the girl's high school record indicated that in all probability she was not retarded. The state court judge who granted the petition ordering sterilization did not hold a hearing, nor appoint counsel or a guardian *ad litem* for the girl, nor notify the girl of the petition or subsequent order. Despite these flagrant violations of due process, the U.S. Supreme Court in 1978 ruled that the state court judge possessed absolute immunity for his acts and could not be held liable for any harm his acts caused.[28]

Judges may frequently have to disqualify themselves from serving as a judge in a given trial. A judge holding policies in an insurance company of which his son-in-law is president and manager is disqualified to sit in an action brought upon premium notes assigned by such company, according to *California State Life Insurance Co. v Kring*.[29] But a judge is not disqualified because of interest in the insurer, even though he holds a life policy issued by the insurer, if it does not appear that the defendant is a mutual company or that the payment or nonpayment of the policy issued upon will directly affect any find in which the judge's policy might participate by way of dividends, as seen in *Kansas City Life Insurance Co. v. Kinkens.*[30]

It is said that judges are inadequately trained to be judges and that the problem relates to "the way to teach" the art of judging.[31] As one writer pointed out, "[W]hen lawyers take their place on the bench, there are things to be unlearned as well, and this is an aspect that is more or less ignored!"[32]

NOTES

1. 466 U.S. 522 (1983).
2. Unreported Judgment COJ-7 (Ala. Ct. Jud. July 18, 1977).
3. Judicial disciplinary proceedings have been described as regulatory in nature, serving a function similar to that of a grand jury. *See* In. Re. Haddad, 627 P.2d 221 (Ariz. 1981).
4. *See* 69 A.B.A.J. (Dec. 1983), at 1808–1809.
5. *See* O'Brien v. Chandler, 496 F.2d 403 (10th Cir. 1974).
6. *See* Garfield v. Palmieri, 297 F.2d 526 (2d Cir. 1962).
7. *See* Kraushaar v. Lavin, 39 N.Y.S.2d 880 (1943).
8. 48 N.E.2d 257 (N.Y. 1943).
9. *See* King County v. United Pacific Insurance Co., 434 P.2d 554 (Wash. 1967).
10. *See* Truesdale v. Bellinger, 172, S.E. 784 (S.C. 1934).
11. *See* Heyn v. Massachusetts Bonding and Insurance Co., 110 S.W.2d, 261 (Tex. 1937).
12. 42 U.S.C. § 1101 (1983).
13. *See* Pierson v. Ray, 87 S. Ct. 1212 (1967).
14. 98 S. Ct. 1099 (1978). The case involved a suit against a state judge for the *ex parte* authorization of the sterilization of a slightly retarded 15-year-old girl. The pertinent state statute contained no express authorization for judicial approval of sterilization. The Court determined that the judge had acted merely in excess, but not in the total absence, of his established jurisdiction.
15. 100 S. Ct. 1967 (1980).
16. *See* Note, 33 Baylor L. Rev. 351 (1981).
17. *Infra* note 14.
18. *Infra* note 16 at 357.
19. *Infra* note 15.
20. *See* ch. 2 in Warren Freedman, Malpractice Liability in the Business Professions (1995).
21. *See* Lopez v. Vanderwater, 620F.2d 1992 (7th Cir. 1980).
22. *Infra* note 16 at 359.

23. **Guidelines for Cases Involving Judicial Disability***

1. *Definition*

Judicial disability exists whenever a physical or mental impairment significantly interferes with a judge's capacity to perform judicial functions and duties.

*Reprinted with permission of the American Judicature Society Center for Judicial Conduct Organizations.

Commentary: Of particular significance are those disabilities that impair a judge's capacity to exercise judgment, discretion, and self-control in the conduct of the judicial office. It has been held in several cases that the presence of willful misconduct is not a prerequisite to finding that a judge is disabled. In fact, in many instances of judicial disability, willful misconduct is not present. Judicial disability can be temporary or permanent and can be caused by physical illness or injury, mental illness, stress, senility and alcohol or drug abuse.

2. *Authority*

A judicial conduct organization should have authority to receive and initiate complaints, investigate, conduct hearings, and make recommendations to a court or take action itself in cases concerning judicial disability.

Commentary: A physical or mental disability that impairs a judge's capacity to perform functions affects the administration of justice no less than does judicial misconduct, and the end result of judicial disability may be misconduct. Therefore, a judicial conduct organization is an appropriate agency to deal with judicial disability and should possess the authority over disability cases that it possesses over conduct cases.

Most states have established a judicial retirement and pension board or similar entity charged with administering a judicial retirement program. This guideline is not intended to affect the administrative authority to such entities in cases of voluntary application for disability retirement made in normal course and pursuant retirement program provisions.

3. *Alertness to Symptoms of Disability*

A judicial conduct organization should be alert to behavior that is symptomatic of judicial disability and should take steps to deal with it to prevent the possible occurrence of misconduct.

Commentary: It is always preferable to prevent misconduct rather than to address it after it occurs. Accordingly, a judicial conduct organization should be sensitive to the symptoms of disability, so that treatment, counselling, or other preventive action can be taken prior to the occurrence of misconduct. The following behavior, particularly when it happens recurringly, may be indicative of a disability:

A. Arrogant conduct
B. Intolerance and lack of patience
C. Harassment of lawyers, litigants, and others
D. Temper flare-ups
E. Tyrannical actions
F. Unsteadiness on the bench
G. Falling asleep on the bench
H. Violent mood changes
I. Severe change in personality
J. Emotionally unstable conduct (crying, inappropriate laughter, etc.)
K. Periodic mental lapses
L. Slurred or halting speech
M. Missing an excessive amount of work
N. Drunkenness
O. Inability to keep up with the work of the court
P. Generally bizarre conduct

The above list of symptoms is by no means exhaustive. A profitable method for members of a judicial conduct organization to become acquainted with a variety of disabling illnesses and their symptoms is to consult with the health professionals, such as physicians, psychologists, and treatment counselors.

4. *Procedures*

In dealing with cases of judicial disability, a judicial conduct organization should follow the same procedures that it follows in discipline cases insofar as those procedures are appropriate to disability cases.

Commentary: Usually, the same procedures used in discipline cases will be appropriate in disability cases. Thus, as a general rule, a judicial conduct organization should follow the same procedures in disability cases as are used in discipline cases. For example, procedures that relate to cross-examining witnesses and to the right to counsel ordinarily should be identical in discipline and disability cases. However, a judicial conduct organization should not be reluctant to modify the procedures used in discipline cases to comport the relevant needs and concerns of disability cases.

5. *Promptness*

In dealing with disability cases, a judicial conduct organization should endeavor to act as promptly as practicable consistent with the dictates of sound decision making and fairness to all concerned parties.

Commentary: Promptness in dealing with disability cases is obviously desirable to prevent judicial misconduct, and, in cases of treatable disability, to encourage the initiation of treatment as soon as possible. The goal of prompt action, however, should not be allowed to override the principles of sound and fair decision making.

6. *Assistance Programs*

Assistance programs should be available to help judges overcome their disabilities.

Commentary: A judicial conduct organization should gather information on programs available to judges and should try to determine which programs have a reputation for success. In instances of disability, judges should be urged to participate in an appropriate program.

The information on available programs should also be disseminated generally among judges. This will encourage use of the programs even where disability does not come to the conduct organization's attention. Also, making known among judges the organization's interest in disability will encourage reporting of problems.

7. . . . .

8. *Notification of State Agencies*

In dealing with cases of judicial disability, a judicial conduct organization should notify at the earliest possible date and should coordinate its efforts with the state agencies, if any, responsible for making judicial assignments and for appointing interim judges.

Commentary: The state court administrative agency or officer (e.g., court administrator, chief judge) should be notified when indications of disability come to the conduct organization's attention. The administrative officer or agency may conclude, with or without further inquiry, that the judge should be relieved of some or all assignments or reassigned to less strenuous or less critical functions. Such action is particularly appropriate where the potential for hardship to the judge or prejudice to litigants is apparent. In cases where such administrative action is not immediately warranted, early notification provides court administrators with an opportunity to monitor the situation and prepare to take steps which become necessary as the case proceeds.

In some states, judicial conduct organizations may be restrained by rules of confidentiality from notifying other state agencies or officers about possible court administrators and chief judges, have a proper interest in knowing such information, it is advisable for rules of confidentiality to be amended to permit such notification. Where notification is allowed, the existing rules of confidentiality should attach to the state agencies and officers who receive notification of possible disability cases.

9. ....

10. Reassessment

Where a disability case is dealt with on an informal basis, the judicial conduct organization should periodically reassess the case to determine whether formal proceedings are necessary.

Commentary: Where the judicial conduct organization and a judge have informally arrived at an arrangement for dealing with the judge's disability, the organization should be careful to periodically reassess the situation. Disabilities may be recurrent or may proceed through stages of progressive impairment. These considerations are especially pertinent in cases of alcoholism and drug abuse. A judge's enrollment in an alcohol or drug treatment program does not always insure that the problem is solved.

This guideline is only applicable where the informal remedy involves continued judicial service or prospective return from a leave of absence and not where the judge permanently leaves office.

11. Formal Proceedings

Where a judicial conduct organization has probable cause to believe that a judge is disabled, it may initiate formal proceedings against the judge, in which case the judge should be temporarily suspended, with pay, from performing judicial functions pending the outcome of the proceedings. The formal proceedings should be conducted as promptly as practicable consistent with the dictates of sound decision making and fairness to all concerned parties.

Commentary: The definition of probable cause in disability cases can be formulated by using analogous definitions from other areas of the law. Probable cause exists where, upon reasonable inquiry, there is found to exist an apparent state of facts which would induce a reasonably intelligent and prudent person to believe that the judge in question is disabled.

If, upon a finding of probable cause, it is determined that formal proceedings are warranted, interim suspension with pay is the most appropriate measure to avoid prejudice to litigants and maintain public confidence in the judiciary. Considerations of fairness and due process dictate that a judge under interim suspension should continue to receive pay pending final resolution of the matter, and that resolution of the charges should be prompt.

12. Medical Examinations and Records

In investigating judicial disability, a judicial conduct organization should request the judge to submit all pertinent medical and other records to the organization. If a judge declines to submit such records, or if further information is needed, the judicial conduct organization should request the judge to submit the independent medical or other examinations at the expense of the organization. Where an independent examination of a judge is made, a copy of its results should be given to the judge.

Commentary: Records pertinent in disability cases, especially medical and psychiatric records, should be made available to the judicial conduct organization during a disability investigation. A judge who submits to an independent examination is entitled to know the results so that those results may be challenged or taken into account in preparing a defense.

24. 567 A.2d 1036 (Pa. 1989).

25. *See generally* Wolfram, Modern Legal Ethics (1986), at 970.

26. *See* Forrester v. White, 484 U.S. 219 (1988).

27. 433 U.S. 349 (1978); also *infra* note 14.

28. *See* Nahmod, *Persons Who Are Not Persons: Absolute Individual Immunity Under Section 1983*, 38 DePaul L. Rev. 1 (1978).

29. 280 S.W. 372 (Tex. App. 1918).

30. 202 S.W. 772 (Tex. App. 1918).

31. *See* Carnahan, *Judges Need a Trade School*, N.Y.L.J. (Apr. 13, 1992), at 15–16.

32. *Id.:* "An additional problem is that there has been a greening of the bench during the last thirty years or so. It used to be that becoming a judge was a cap to an experienced lawyer's career. After a quarter of a century of watching other judges, most lawyers, once on the bench, could get the hang of things quickly. Furthermore, lawyers used to have a broader practice background as well; the trend towards legal specialization also has produced a specialized bench."

Chapter 4

Law Librarians

While the probabilities of a reference librarian being sued for malpractice are nil, nevertheless, as a professional, he or she might find himself or herself the victim of a lawsuit because he or she did not provide all the answers a patron feels were required by a request for assistance. Of course, what damages ensued are conjectural, although, in a given hypothetical suit against the librarian, the property damages can be defined. For example, suppose that the plaintiff requested the librarian to recommend a book on how to build a patio.[1] The patron became disgruntled when the structure collapsed, causing great property damage. Plaintiff alleges that the recommended book was not only outdated but inadequate. There can be little doubt that those who use professional librarian services have found that professionals have often promised society more than their training and talent can deliver!

The law librarian is frequently the victim of the law library's efforts to increase patronage; but more and more patrons, lawyers and nonlawyers, if unhappy for any reason may take out their ire on the law librarian. A law librarian is a "specialist in legal and non-legal bibliography and an invaluable reference assistant" and therefore vulnerable to the malpractice lawsuit,[2] especially when the law librarian is asked to provide assistance to the lay public, a group other than those for whom the law library was originally intended. In 1927, one judge opined that the law library should be a general library open to the public when a community lacked a general library so that the people might better understand the causes and results of momentous events and that "the work behind the changes is to be governed not by force but by law, by justice, and righteousness."[3] Indeed, Section 247 of the New

York Education Law opened the law library "for consultation to every citizen of the state at all hours when the state library is open" but limiting the "borrowing of books to every duly-admitted lawyer residing in the State of New York."[4]

The U.S. Supreme Court in *Faretta v. California*[5] found that the prisoner had been deprived of his "constitutional right to proceed with counsel when he voluntarily and intelligently elected to do so." Thus, by implication the highest court in 1975 opined that law libraries should be open to the general public.

Unauthorized legal practice by law librarians is a cause of action, as illustrated by the Professional Code of Ethics,[6] which provides, in part, that "law librarians, while engaged in their professional work, have a duty not to solicit an attorney/client relationship." Note E.C. 3–5 of Canon 3 of the Professional Code of Responsibility:

> It is neither necessary nor desirable to attempt the formulation of a single, specific definition of what constitutes the practice of law. *Functionally, the practice of law relates to the rendition of services for others that call for the professional judgment of a lawyer. The essence of the professional judgment of the lawyer is his educated ability to relate the general body and philosophy of law to a specific legal problem of a client;* and thus, the public interest will be better served if only lawyers are permitted to act in matters involving professional judgment. Where this professional judgment is not involved, nonlawyers, such as court clerks, police officers, abstracters, and many governmental employees, may engage in occupations that require a special knowledge of law in certain areas. But the services of a lawyer are essential in the public interest whenever the exercise of professional legal judgment is required. [Italics supplied]

No wonder members of the legal profession have been concerned with reference librarians assisting a patron without practicing law, without violating the canons of ethics or responsibility. In *Johnson v. Avery*,[7] the highest court emphasized that "the power of the states to control the practice of law cannot be exercised so as to abrogate federally protected rights." Mr. Justice Douglas in a concurring opinion pointed out: "Laymen—in and out of prison—should be allowed as 'next friend' to any person in the preparation of any paper or document or claim, so long as he does not hold himself out as practicing law or as being a member of the Bar. The cooperation and help of laymen, as well as of lawyers, is necessary, if the right of reasonable access to the courts' (citing cases) is to be available to the indigent."

Thus, the patron who is refused access to the courts or is refused entrance to a public library would have a cause of action.[8] As the writer expressed the dilemma:

> Since it is established that the person has a right to library material, the library and its librarians have a correlative duty to make the material accessible. Despite this coextensive relationship, we are still in the unsatisfactorily nebulous position of being unable to describe adequately that reciprocal function. Except for the general statements about the attitude of a librarian or reference person, we have seen that there is no satisfactory description of how extensive is the performance of that duty. There is only the limita-

> tion that it must not exceed the boundary which will metamorphose assistance into unauthorized practice. Though this is conceded, it is hardly a satisfactory measure. We must assume the purpose of the patron is not to create a litigious situation but a sincere attempt to satisfy a personal need and that an unauthorized judgment is probably the very last end the patron would want.
>
> Therefore it would appear that any liability that might accrue would result from the relation of the parties, the undertaking by the librarian to assist the patron, since it is hardly conceivable that the former would "intend" to give the patron any less than requested or to substitute an irrelevance and represent it as the essence.[9] [Citations omitted]

The same writer concluded: "One can hardly feel that pro se assertions of any malpractice claims against a law librarian would not have great difficulty of being established. Nonetheless, it appears the best course for a librarian would be to know one's subject thoroughly; to offer as much assistance as a patron might reasonably need to feel comfortable in a strange environment and not to be antagonistic to a pro se's aspirations, no matter how capricious they might appear."

The 4,500 librarians, including those in academic life, law firms, corporations, bar associations, courts, and the like, do have membership in the American Association of Law Libraries,[10] which promulgated the Code of Ethics[11] shown in the Appendix to Chapter 4.

NOTES

1. *See generally* Leone, *Malpractice Liability of a Law Librarian?* 73 L. Libr. J. 45 (1991).
2. *See* Marke, *The Librarian and You: Are You Missing the Boat?* 40 N.Y.S Bar J. 340 (1968), at 344.
3. *Note* Riddell, *Address of Welcome* (A.A.L.L. 22d Annual Meeting), 20 L. Libr. J. 93 (1927), at 94.
4. *See* American Commuters' Assn. v. Levitt, 279 F. Supp. 40 (S.D.N.Y. 1967).
5. 422 U.S. 806 (1975).
6. *See* 10 A.A.L.L. Newsletter 43 (Jan. 1979).
7. 393 U.S. 483 (1968).
8. *Infra* note 1 at 59.
9. *Id.* at 58.
10. *Id.* at 65.
11. Located at 58 West Jackson Boulevard, Chicago, Ill. 60604. Additional security for law librarians was advocated after a murder/suicide on June 1, 1992, in Los Angeles County, California, according to N.L.J. (June 15, 1992), at 2. A lawyer was shot in the law library by his client, who then immediately shot himself. The particular gunman had apparently been coming to the law library for 20 years; he was a litigious individual, to say the least!

APPENDIX TO CHAPTER 4

CODE OF ETHICS*

The American Association of Law Libraries espouses the statement of professional ethics promulgated by the American Library Association, which states that:

"A librarian:

—has a special responsibility to maintain the principles of the Library Bill of Rights.

—should learn and faithfully execute the policies of the institution of which one is a part and should endeavor to change those which conflict with the spirit of the Library Bill of Rights.

—must protect the essential confidential relationship which exists between a library user and the library.

—must avoid any possibility of personal financial gain at the expense of the employing institution.

—has an obligation to insure equality of opportunity and fair judgment of competence in actions dealing with staff appointments, retentions and promotions.

—has an obligation when making appraisal of the qualification of any individual to report the facts clearly, accurately, and without prejudice, according to generally accepted guidelines concerning the disclosure of personal information."

*Reprinted with permission of the American Association of Law Libraries.

In addition, the Association, in light of the special character and mission of its membership, espouses the principles that law librarians, while engaged in their professional work:

—have a duty *neither to engage in the unauthorized practice of law nor to solicit an attorney/client relationship*.

—have a duty to avoid any situations posing a possible *undisclosed* conflict of interest.

—have a special duty, given the nature of their patron base, to treat confidentially any private information obtained through contact with library patrons and not to divulge any confidential information to persons representing adverse interests.

—have a duty to exercise scrupulous care in avoiding any acts, or even the appearance, of misappropriating the work product of library patrons or professional colleagues to their own credit or profit.

—have a duty actively to *promote* free and effective access to legal information.

—have a duty to society and the legal profession to work both individually and through their professional organizations toward *improving* the quality and *minimizing* the cost of the library component of the delivery of legal services.

Chapter 5

Lobbyists

There can be little doubt that of all professionals, lawyers frequently wear many "hats," and the art of lobbying is but one of the many hats worn by lawyers. As a lobbyist, the lawyer has been named as a defendant or a co-conspirator with trade associations,[1] particularly in toxic tort and products liability litigation. The injured parties have sought to hold lawyers and trade associations liable for product-related injuries, based on a variety of theories including negligent certification of product safety, fraud and misrepresentation,[2] enterprise liability, and concert of action or conspiracy to conceal the alleged dangers associated with the product. Generally these lobbying cases have been dismissed on the ground that such activities are privileged as lawful "petitioning" protected by the First Amendment.[3]

But in *Cippolone* v. *Liggett Group, Inc.*,[4] the federal district court in New Jersey denied the motion ***in limine*** to exclude evidence that defendant lawyers and defendant tobacco industry provided false and misleading information to Congress and offered jobs to members of Congress who voted favorably on tobacco legislation.[5] However, in *Ford Motor Co. v. Durrill*[6] evidence that the president and counsel of Ford and the chief executive officer (CEO) of another automobile manufacturer lobbied President Richard Nixon concerning automobile safety regulations that they considered to be too expensive was held to be relevant to the claim that the defendants acted with conscious indifference to the rights and safety of the public in the design of the automobiles.

But the doctrine of antitrust immunity for legislative activities appears to be widely accepted, especially following the U.S. Supreme Court decision[7] that even deceptive or fraudulent campaign practices do not bring legislative or political lobbying activities under the Sherman Act, which act is a "code that condemns trade restraints, not political activity. . . . [A] publicity campaign to influence governmental action falls clearly into the category of political activity." But in *McDonald v. Smith*[8] the highest court in 1986 held that First Amendment immunity from tort liability for false statements of fact contained in petitions to government does not extend to "intentionally and reckless falsehoods."

It should be observed that lobbying by attorneys and others is subject to registration and reporting requirements under the Federal Regulation of Lobbying Act of 1946.[9] The act requires registration and reporting by a person who "solicits, collects, or receives" contributions "to be used principally" to influence or bring about the passage or defeat of any legislation by Congress. Contracts with federal administrative officials are governed by the government in the Sunshine Act,[10] which bars *ex parte* contacts between interested parties and agency officials in formal rule makings and adjudications.

According to the *American Bar Association Journal* (May 1993),[11] the State Bar of California has since 1990 allowed its members to withhold more than $250,000 in dues to avoid funding some of the bar's objectionable lobbying and political activities. In short, lawyers have been lobbyists and political activists and could be guilty of malpractice for such lobbying and political activities. It should be noted that the U.S. Supreme Court in 1990 in *Keller v. State Bar*[12] had ruled that mandatory or "unified" state bars may not force lawyers to fund through mandatory dues the political or ideological activities not germane to the bar's central purposes. As a result, lobbying activities by lawyers have been radically curbed or curtailed. But in Michigan, more than 5,000 lawyers have withheld $18 each for a total of $91,620 during the past fiscal years; in California, 13,016 lawyers have withheld $3 each, and in Wisconsin, more than 5,300 lawyers have withheld $5 for a total of $26,530 in 1991–1992.

NOTES

1. *See* Vorhees, *Product Liability Risks Faced by Trade Associations That Lobby the Government on Health and Safety Issues*, J. PROD. & TOXIC LIAB. 15 (1993), at 55–80.

2. *See* WARREN FREEDMAN, THE BUSINESS TORT OF FRAUD AND MISREPRESENTATION (1989), at Section 7.4 thereof.

3. *See* Eastern Railroad Presidents Conference v. Noerr Motor Freight, Inc., 365 U.S. 127 (1961).

4. 688 F. Supp. 408 (N.J. 1987).

5. *Infra* note 1 at 56.

6. 714 S.W.2d 339 (Tex. App. 1986).

7. *Infra* note 3.

8. 472 U.S. 479 (1986).
9. 2 U.S.C. §§ 261–270 (1988).
10. 5 U.S.C. § 556(d) and 5 U.S.C. § 557(d) (1988).
11. At 30.
12. 496 U.S. 1 (1990).

Chapter 6

Mediators and Arbitrators

The art of mediation and arbitration has brought to the fore the professionalism of its leadership by its widespread acceptance in legal circles. The American Arbitration Association,[1] founded in 1926, has a membership of almost 7,000 businesses, unions, trade and educational associations, law firms, and other interested individuals. Its national panel of arbitrators has more than 60,000 individuals listed to mediate or to arbitrate. The Code of Ethics for Arbitrators in Commercial Disputes is especially thorough as shown in Appendix A of this chapter. Note also Appendix B, the code of Professional Responsibility for Arbitrators of Labor-Management Disputes.

The Society of Professionals in Dispute Resolution[2] comprises arbitrators, mediators, ombudsmen, fact-finders, conciliators, trial examiners, hearing officers, and educators of dispute resolution process. Note its Ethical Standards of Professional Conduct in Appendix C.

It should be observed that court-appointed mediators and arbitrators are given judicial immunity for performing judicial assignments.[3] Mediators, in particular, have been used increasingly in all types of civil and criminal cases, from divorces to complex civil litigation.[4] Indeed, more than 40 states have statutes conferring some measure of confidentiality upon the mediation process.[5] One writer[6] has observed that "[o]ne of the central functions of mediation is to encourage the parties to speak candidly about their interests, needs, fears, and desires. If a party has any concern over whether what it tells the mediator in confidence, or what it does in the negotiations, might be revealed to its detriment, any rational party would not be as forthcoming." Indeed, parties' trust in the mediator as an impartial person would be threatened if the mediator could freely testify subsequently about the substance of the mediator discussions with the parties.[7]

It should be noted historically that mediation is deeply rooted in the tradition of many lands and cultures.[8] Perhaps the congressional enactment of the Dispute Resolution Act of 1980 is but a fulfillment of that tradition.[9] Mediation has been defined as "a process whereby a neutral third party acts to encourage and facilitate the resolution of a dispute without prescribing what it should be. It is an informal and nonadversarial process with the objective of helping the disputing parties reach a mutually acceptable agreement."[10] Actions against mediators may take the form of tort, contract, or breach of fiduciary duty,[11] but each of these legal theories must first surmount the difficulty of proving a breach of duty and damages before a mediator can be found liable.[12] Proving damages is precarious, as disgruntled participants in the mediation must estimate what they would have obtained in another dispute resolution procedure or what economic consequences were the unique result of the fault of the mediator.[13]

In Florida, for example, broad immunities have been granted to court-appointed mediators.[14] But whether absolute immunity is necessary is an open question. In *Butz v. Economou*[15] the U.S. Supreme Court laid down a two-part test for determining the need for absolute immunity, to wit: If the officials function is judicial in nature, and a disgruntled party's constitutional rights are protected by safeguards built into the regulatory framework, then the officer's conduct will be immune from civil liability. Court-appointed mediators would qualify under the test. The states have also addressed this issue, and at least 13 states have granted some form of immunity to mediators.[16]

Performance appraisal of mediators might identify, measure, and provide improvement techniques for relevant desired behaviors and outputs.[17]

NOTES

1. Located at 140 West 51st Street, New York, N.Y. 10020–1203.
2. Located at 1730 Rhode Island Avenue, N.W., Washington, D.C. 20036. *Also note* the Academy of Family Mediators, P.O. Box 10501, Eugene, Oregon 97440, comprising over 1,000 members with backgrounds in behavior science, conflict resolution, and the law, specializing in mediating family disputes and divorce. The academy's Standards of Practice for Family and Divorce Mediation appear in Appendix D.

See Friedman, *Punitive Damages in Securities Cases*, N.Y.L.J. (May 2, 1991), at 3 and 30, where the author commented on the arbitrator's authority to award punitive damages. In citing Shearson/American Express v. McMahon Inc., 482 U.S. 220 (1987), the writer observed that the U.S. Supreme Court found that RICO claims were specifically arbitrable.

> Whether arbitrators could award treble damages under RICO was answered in the affirmative by the Second Circuit in Kerr-McGee Refining Corp. v. Triumph Tankers. While Kerr-McGee did not pertain to a securities case, the connection between that case

and McMahon is worth noting because the court, in dictum, observed that in an appropriate case, the arbitrators could "enhance" their award by punitive damages (citing Bonar, *supra*).

The bottom line, pending on the outcome of the pending appeals in Fahnestock and Barbier, or some legislative enactment, seems to be that where interstate commerce is present, arbitrators are permitted to award punitive damages in New York, despite a New York choice of law provision. The likelihood of a punitive damage award being upheld, however, is increased under a broad clause or where the arbitration association's rules are used. Until the situation becomes clarified, however, such an award may be challenged by a losing party, albeit without success.

The arbitration association's rules do not address punitive damages, which seems to be acceptable to at least a majority of association users. . . .

Should punitive damages be awardable in securities arbitration? Given the fact that McMahon, *supra*, and the later Supreme Court decision in Rodriguez de Quijas v. Shearson/American Express Inc. for all intents and purposes allow arbitrators to decide statutory securities issues, the answer seems to be yes. If the sole avenue of recourse for aggrieved investors is arbitration, it would seem appropriate that arbitration be permitted to offer complete relief, or at least the same relief they would be able to obtain in court. From another perspective, denying arbitrators the authority to award punitive damages in securities cases could serve to encourage or condone unscrupulous conduct by brokers, who might believe that damages would be limited to the compensatory type.

3. *See* Mills v. Killebrew, 765 F.2d 69 (6th Cir. 1985).

4. *See* Green, *A Heretical View of the Mediation Privilege*, 2 Ohio St. J. Disp. Resol. 1 (1986).

5. See Note, 105 Harv. L. Rev. 1339 (1992), at 1355. *Also see* Rogers and McEwen, Mediation: Law, Policy and Practice (1989), at Section 8.33 thereof.

6. *See* Harter, *Neither Cop Nor Collection Agent: Encouraging Administrative Settlements by Ensuring Mediator Confidentiality*, 41 Admin. L. Rev. 315 (1989), at 324.

7. *See* NLRB v. Joseph Macaluso, Inc., 618 F.2d 51 (9th Cir. 1980).

8. *See* Folberg and Taylor, Mediation (1984), at 1–7.

9. 28 U.S.C. App II (1980).

10. Section 44.301(1) of Fla. Stat. (1989).

11. *See* Note, *Judicial Immunity for Mediators*, 17 Fla. St. U.L. Rev. 623 (1990).

12. *Infra* note 8 at 281.

13. *Infra* note 11.

14. *See* Section 44.307 of Fla. Stat. (1989).

15. 438 U.S. 478 (1978).

16. *Note*: *Colorado*: Colo. Rev. Stat. § 13–22–305 (Supp. 1988) (limiting qualified immunity to willful or wanton misconduct); *Iowa*: Iowa Code § 679.13 (1987) (limiting immunity to actions by dispute resolution center mediators made "in bad faith, with malicious purpose or in a manner exhibiting willful and wanton disregard of human rights, safety or property"); *Maine*: Me. Rev. Stat. Ann. tit. 4, § 18(2–A) (1964) and tit. 14, § 8111(1) (Supp. 1988) (providing immunity for negligent performance of ministerial acts or discretionary functions by mediators under contract with the judicial department); *Minnesota*: Minn. Stat. Ann. § 583.26(7) (West 1988) (providing immunity for actions within the scope of farm-lender mediation panel); *Mississippi*: Miss. Code Ann. § 69–2–49 (Supp. 1988) (providing immunity for actions within the scope of the farm debt mediation services); *Montana*: Mont. Code

ANN. § 27–6–106 (1987) (providing absolute immunity for medical malpractice mediators); *New Jersey*: N.J. REV. STAT. § 2A:23A-9(d) (1987) (providing immunity for wrongful conduct of a dispute resolution umpire); *North Carolina*: N.C. GEN. STAT. §§ 1–539.10 to –539.11 (Supp. 1988) (limiting qualified immunity to uninsured volunteer mediators serving with uninsured nonprofit charitable organizations); *Oklahoma*: OKLA. STAT. ANN. tit. 12, § 1805(E) (West Supp. 1989) (providing immunity for "gross negligence with malicious purpose or . . . willful disregard of the rights, safety, or property of any party to the mediation"); *Virginia:* VA. CODE ANN. § 8.01–581.23 (Supp. 1988) (limiting qualified immunity to acts or omissions done or made in good faith during mediation); *Washington*: WASH. REV. CODE ANN. § 7.75.100 (Supp. 1989) (limiting qualified immunity to dispute resolution center directors and mediators acting in good faith); *Wisconsin*: WISC. STAT. ANN. § 93.50(2)(c) (West Supp. 1988) (providing immunity for any acts or omissions within the scope of Department of Agriculture, Trade and Consumer Protection mediation duties); WISC. STAT. ANN. § 655.465(6) (West Supp. 1988) (limiting qualified immunity to medical malpractice mediators acting in good faith): *Wyoming:* WYO. STAT. § 11–41–105 (Supp. 1989) (limiting qualified immunity).

17. *See generally* KOLB, THE MEDIATORS (1983); and Note, 9 LABOR L.J. (1958), at 758.

APPENDIX A

Code of Ethics for Arbitrators in Commercial Disputes*

PREAMBLE

The use of commercial arbitration to resolve a wide variety of disputes has grown extensively and forms a significant part of the system of justice which our society relies upon for the fair determination of legal rights. Persons who act as commercial arbitrators therefore undertake serious responsibilities to the public as well as to the parties. These responsibilities include important ethical obligations.

Few cases of unethical behavior by commercial arbitrators have arisen. Nevertheless, the American Bar Association and the American Arbitration Association believe that it is in the public interest to set forth generally accepted standards of ethical conduct for the guidance of arbitrators and parties in commercial disputes. By establishing this Code, the sponsors hope to contribute to the maintenance of high standards and continued confidence in the process of arbitration.

There are many different types of commercial arbitration. Some cases are conducted under arbitration rules established by various organizations and trade associations, while others are carried on without such rules. Although most cases are arbitrated pursuant to voluntary agreement of the parties, certain types of disputes are submitted to arbitration by reason of particular laws. This Code is intended to apply to all such proceedings in which disputes or claims are submitted for decision to one or more arbitrators appointed in a manner provided by an agreement of the parties, by applicable arbitration rules or by law. In all such cases the persons who have the power to decide should observe fundamental standards of ethical conduct. In this Code all such persons are called "arbitrators," although in some types of cases they may be called "umpires" or may have some other title.

Various aspects of the conduct of arbitrators, including some matters covered by this Code, may be governed by agreements of the parties, by arbitration rules to which the parties have agreed, or by applicable law. This Code does not take the place of, or supersede, any such agreements, rules and laws and does not establish any new or additional grounds for judicial review of arbitration awards.

While this Code is intended to provide ethical guidelines in many types of arbitration, it does not form part of the arbitration rules of the American Arbitration Association or of any other organization, nor is it intended to apply to mediation or conciliation. Labor arbitrations are governed by the "Code of Professional Responsibility for Arbitrators of Labor-Management Disputes," not by this Code.

Arbitrators, like judges, have the power to decide cases. However, unlike full-time judges, arbitrators are usually engaged in other occupations before, during and after the time they serve as arbitrators. Often arbitrators are purposely chosen from the same trade or industry as the parties in order to bring special knowledge to the task of deciding. This Code recognizes these fundamental differences between arbitrators and judges.

In some types of arbitration there are three, or more, arbitrators. In these cases, it is sometimes the practice for each party, acting alone, to appoint one arbitrator and for the other arbitrator(s) to be designated by those two, or by the parties, or by an independent

*Reprinted with permission of the American Arbitration Association.

institution or individual. The sponsors of this Code believe that it is preferable for parties to agree that all arbitrators should comply with the same ethical standards. However, it is recognized that there is a long-established practice in some types of arbitration for those arbitrators who are appointed by one party, acting alone, to be governed by special ethical considerations. Those special considerations are set forth in the last section of the Code, headed "Ethical Considerations Relating to Arbitrators Appointed By One Party."

Although this Code is sponsored by the American Arbitration Association and the American Bar Association, its use is not limited to arbitrations administered by the AAA or to cases in which the arbitrators are lawyers. Rather, it is presented as a public service to provide guidance in all types of commercial arbitration.

CANON I

AN ARBITRATOR SHOULD UPHOLD THE INTEGRITY AND FAIRNESS OF THE ARBITRATION PROCESS

A. Fair and just processes for resolving disputes are indispensable in our society. Commercial arbitration is an important method for deciding many types of disputes. In order for commercial arbitration to be effective, there must be broad public confidence in the integrity and fairness of the process. Therefore, an arbitrator has a responsibility not only to the parties but also to the process of arbitration itself, and must observe high standards of conduct so that the integrity and fairness of the process will be preserved. Accordingly, an arbitrator should recognize a responsibility to the public, to the parties whose rights will be decided, and to all other participants in the proceeding. The provisions of this Code should be construed and applied to further these objectives.

B. It is inconsistent with the integrity of the arbitration process for persons to solicit appointment for themselves. However, a person may indicate a general willingness to serve as an arbitrator.

C. Persons should accept appointment as arbitrators only if they believe that they can be available to conduct the arbitration promptly.

D. After accepting appointment and while serving as an arbitrator, a person should avoid entering into any financial, business, professional, family or social relationship, or acquiring any financial or personal interest, which is likely to affect impartiality or which might reasonably create the appearance of partiality or bias. For a reasonable period of time after the decision of a case, persons who have served as arbitrators should avoid entering into any such relationship, or acquiring any such interest, in circumstances which might reasonably create the appearance that they had been influenced in the arbitration by the anticipation or expectation of the relationship or interest.

E. Arbitrators should conduct themselves in a way that is fair to all parties and should not be swayed by outside pressure, by public clamor, or fear of criticism or by self-interest.

F. When an arbitrator's authority is derived from an agreement of the parties, the arbitrator should neither exceed that authority nor do less than is required to exercise that authority completely. Where the agreement of the parties sets forth procedures to be followed in conducting the arbitration or refers to rules to be followed, it is the obligation of the arbitrator to comply with such procedures or rules.

G. An arbitrator should make all reasonable efforts to prevent delaying tactics, harassment of parties or other participants, or other abuse or disruption of the arbitration process.

H. The ethical obligations of an arbitrator begin upon acceptance of the appointment and continue throughout all stages of the proceeding. In addition, wherever specifically set forth in this Code, certain ethical obligations begin as soon as a person is requested to serve as an arbitrator and certain ethical obligations continue even after the decision in the case has been given to the parties.

CANON II

AN ARBITRATOR SHOULD DISCLOSE ANY INTEREST OR RELATIONSHIP LIKELY TO AFFECT IMPARTIALITY OR WHICH MIGHT CREATE AN APPEARANCE OF PARTIALITY OR BIAS

Introductory Note:

This Code reflects the prevailing principle that arbitrators should disclose the existence of any interests or relationships which are likely to affect their impartiality or which might reasonably create the appearance that they are biased against one party or favorable to another. These provisions of the Code are intended to be applied realistically so that the burden of detailed disclosure does not become so great that it is impractical for persons in the business world to be arbitrators, thereby depriving parties of the services of those who might be best informed and qualified to decide particular types of cases.*

This Code does not limit the freedom of parties to agree on anyone they choose as an arbitrator. When parties, with knowledge of a person's interests and relationships, nevertheless desire that individual to serve as an arbitrator, that person may properly serve.

Disclosure:

A. Persons who are requested to serve as arbitrators should, before accepting, disclose:

(1) Any direct or indirect financial or personal interest in the outcome of the arbitration;

(2) Any existing or past financial, business, professional, family or social relationships which are likely to affect impartiality or which might reasonably create an appearance of partiality or bias. Persons requested to serve as arbitrators should disclose any such relationships which they personally have

*In applying the provisions of this Code relating to disclosure, it may be helpful to recall the words of the concurring opinion in a case decided by the United States Supreme Court, that arbitrators "should err on the side of disclosure" because "it is better that the relationship be disclosed at the outset when the parties are free to reject the arbitrator or accept him with knowledge of the relationship." At the same time, it must be recognized that "an arbitrator's business relationships may be diverse indeed, involving more or less remote commercial connections with great numbers of people." Accordingly, an arbitrator "cannot be expected to provide the parties with his complete and unexpurgated business biography," nor is an arbitrator called upon to disclose interests or relationships which are merely "trivial." (Concurring opinion in *Commonwealth Coatings Corp. v. Continental Casualty Co.*, 393 US 145, 151-152, 1968.)

with any party or its lawyer, or with any individual whom they have been told will be a witness. They should also disclose any such relationships involving members of their families or their current employers, partners or business associates.

B. Persons who are requested to accept appointment as arbitrators should make a reasonable effort to inform themselves of any interests or relationships described in Paragraph A above.

C. The obligation to disclose interests or relationships described in Paragraph A above is a continuing duty which requires a person who accepts appointment as an arbitrator to disclose, at any stage of the arbitration, any such interests or relationships which may arise, or which are recalled or discovered.

D. Disclosure should be made to all parties unless other procedures for disclosure are provided in the rules or practices of an institution which is administering the arbitration. Where more than one arbitrator has been appointed, each should inform the others of the interests and relationships which have been disclosed.

E. In the event that an arbitrator is requested by all parties to withdraw, the arbitrator should do so. In the event that an arbitrator is requested to withdraw by less than all of the parties because of alleged partiality or bias, the arbitrator should withdraw unless either of the following circumstances exists:

(1) If an agreement of the parties, or arbitration rules agreed to by the parties, establishes procedures for determining challenges to arbitrators, then those procedures should be followed; or

(2) If the arbitrator, after carefully considering the matter, determines that the reason for the challenge is not substantial, and that he or she can nevertheless act and decide the case impartially and fairly, and that withdrawal would cause unfair delay or expense to another party or would be contrary to the ends of justice.

CANON III

AN ARBITRATOR IN COMMUNICATING WITH THE PARTIES SHOULD AVOID IMPROPRIETY OR THE APPEARANCE OF IMPROPRIETY

A. If an agreement of the parties, or any applicable arbitration rules referred to in that agreement, establishes the manner or content of communications between the arbitrator and the parties, the arbitrator should follow those procedures notwithstanding any contrary provisions of the following Paragraphs B and C.

B. Unless otherwise provided in applicable arbitration rules or in an agreement of the parties, arbitrators should not discuss a case with any party in the absence of each other party, except in any of the following circumstances:

(1) Discussions may be had with a party concerning such matters as setting the time and place of hearings or making other arrangements for the conduct of the proceedings. However, the arbitrator should promptly inform each other party of the discussion and should not make any final determination concerning the matter discussed before giving each absent party an opportunity to express its views.

(2) If a party fails to be present at a hearing after having been given due notice, the arbitrator may discuss the case with any party who is present.
(3) If all parties request or consent that such discussion take place.

C. Unless otherwise provided in applicable arbitration rules or in an agreement of the parties, whenever an arbitrator communicates in writing with one party, the arbitrator should at the same time send a copy of the communication to each other party. Whenever an arbitrator receives any written communication concerning the case from one party which has not already been sent to each other party, the arbitrator should do so.

CANON IV

AN ARBITRATOR SHOULD CONDUCT THE PROCEEDINGS FAIRLY AND DILIGENTLY

A. An arbitrator should conduct the proceedings in an evenhanded manner and treat all parties with equality and fairness at all stages of the proceedings.

B. An arbitrator should perform duties diligently and conclude the case as promptly as the circumstances reasonably permit.

C. An arbitrator should be patient and courteous to the parties, to their lawyers and to the witnesses and should encourage similar conduct by all participants in the proceedings.

D. Unless otherwise agreed by the parties or provided in arbitration rules agreed to by the parties, an arbitrator should accord to all parties the right to appear in person and to be heard after due notice of the time and place of hearing.

E. An arbitrator should not deny any party the opportunity to be represented by counsel.

F. If a party fails to appear after due notice, an arbitrator should proceed with the arbitration when authorized to do so by the agreement of the parties, the rules agreed to by the parties or by law. However, an arbitrator should do so only after receiving assurance that notice has been given to the absent party.

G. When an arbitrator determines that more information than has been presented by the parties is required to decide the case, it is not improper for the arbitrator to ask questions, call witnesses, and request documents or other evidence.

H. It is not improper for an arbitrator to suggest to the parties that they discuss the possibility of settlement of the case. However, an arbitrator should not be present or otherwise participate in the settlement discussions unless requested to do so by all parties. An arbitrator should not exert pressure on any party to settle.

I. Nothing in this Code is intended to prevent a person from acting as a mediator or conciliator of a dispute in which he or she has been appointed as arbitrator, if requested to do so by all parties or where authorized or required to do so by applicable laws or rules.

J. When there is more than one arbitrator, the arbitrators should afford each other the full opportunity to participate in all aspects of the proceedings.

CANON V

AN ARBITRATOR SHOULD MAKE DECISIONS IN A JUST, INDEPENDENT AND DELIBERATE MANNER

A. An arbitrator should, after careful deliberation, decide all issues submitted for determination. An arbitrator should decide no other issues.

B. An arbitrator should decide all matters justly, exercising independent judgment, and should not permit outside pressure to affect the decision.

C. An arbitrator should not delegate the duty to decide to any other person.

D. In the event that all parties agree upon a settlement of the issues in dispute and request an arbitrator to embody that agreement in an award, an arbitrator may do so, but is not required to do so unless satisfied with the propriety of the terms of settlement. Whenever an arbitrator embodies a settlement by the parties in an award, the arbitrator should state in the award that it is based on an agreement of the parties.

CANON VI

AN ARBITRATOR SHOULD BE FAITHFUL TO THE RELATIONSHIP OF TRUST AND CONFIDENTIALITY INHERENT IN THAT OFFICE

A. An arbitrator is in a relationship of trust to the parties and should not, at any time, use confidential information acquired during the arbitration proceeding to gain personal advantage or advantage for others, or to affect adversely the interest of another.

B. Unless otherwise agreed by the parties, or required by applicable rules or law, an arbitrator should keep confidential all matters relating to the arbitration proceedings and decision.

C. It is not proper at any time for an arbitrator to inform anyone of the decision in advance of the time it is given to all parties. In a case in which there is more than one arbitrator, it is not proper at any time for an arbitrator to inform anyone concerning the deliberations of the arbitrators. After an arbitration award has been made, it is not proper for an arbitrator to assist in any post-arbitration proceedings, except as may be required by law.

D. In many types of arbitration it is customary practice for the arbitrators to serve without pay. However, in some types of cases it is customary for arbitrators to receive compensation for their services and reimbursement for their expenses. In cases in which any such payments are to be made, all persons who are requested to serve, or who are serving as arbitrators, should be governed by the same high standards of integrity and fairness as apply to their other activities in the case. Accordingly, such persons should scrupulously avoid bargaining with parties over the amount of payments or engaging in any communications concerning payments which would create an appearance of coercion or other impropriety. In the absence of governing provisions in the agreement of the parties or in rules agreed to by the parties or in applicable law, certain practices relating to payments are generally recognized as being preferable in order to preserve the integrity and fairness of the arbitration process. These practices include:

(1) It is preferable that before the arbitrator finally accepts appointment the basis of payment be established and that all parties be informed thereof in writing.

(2) In cases conducted under the rules or administration of an institution which is available to assist in making arrangements for payments, the payments should

be arranged by the institution to avoid the necessity for communication by the arbitrators directly with the parties concerning the subject.

(3) In cases where no institution is available to assist in making arrangements for payments, it is preferable that any discussions with arbitrators concerning payments should take place in the presence of all parties.

CANON VII

ETHICAL CONSIDERATIONS RELATING TO ARBITRATORS APPOINTED BY ONE PARTY

Introductory Note:

In some types of arbitration in which there are three arbitrators it is customary for each party, acting alone, to appoint one arbitrator. The third arbitrator is then appointed either by agreement of the parties or of the two arbitrators, or, failing such agreement, by an independent institution or individual. In some of these types of arbitration, all three arbitrators are customarily considered to be neutral and are expected to observe the same standards of ethical conduct. However, there are also many types of tripartite arbitration in which it has been the practice that the two arbitrators appointed by the parties are not considered to be neutral and are expected to observe many—but not all—of the same ethical standards as the neutral third arbitrator. For the purposes of this Code, an arbitrator appointed by one party who is not expected to observe all of the same standards as the third arbitrator is referred to as a "non-neutral arbitrator." This Canon VII describes the ethical obligations which non-neutral party-appointed arbitrators should observe and those which are not applicable to them.

In all arbitrations in which there are two or more party-appointed arbitrators, it is important for everyone concerned to know from the start whether the party-appointed arbitrators are expected to be neutrals or non-neutrals. In such arbitrations, the two party-appointed arbitrators should be considered non-neutrals unless both parties inform the arbitrators that all three arbitrators are to be neutral, or unless the contract, the applicable arbitration rules, or any governing law requires that all three arbitrators are to be neutral.

It should be noted that in cases where the arbitration is conducted outside the United States the applicable law may require that all arbitrators be neutral. Accordingly, in such cases the governing law should be considered before applying any of the following provisions relating to non-neutral party-appointed arbitrators.

A. Obligations Under Canon I:

Non-neutral party-appointed arbitrators should observe all of the obligations of Canon I to uphold the integrity and fairness of the arbitration process, subject only to the following provisions:

(1) Non-neutral arbitrators may be predisposed toward the party who appointed them but in all other respects are obligated to act in good faith and with integrity and fairness. For example, non-neutral arbitrators should not engage in delaying tactics or harassment of any party or witness and should not knowingly make untrue or misleading statements to the other arbitrators.

(2) The provisions of Canon I-D relating to relationships and interests are not applicable to non-neutral arbitrators.

B. Obligations Under Canon II:

Non-neutral party-appointed arbitrators should disclose to all parties, and to the other arbitrators, all interests and relationships which Canon II requires be disclosed. Disclosure as required by Canon II is for the benefit not only of the party who appointed the non-neutral arbitrator, but also for the benefit of the other parties and arbitrators so that they may know of any bias which may exist or appear to exist. However, this obligation is subject to the following provisions:

(1) Disclosure by non-neutral arbitrators should be sufficient to describe the general nature and scope of any interest or relationship, but need not include as detailed information as is expected from persons appointed as neutral arbitrators.
(2) Non-neutral arbitrators are not obligated to withdraw if requested to do so by the party who did not appoint them, notwithstanding the provisions of Canon II-E.

C. Obligations Under Canon III:

Non-neutral party-appointed arbitrators should observe all of the obligations of Canon III concerning communications with the parties, subject only to the following provisions:

(1) In an arbitration in which the two party-appointed arbitrators are expected to appoint the third arbitrator, non-neutral arbitrators may consult with the party who appointed them concerning the acceptability of persons under consideration for appointment as the third arbitrator.
(2) Non-neutral arbitrators may communicate with the party who appointed them concerning any other aspect of the case, provided they first inform the other arbitrators and the parties that they intend to do so. If such communication occurred prior to the time the person was appointed as arbitrator, or prior to the first hearing or other meeting of the parties with the arbitrators, the non-neutral arbitrator should at the first hearing or meeting, disclose the fact that such communication has taken place. In complying with the provisions of this paragraph, it is sufficient that there be disclosure of the fact that such communication has occurred without disclosing the content of the communication. It is also sufficient to disclose at any time the intention to follow the procedure of having such communications in the future and there is no requirement thereafter that there be disclosure before each separate occasion on which such a communication occurs.
(3) When non-neutral arbitrators communicate in writing with the party who appointed them concerning any matter as to which communication is permitted under this Code, they are not required to send copies of any such written communications to any other party or arbitrator.

D. Obligations Under Canon IV:

Non-neutral party-appointed arbitrators should observe all of the obligations of Canon IV to conduct the proceedings fairly and diligently.

E. Obligations Under Canon V:

Non-neutral party-appointed arbitrators should observe all of the obligations of Canon V concerning making decisions, subject only to the following provision:

(1) Non-neutral arbitrators are permitted to be predisposed toward deciding in favor of the party who appointed them.

F. Obligations Under Canon VI:

Non-neutral party-appointed arbitrators should observe all of the obligations of Canon VI to be faithful to the relationship of trust inherent in the office of arbitrator, subject only to the following provision:

(1) Non-neutral arbitrators are not subject to the provisions of Canon VI-D with respect to any payments by the party who appointed them.

APPENDIX B

Code of Professional Responsibility for Arbitrators of Labor-Management Disputes*

FOREWORD

Reasons for Code revision should be noted briefly. Ethical considerations and procedural standards are sufficiently intertwined to warrant combining the subject matter of Parts I and II of the 1951 Code under the caption of "Professional Responsibility." It has seemed advisable to eliminate admonitions to the parties (Part III of the 1951 Code) except as they appear incidentally in connection with matters primarily involving responsibilities of arbitrators. Substantial growth of third party participation in dispute resolution in the public sector requires consideration. It appears that arbitration of new contract terms may become more significant. Finally, during the interval of more than two decades, new problems have emerged as private sector grievance arbitration has matured and has become more diversified.

PREAMBLE

Background

Voluntary arbitration rests upon the mutual desire of management and labor in each collective bargaining relationship to develop procedures for dispute settlement which meet their own particular needs and obligations. No two voluntary systems, therefore, are likely to be identical in practice. Words used to describe arbitrators (Arbitrator, Umpire, Impartial Chairman, Chairman of Arbitration Board, etc.) may suggest typical approaches but actual differences within any general type of arrangement may be as great as distinctions often made among the several types.

Some arbitration and related procedures, however, are not the product of voluntary agreement. These procedures, primarily but not exclusively applicable in the public sector, sometimes utilize other third party titles (Fact Finder, Impasse Panel, Board of Inquiry, etc.). These procedures range all the way from arbitration prescribed by statute to arrangements substantially indistinguishable from voluntary procedures.

The standards of professional responsibility set forth in this Code are designed to guide the impartial third party serving in these diverse labor-management relationships.

Scope of Code

This Code is a privately developed set of standards of professional behavior. It applies to voluntary arbitration of labor-management grievance disputes and of disputes

*Reprinted with permission of the American Arbitration Association.

concerning new or revised contract terms. Both "ad hoc" and "permanent" varieties of voluntary arbitration, private and public sector, are included. To the extent relevant in any specific case, it also applies to advisory arbitration, impasse resolution panels, arbitration prescribed by statutes, fact-finding, and other special procedures.

The word "arbitrator," as used hereinafter in the Code, is intended to apply to any impartial person, irrespective of specific title, who serves in a labor-management dispute procedure in which there is conferred authority to decide issues or to make formal recommendations.

The Code is not designed to apply to mediation or conciliation, as distinguished from arbitration, nor to other procedures in which the third party is not authorized in advance to make decisions or recommendations. It does not apply to partisan representatives on tripartite boards. It does not apply to commercial arbitration or to other uses of arbitration outside the labor-management dispute area.

Format of Code

Bold Face type, sometimes including explanatory material, is used to set forth general principles. *Italics* are used for amplification of general principles. Ordinary type is used primarily for illustrative or explanatory comment.

Application of Code

Faithful adherence by an arbitrator to this Code is basic to professional responsibility.

The National Academy of Arbitrators will expect its members to be governed in their professional conduct by this Code and stands ready, through its Committee on Ethics and Grievances, to advise its members as to the Code's interpretation. The American Arbitration Association and the Federal Mediation and Conciliation Service will apply the Code to the arbitrators on their rosters in cases handled under their respective appointment or referral procedures. Other arbitrators and administrative agencies may, of course, voluntarily adopt the Code and be governed by it.

In interpreting the Code and applying it to charges of professional misconduct, under existing or revised procedures of the National Academy of Arbitrators and of the administrative agencies, it should be recognized that while some of its standards express ethical principles basic to the arbitration profession, others rest less on ethics than on considerations of good practice. Experience has shown the difficulty of drawing rigid lines of distinction between ethics and good practice and this Code does not attempt to do so. Rather, it leaves the gravity of alleged misconduct and the extent to which ethical standards have been violated to be assessed in the light of the facts and circumstances of each particular case.

1
ARBITRATOR'S QUALIFICATIONS AND RESPONSIBILITIES TO THE PROFESSION

A. General Qualifications

1. Essential personal qualifications of an arbitrator include honesty, integrity, impartiality and general competence in labor relations matters.

An arbitrator must demonstrate ability to exercise these personal qualities faithfully and with good judgment, both in procedural matters and in substantive decisions.

a. Selection by mutual agreement of the parties or direct designation by an administrative agency are the effective methods of appraisal of this combination of an individual's potential and performance, rather than the fact of placement on a roster of an administrative agency or membership in a professional association of arbitrators.

2. An arbitrator must be as ready to rule for one party as for the other on each issue, either in a single case or in a group of cases. Compromise by an arbitrator for the sake of attempting to achieve personal acceptability is unprofessional.

B. Qualifications for Special Cases

1. An arbitrator must decline appointment, withdraw, or request technical assistance when he or she decides that a case is beyond his or her competence.

a. An arbitrator may be qualified generally but not for specialized assignments. Some types of incentive, work standard, job evaluation, welfare program, pension, or insurance cases may require specialized knowledge, experience or competence. Arbitration of contract terms also may require distinctive background and experience.

b. Effective appraisal by an administrative agency or by an arbitrator of the need for special qualifications requires that both parties make known the special nature of the case prior to appointment of the arbitrator.

C. Responsibilities to the Profession

1. An arbitrator must uphold the dignity and integrity of the office and endeavor to provide effective service to the parties.

a. To this end, an arbitrator should keep current with principles, practices and developments that are relevant to his or her own field of arbitration practice.

2. An experienced arbitrator should cooperate in the training of new arbitrators.

3. An arbitrator must not advertise or solicit arbitration assignments.

a. It is a matter of personal preference whether an arbitrator includes "Labor Arbitrator" or similar notation on letterheads, cards, or announcements. *It is inappropriate, however, to include memberships or offices held in professional societies or listings on rosters of administrative agencies.*

b. *Information provided for published biographical sketches, as well as that supplied to administrative agencies, must be accurate.* Such information may include membership in professional organizations (including reference to significant offices held), and listings on rosters of administrative agencies.

2
RESPONSIBILITIES TO THE PARTIES

A. Recognition of Diversity in Arbitration Arrangements

1. An arbitrator should conscientiously endeavor to understand and observe, to the extent consistent with professional responsibility, the significant principles governing each arbitration system in which he or she serves.

a. Recognition of special features of a particular arbitration arrangement can be essential with respect to procedural matters and may influence other aspects of the arbitration process.

2. Such understanding does not relieve an arbitrator from a corollary responsibility to seek to discern and refuse to lend approval or consent to any collusive attempt by the parties to use arbitration for an improper purpose.

B. Required Disclosures

1. Before accepting an appointment, an arbitrator must disclose directly or through the administrative agency involved, any current or past managerial, representational, or consultative relationship with any company or union involved in a proceeding in which he or she is being considered for appointment or has been tentatively designated to serve. Disclosure must also be made of any pertinent pecuniary interest.

a. The duty to disclose includes membership on a Board of Directors, full-time or part-time service as a representative or advocate, consultation work for a fee, current stock or bond ownership (other than mutual fund shares or appropriate trust arrangements) or any other pertinent form of managerial, financial or immediate family interest in the company or union involved.

2. When an arbitrator is serving concurrently as an advocate for or representative of other companies or unions in labor relations matters, or has done so in recent years, he or she must disclose such activities before accepting appointment as an arbitrator.

An arbitrator must disclose such activities to an administrative agency if he or she is on that agency's active roster or seeks placement on a roster. Such disclosure then satisfies this requirement for cases handled under that agency's referral.

a. It is not necessary to disclose names of clients or other specific details. It is necessary to indicate the general nature of the labor relations advocacy or representational work involved, whether for companies or unions or both, and a reasonable approximation of the extent of such activity.

b. *An arbitrator on an administrative agency's roster has a continuing obligation to notify the agency of any significant changes pertinent to this requirement.*

c. When an administrative agency is not involved, an arbitrator must make such disclosure directly unless he or she is certain that both parties to the case are fully aware of such activities.

3. An arbitrator must not permit personal relationships to affect decision-making.

Prior to acceptance of an appointment, an arbitrator must disclose to the parties or to the administrative agency involved any close personal relationship or other circumstance, in addition to those specifically mentioned earlier in this section, which might reasonably raise a question as to the arbitrator's impartiality.

a. Arbitrators establish personal relationships with many company and union representatives, with fellow arbitrators, and with fellow members of various professional associations. There should be no attempt to be secretive about such friendships or acquaintances but disclosure is not necessary unless some feature of a particular relationship might reasonably appear to impair impartiality.

4. If the circumstances requiring disclosure are not known to the arbitrator prior to acceptance of appointment, disclosure must be made when such circumstances become known to the arbitrator.

5. The burden of disclosure rests on the arbitrator. After appropriate disclosure, the arbitrator may serve if both parties so desire. If the arbitrator believes or perceives that there is a clear conflict of interest, he or she should withdraw, irrespective of the expressed desires of the parties.

C. Privacy of Arbitration

1. All significant aspects of an arbitration proceeding must be treated by the arbitrator as confidential unless this requirement is waived by both parties or disclosure is required or permitted by law.

a. Attendance at hearings by persons not representing the parties or invited by either or both of them should be permitted only when the parties agree or when an applicable law requires or permits. Occasionally, special circumstances may require that an arbitrator rule on such matters as attendance and degree of participation of counsel selected by a grievant.

b. *Discussion of a case at any time by an arbitrator with persons not involved directly should be limited to situations where advance approval or consent of both parties is obtained or where the identity of the parties and details of the case are sufficiently obscured to eliminate any realistic probability of identification.*

A commonly recognized exception is discussion of a problem in a case with a fellow arbitrator. *Any such discussion does not relieve the arbitrator who is acting in the case from sole responsibility for the decision and the discussion must be considered as confidential.*

Discussion of aspects of a case in a classroom without prior specific approval of the parties is not a violation provided the arbitrator is satisfied that there is no breach of essential confidentiality.

c. *It is a violation of professional responsibility for an arbitrator to make public an award without the consent of the parties.*

An arbitrator may ask the parties whether they consent to the publication of the award either at the hearing or at the time the award is issued.

(1) *If such question is asked at the hearing it should be asked in writing as follows:*

"Do you consent to the submission of the award in this matter for publication?

( ) YES *( ) NO*

If you consent you have the right to notify the arbitrator within 30 days after the date of the award that you revoke your consent."

It is desirable but not required that the arbitrator remind the parties at the time of the issuance of the award of their right to withdraw their consent to publication.

(2) If the question of consent to the publication of the award is raised at the time the award is issued, the arbitrator may state in writing to each party that failure to answer the inquiry within 30 days will be considered an implied consent to publish.

d. It is not improper for an arbitrator to donate arbitration files to a library of a college, university or similar institution without prior consent of all the parties involved. When the circumstances permit, there should be deleted from such donations any cases concerning which one or both of the parties have expressed a desire for privacy. As an additional safeguard, an arbitrator may also decide to withhold recent cases or indicate to the donee a time interval before such cases can be made generally available.

e. *Applicable laws, regulations, or practices of the parties may permit or even require exceptions to the above noted principles of privacy.*

D. Personal Relationships with the Parties

1. An arbitrator must make every reasonable effort to conform to arrangements required by an administrative agency or mutually desired by the parties regarding communications and personal relationships with the parties.

a. *Only an "arm's-length" relationship may be acceptable to the parties in some arbitration arrangements or may be required by the rules of an administrative agency. The arbitrator should then have no contact of consequence with representatives of either party while handling a case without the other party's presence or consent.*

b. *In other situations, both parties may want communications and personal relationships to be less formal. It is then appropriate for the arbitrator to respond accordingly.*

E. Jurisdiction

1. An arbitrator must observe faithfully both the limitations and inclusions of the jurisdiction conferred by an agreement or other submission under which he or she serves.

2. A direct settlement by the parties of some or all issues in a case, at any stage of the proceedings, must be accepted by the arbitrator as relieving him or her of further jurisdiction over such issues.

F. Mediation by an Arbitrator

1. When the parties wish at the outset to give an arbitrator authority both to mediate and to decide or submit recommendations regarding residual issues, if any, they should so advise the arbitrator prior to appointment. If the appointment is accepted, the arbitrator must perform a mediation role consistent with the circumstances of the case.

a. Direct appointments, also, may require a dual role as mediator and arbitrator of residual issues. This is most likely to occur in some public sector cases.

2. When a request to mediate is first made after appointment, the arbitrator may either accept or decline a mediation role.

a. *Once arbitration has been invoked, either party normally has a right to insist that the process be continued to decision.*

b. *If one party requests that the arbitrator mediate and the other party objects, the arbitrator should decline the request.*

c. *An arbitrator is not precluded from making a suggestion that he or she mediate. To avoid the possibility of improper pressure, the arbitrator should not so suggest unless it can be discerned that both parties are likely to be receptive. In any event, the arbitrator's suggestion should not be pursued unless both parties readily agree.*

G. Reliance by an Arbitrator on Other Arbitration Awards or on Independent Research

1. An arbitrator must assume full personal responsibility for the decision in each case decided.

a. *The extent, if any, to which an arbitrator properly may rely on precedent, on guidance of other awards, or on independent research is dependent primarily on the policies of the parties on these matters, as expressed in the contract, or other agreement, or at the hearing.*

b. When the mutual desires of the parties are not known or when the parties express differing opinions or policies, the arbitrator may exercise discretion as to these matters, consistent with acceptance of full personal responsibility for the award.

H. Use of Assistants

1. An arbitrator must not delegate any decision-making function to another person without consent of the parties.

a. *Without prior consent of the parties, an arbitrator may use the services of an assistant for research, clerical duties, or preliminary drafting under the direction of the arbitrator, which does not involve the delegation of any decision-making function.*

b. *If an arbitrator is unable, because of time limitations or other reasons, to handle all decision-making aspects of a case, it is not a violation of professional responsibility to suggest to the parties an allocation of responsibility between the arbitrator and an assistant or associate. The arbitrator must not exert pressure on the parties to accept such a suggestion.*

I. Consent Awards

1. Prior to issuance of an award, the parties may jointly request the arbitrator to include in the award certain agreements between them, concerning some or all of the issues. If the arbitrator believes that a suggested award is proper, fair, sound, and lawful, it is consistent with professional responsibility to adopt it.

a. *Before a complying with such a request, an arbitrator must be certain that he or she understands the suggested settlement adequately in order to be able to appraise its terms. If it appears that pertinent facts or circumstances may not have been disclosed, the arbitrator should take the initiative to assure that all significant aspects of the case are fully understood. To this end, the arbitrator may request additional specific information and may question witnesses at a hearing.*

J. Avoidance of Delay

1. It is a basic professional responsibility of an arbitrator to plan his or her work schedule so that present and future commitments will be fulfilled in a timely manner.

a. *When planning is upset for reasons beyond the control of the arbitrator, he or she, nevertheless, should exert every reasonable effort to fulfill all commitments. If this is not possible, prompt notice at the arbitrator's initiative should be given to all parties affected. Such notices should include reasonably accurate estimates of any additional time required. To the extent possible, priority should be given to cases in process so that other parties may make alternative arbitration arrangements.*

2. An arbitrator must cooperate with the parties and with any administrative agency involved in avoiding delays.

a. *An arbitrator on the active roster of an administrative agency must take the initiative in advising the agency of any scheduling difficulties that he or she can foresee.*

b. *Requests for services, whether received directly or through an administrative agency, should be declined if the arbitrator is unable to schedule a hearing as soon as the parties wish. If the parties, nevertheless, jointly desire to obtain the services of the arbitrator and the arbitrator agrees, arrangements should be made by agreement that the arbitrator confidently expects to fulfill.*

c. *An arbitrator may properly seek to persuade the parties to alter or eliminate arbitration procedures or tactics that cause unnecessary delay.*

3. Once the case record has been closed, an arbitrator must adhere to the time limits for an award, as stipulated in the labor agreement or as provided by regulation of an administrative agency or as otherwise agreed.

a. *If an appropriate award cannot be rendered within the required time, it is incumbent on the arbitrator to seek an extension of time from the parties.*

b. If the parties have agreed upon abnormally short time limits for an award after a case is closed, the arbitrator should be so advised by the parties or by the administrative agency involved, prior to acceptance of appointment.

K. Fees and Expenses

1. An arbitrator occupies a position of trust in respect to the parties and the administrative agencies. In charging for services and expenses, the arbitrator must be governed by the same high standards of honor and integrity that apply to all other phases of his or her work.

An arbitrator must endeavor to keep total charges for services and expenses reasonable and consistent with the nature of the case or cases decided.

Prior to appointment, the parties should be aware of or be able readily to determine all significant aspects of an arbitrator's bases for charges for fees and expenses.

a. *Services Not Primarily Chargeable on a Per Diem Basis*

By agreement with the parties, the financial aspects of many "permanent" arbitration assignments, of some interest disputes, and of some "ad hoc" grievance assignments do not include a per diem fee for services as a primary part of the total understanding. *In such situations, the arbitrator must adhere faithfully to all agreed-upon arrangements governing fees and expenses.*

b. *Per Diem Basis for Charges for Services*

(1) *When an arbitrator's charges for services are determined primarily by a stipulated per diem fee, the arbitrator should establish in advance his or her bases for application of such per diem fee and for determination of reimbursable expenses.*

Practices established by an arbitrator should include the basis for charges, if any, for:

(a) hearing time, including the application of the stipulated basic per diem hearing fee to hearing days of varying lengths;

(b) study time;

(c) necessary travel time when not included in charges for hearing time;

3
RESPONSIBILITIES TO ADMINISTRATIVE AGENCIES

A. General Responsibilities

1. An arbitrator must be candid, accurate, and fully responsive to an administrative agency concerning his or her qualifications, availability, and all other pertinent matters.

2. An arbitrator must observe policies and rules of an administrative agency in cases referred by that agency.

3. An arbitrator must not seek to influence an administrative agency by any improper means, including gifts or other inducements to agency personnel.

a. It is not improper for a person seeking placement on a roster to request references from individuals having knowledge of the applicant's experience and qualifications.

b. Arbitrators should recognize that the primary responsibility of an administrative agency is to serve the parties.

4
PREHEARING CONDUCT

1. All prehearing matters must be handled in a manner that fosters complete impartiality by the arbitrator.

a. The primary purpose of prehearing discussions involving the arbitrator is to obtain agreement on procedural matters so that the hearing can proceed without unnecessary obstacles. If differences of opinion should arise during such discussions and, particularly, if such differences appear to impinge on substantive matters, the circumstances will suggest whether the matter can be resolved informally or may require a prehearing conference or, more rarely, a formal preliminary hearing. When an administrative agency handles some or all aspects of the arrangements prior to a hearing, the arbitrator will become involved only if differences of some substance arise.

b. *Copies of any prehearing correspondence between the arbitrator and either party must be made available to both parties.*

5
HEARING CONDUCT

A. General Principles

1. An arbitrator must provide a fair and adequate hearing which assures that both parties have sufficient opportunity to present their respective evidence and argument.

a. *Within the limits of this responsibility, an arbitrator should conform to the various types of hearing procedures desired by the parties.*

b. An arbitrator may: encourage stipulations of fact; restate the substance of issues or arguments to promote or verify understanding; question the parties' representatives or witnesses, when necessary or advisable, to obtain additional pertinent information; and request that the parties submit additional evidence, either at the hearing or by subsequent filing.

(d) postponement or cancellation of hearings by the parties and the circumstances in which such charges will normally be assessed or waived;

(e) office overhead expenses (secretarial, telephone, postage, etc.);

(f) the work of paid assistants or associates.

(2) *Each arbitrator should be guided by the following general principles:*

(a) *Per diem charges for a hearing should not be in excess of actual time spent or allocated for the hearing.*

(b) *Per diem charges for study time should not be in excess of actual time spent.*

(c) *Any fixed ratio of study days to hearing days, not agreed to specifically by the parties, is inconsistent with the per diem method of charges for services.*

(d) *Charges for expenses must not be in excess of actual expenses normally reimbursable and incurred in connection with the case or cases involved.*

(e) *When time or expense charges are involved for two or more sets of parties on the same day or trip, such time or expense charges should be appropriately prorated.*

(f) *An arbitrator may stipulate in advance a minimum charge for a hearing without violation of (a) or (e) above.*

(3) *An arbitrator on the active roster of an administrative agency must file with the agency his or her individual bases for determination of fees and expenses if the agency so requires. Thereafter, it is the responsibility of each such arbitrator to advise the agency promptly of any change in any basis for charges.*

Such filing may be in the form of answers to a questionnaire devised by an agency or by any other method adopted by or approved by an agency.

Having supplied an administrative agency with the information noted above, an arbitrator's professional responsibility of disclosure under this Code with respect to fees and expenses has been satisfied for cases referred by that agency.

(4) *If an administrative agency promulgates specific standards with respect to any of these matters which are in addition to or more restrictive than an individual arbitrator's standards, an arbitrator on its active roster must observe the agency standards for cases handled under the auspices of that agency, or decline to serve.*

(5) *When an arbitrator is contacted directly by the parties for a case or cases, the arbitrator has a professional responsibility to respond to questions by submitting his or her bases for charges for fees and charges.*

(6) *When it is known to the arbitrator that one or both of the parties cannot afford normal charges, it is consistent with professional responsibility to charge lesser amounts to both parties or to one of the parties if the other party is made aware of the difference and agrees.*

(7) *If an arbitrator concludes that the total of charges derived from his or her normal basis of calculation is not compatible with the case decided, it is consistent with professional responsibility to charge lesser amounts to both parties.*

2. An arbitrator must maintain adequate records to support charges for services and expenses and must make an accounting to the parties or to an involved administrative agency on request.

c. *An arbitrator should not intrude into a party's presentation so as to prevent that party from putting forward its case fairly and adequately.*

B. Transcripts or Recordings

1. Mutual agreement of the parties as to use or non-use of a transcript must be respected by the arbitrator.

a. *A transcript is the official record of a hearing only when both parties agree to a transcript or an applicable law or regulation so provides.*

b. An arbitrator may seek to persuade the parties to avoid use of a transcript, or to use a transcript if the nature of the case appears to require one. *However, if an arbitrator intends to make his or her appointment to a case contingent on mutual agreement to a transcript, that requirement must be made known to both parties prior to appointment.*

c. If the parties do not agree to a transcript, an arbitrator may permit one party to take a transcript at its own cost. The arbitrator may also make appropriate arrangements under which the other party may have access to a copy, if a copy is provided to the arbitrator.

d. Without prior approval, an arbitrator may seek to use his or her own tape recorder to supplement note taking. The arbitrator should not insist on such a tape recording if either or both parties object.

C. Ex Parte Hearings

1. In determining whether to conduct an ex parte hearing, an arbitrator must consider relevant legal, contractual, and other pertinent circumstances.

2. An arbitrator must be certain, before proceeding ex parte, that the party refusing or failing to attend the hearing has been given adequate notice of the time, place, and purposes of the hearing.

D. Plant Visits

1. An arbitrator should comply with a request of any party that he or she visit a work area pertinent to the dispute prior to, during, or after a hearing. An arbitrator may also initiate such a request.

a. *Procedures for such visits should be agreed to by the parties in consultation with the arbitrator.*

E. Bench Decisions or Expedited Awards

1. When an arbitrator understands, prior to acceptance of appointment, that a bench decision is expected at the conclusion of the hearing, the arbitrator must comply with the understanding unless both parties agree otherwise.

a. *If notice of the parties' desire for a bench decision is not given prior to the arbitrator's acceptance of the case, issuance of such a bench decision is discretionary.*

b. *When only one party makes the request and the other objects, the arbitrator should not render a bench decision except under most unusual circumstances.*

2. When an arbitrator understands, prior to acceptance of appointment, that a concise written award is expected within a stated time period after the hearing, the arbitrator must comply with the understanding unless both parties agree otherwise.

c. *An arbitrator should not intrude into a party's presentation so as to prevent that party from putting forward its case fairly and adequately.*

B. Transcripts or Recordings

1. Mutual agreement of the parties as to use or non-use of a transcript must be respected by the arbitrator.

a. *A transcript is the official record of a hearing only when both parties agree to a transcript or an applicable law or regulation so provides.*

b. An arbitrator may seek to persuade the parties to avoid use of a transcript, or to use a transcript if the nature of the case appears to require one. *However, if an arbitrator intends to make his or her appointment to a case contingent on mutual agreement to a transcript, that requirement must be made known to both parties prior to appointment.*

c. If the parties do not agree to a transcript, an arbitrator may permit one party to take a transcript at its own cost. The arbitrator may also make appropriate arrangements under which the other party may have access to a copy, if a copy is provided to the arbitrator.

d. Without prior approval, an arbitrator may seek to use his or her own tape recorder to supplement note taking. The arbitrator should not insist on such a tape recording if either or both parties object.

C. Ex Parte Hearings

1. In determining whether to conduct an ex parte hearing, an arbitrator must consider relevant legal, contractual, and other pertinent circumstances.

2. An arbitrator must be certain, before proceeding ex parte, that the party refusing or failing to attend the hearing has been given adequate notice of the time, place, and purposes of the hearing.

D. Plant Visits

1. An arbitrator should comply with a request of any party that he or she visit a work area pertinent to the dispute prior to, during, or after a hearing. An arbitrator may also initiate such a request.

a. *Procedures for such visits should be agreed to by the parties in consultation with the arbitrator.*

E. Bench Decisions or Expedited Awards

1. When an arbitrator understands, prior to acceptance of appointment, that a bench decision is expected at the conclusion of the hearing, the arbitrator must comply with the understanding unless both parties agree otherwise.

a. *If notice of the parties' desire for a bench decision is not given prior to the arbitrator's acceptance of the case, issuance of such a bench decision is discretionary.*

b. *When only one party makes the request and the other objects, the arbitrator should not render a bench decision except under most unusual circumstances.*

2. When an arbitrator understands, prior to acceptance of appointment, that a concise written award is expected within a stated time period after the hearing, the arbitrator must comply with the understanding unless both parties agree otherwise.

APPENDIX C

Ethical Standards of Professional Conduct*

INTRODUCTION

The Society for Professionals in Dispute Resolution was established in 1973 to promote the peaceful resolution of disputes. Members of the society believe that resolving disputes through negotiation, mediation, arbitration, and other neutral interventions can be of great benefit to disputing parties and to society. In 1983, the SPIDR Board charged the Ethics Committee with the task of developing ethical standards of professional responsibility. The committee membership represented all the various sectors and disciplines within SPIDR. This document, adopted by the Board on June 2, 1986, is the result of that charge.

The purpose of this document is to promote among SPIDR members and associates ethical conduct and a high level of competency among SPIDR members, including honesty, integrity, impartiality, and the exercise of good judgment in their dispute resolution efforts. It is hoped that this document also will help to (1) define the profession of dispute resolution, (2) educate the public, and (3) inform users of dispute resolution services.

APPLICATION OF STANDARDS

Adherence to these ethical standards by SPIDR members and associates is basic to professional responsibility. SPIDR members and associates commit themselves to be guided in their professional conduct by these standards. The SPIDR Board of Directors or its designee is available to advise members and associates about interpretation of these standards. Other neutral practitioners and organizations are welcome to follow these standards.

SCOPE

It is recognized that SPIDR members and associates resolve disputes in various sectors within the disciplines of dispute resolution and have their own codes of professional conduct. These standards have been developed as general guidelines of practice for neutral disciplines represented in the SPIDR membership. Ethical considerations relevant to some, but not to all, of these disciplines are not covered by these standards.

GENERAL RESPONSIBILITIES

Neutrals have a duty to the parties, to the profession, and to themselves. They should be honest and unbiased, act in good faith, be diligent, and not seek to advance their own interests at the expense of the parties.

---

*Originally published in *Dispute Resolution FORUM*, March 1987, a publication of the National Institute for Dispute Resolution. Reprinted with permission from the Society of Professionals in Dispute Resolution, Inc.

Neutrals must act fairly in dealing with the parties, have no personal interest in the terms of the settlement, show no bias toward individuals and institutions involved in the dispute, be reasonably available as requested by the parties, and be certain that the parties are informed of the process in which they are involved.

RESPONSIBILITIES TO THE PARTIES

1. IMPARTIALITY

The neutral must maintain impartiality toward all parties. Impartiality means freedom from favoritism or bias either by word or by action, and a commitment to serve all parties as opposed to a single party.

2. INFORMED CONSENT

The neutral has an obligation to assure that all parties understand the nature of the process, the procedures, the particular role of the neutral, and the parties' relationship to the neutral.

3. CONFIDENTIALITY

Maintaining confidentiality is critical to the dispute resolution process. Confidentiality encourages candor, a full exploration of the issues, and a neutral's acceptability. There may be some types of cases, however, in which confidentiality is not protected. In such cases, the neutral must advise the parties, when appropriate in the dispute resolution process, that the confidentiality of the proceedings cannot necessarily be maintained. Except in such instances, the neutral must resist all attempts to cause him or her to reveal any information outside the process. A commitment by the neutral to hold information in confidence within the process also must be honored.

4. CONFLICT OF INTEREST

The neutral must refrain from entering or continuing in any dispute if he or she believes or perceives that participation as a neutral would be a clear conflict of interest. The neutral also must disclose any circumstances that may create or give the appearance of a conflict of interest and any circumstances that may reasonably raise a question as to the neutral's impartiality.

The duty to disclose is a continuing obligation throughout the process.

5. PROMPTNESS

The neutral shall exert every reasonable effort to expedite the process.

6. THE SETTLEMENT AND ITS CONSEQUENCES

The dispute resolution process belongs to the parties. The neutral has no vested interest in the terms of a settlement, but must be satisfied that agreements in which he or she has participated will not impugn the integrity of the process. The neutral has a responsibility to see that the parties consider the terms of a settlement. If the neutral is concerned about the possible consequences of a proposed agreement, and the needs of the parties dictate, the neutral must inform the parties of that concern. In adhering to this standard, the neutral may find it advisable to educate the parties, to refer one or more parties for specialized advice, or to withdraw from the case. In no case, however, shall the neutral violate section 3 above, Confidentiality, of these standards.

UNREPRESENTED INTERESTS

The neutral must consider circumstances where interests are not represented in the process. The neutral has an obligation, where in his or her judgment the needs of the parties dictate, to assure that such interests have been considered by the principal parties.

USE OF MULTIPLE PROCEDURES

The use of more than one dispute resolution procedure by the same neutral involves additional responsibilities. Where the use of more than one procedure is initially contemplated, the neutral must take care at the outset to advise the parties of the nature of the procedures and the consequences of revealing information during any one procedure which the neutral may later use for decision making or may share with another decision maker. Where the use of more than one procedure is contemplated after the initiation of the dispute resolution process, the neutral must explain the consequences and afford the parties an opportunity to select another neutral for the subsequent procedures. It is also incumbent upon the neutral to advise the parties of the transition from one dispute resolution process to another.

BACKGROUND AND QUALIFICATIONS

A neutral should accept responsibility only in cases where the neutral has sufficient knowledge regarding the appropriate process and subject matter to be effective. A neutral has a responsibility to maintain and improve his or her professional skills.

DISCLOSURE OF FEES

It is the duty of the neutral to explain to the parties at the outset of the process, the bases of compensation, fees, and charges, if any.

SUPPORT OF THE PROFESSION

The experienced neutral should participate in the development of new practitioners in the field and engage in efforts to educate the public about the value and use of neutral dispute resolution procedures. The neutral should provide pro bono services, as appropriate.

RESPONSIBILITIES OF NEUTRALS WORKING ON THE SAME CASE

In the event that more than one neutral is involved in the resolution of a dispute, each has an obligation to inform the others regarding his or her entry in the case. Neutrals working with the same parties should maintain an open and professional relationship with each other.

ADVERTISING AND SOLICITATION

A neutral must be aware that some forms of advertising and solicitations are inappropriate and in some conflict resolution disciplines, such as labor arbitration, are impermissible. All advertising must honestly represent the services to be rendered. No claims of specific results or promises which imply favor of one side over another for the purpose of obtaining business should be made. No commissions, rebates, or other similar forms of remuneration should be given or received by a neutral for the referral of clients.

APPENDIX D

Standards of Practice for Family and Divorce Mediation*

PREAMBLE

Mediation is a family-centered conflict resolution process in which an impartial third party assists the participants to negotiate a consensual and informed settlement. In mediation, whether private or public, decision-making authority rests with the parties. The role of the mediator includes reducing the obstacles to communication, maximizing the exploration of alternatives, and addressing the needs of those it is agreed are involved or affected.

Mediation is based on principles of problem solving that focus on the needs and interests of the participants; fairness; privacy; self determination; and the best interests of all family members.

These standards are intended to assist and guide public, private, voluntary, and mandatory mediation. It is understood that the manner of implementation and mediator adherence to these standards may be influenced by local law or court rule.

INITIATING THE PROCESS

DEFINITION AND DESCRIPTION OF MEDIATION

The mediator shall define mediation and describe the differences and similarities between mediation and other procedures for dispute resolution. In defining the process, the mediator shall delineate it from therapy, counseling, custody evaluation, arbitration, and advocacy.

IDENTIFICATION OF ISSUES

The mediator shall elicit sufficient information from the participants so that they can mutually define and agree on the issues to be resolved in mediation.

APPROPRIATENESS OF MEDIATION

The mediator shall help the participants evaluate the benefits, risks, and costs of mediation and the alternatives available to them.

MEDIATOR'S DUTY OF DISCLOSURE

Biases

The mediator shall disclose to the participants any biases or strong views relating to the issues to be mediated.

---

*Reprinted with permission of the Academy of Family Mediators.

Training and Experience

The mediator's education, training, and experience to mediate the issues should be accurately described to the participants.

PROCEDURES

The mediator shall reach an understanding with the participants regarding the procedures to be followed in mediation. This includes but is not limited to the practice as to separate meetings between a participant and the mediator, confidentiality, use of legal services, the involvement of additional parties, and conditions under which mediation may be terminated.

MUTUAL DUTIES AND RESPONSIBILITIES

The mediator and the participants shall agree upon the duties and responsibilities that each is accepting in the mediation process. This may be a written or verbal agreement.

IMPARTIALITY AND NEUTRALITY

IMPARTIALITY

The mediator is obligated to maintain impartiality toward all participants. *Impartiality* means freedom from favoritism or bias, either in word or action. Impartiality implies a commitment to aid all participants, as opposed to a single individual, in reaching a mutually satisfactory agreement. *Impartiality* means that a mediator will not play an adversarial role.

The mediator has a responsibility to maintain impartiality while raising questions for the parties to consider as to the fairness, equity, and feasibility of proposed options for settlement.

NEUTRALITY

Neutrality refers to the relationship that the mediator has with the disputing parties. If the mediator feels, or any one of the participants states, that the mediator's background or personal experiences would prejudice the mediator's performance, the mediator should withdraw from mediation unless all agree to proceed.

Prior Relationships

A mediator's actual or perceived impartiality may be compromised by social or professional relationships with one of the participants at any point in time. The mediator shall not proceed if previous legal or counseling services have been provided to one of the participants. If such services have been provided to both participants, mediation shall not proceed unless the prior relationship has been discussed, the role of the mediator made distinct from the earlier relationship, and the participants given the opportunity to freely choose to proceed.

Relationship to Participants

The mediator should be aware that postmediation professional or social relationships may compromise the mediator's continued availability as a neutral third party.

Conflicts of Interest

A mediator should disclose any circumstance to the participants that might cause a conflict of interest.

COSTS AND FEES

EXPLANATION OF FEES

The mediator shall explain the fees to be charged for mediation and any related costs and shall agree with the participants on how the fees will be shared and the manner of payment.

REASONABLE FEES

When setting fees, the mediator shall ensure that they are explicit, fair, reasonable, and commensurate with the service to be performed. Unearned fees should be promptly returned to the clients.

CONTINGENT FEES

It is inappropriate for a mediator to charge contingent fees or to base fees on the outcome of mediation.

REFERRALS AND COMMISSIONS

No commissions, rebates, or similar forms of remuneration shall be given or received for referral of clients for mediation services.

CONFIDENTIALITY AND EXCHANGE OF INFORMATION

CONFIDENTIALITY

Confidentiality relates to the full and open disclosure necessary for the mediation process. A mediator shall foster the confidentiality of the process.

Limits of Confidentiality

The mediator shall inform the parties at the initial meeting of limitations on confidentiality, such as statutorily or judicially mandated reporting.

Appearing in Court

The mediator shall inform the parties of circumstances under which mediators may be compelled to testify in court.

Consequences of Disclosure of Facts Between Parties

The mediator shall discuss with the participants the potential consequences of their disclosure of facts to each other during the mediation process.

RELEASE OF INFORMATION

The mediator shall obtain the consent of the participants prior to releasing information to others. The mediator shall maintain confidentiality and render anonymous all identifying information when materials are used for research or training purposes.

CAUCUS

The mediator shall discuss policy regarding confidentiality for individual caucuses. In the event that a mediator, on consent of the participants, speaks privately with any person not represented in mediation, including children, the mediator shall define how information received will be used.

STORAGE AND DISPOSAL OF RECORDS

The mediator shall maintain confidentiality in the storage and disposal of records.

FULL DISCLOSURE

The mediator shall require disclosure of all relevant information in the mediation process, as would reasonably occur in the judicial discovery process.

SELF-DETERMINATION

RESPONSIBILITIES OF THE PARTICIPANTS AND THE MEDIATOR

The primary responsibility for the resolution of a dispute rests with the participants. The mediator's obligation is to assist the disputants in reaching an informed and voluntary settlement. At no time shall a mediator coerce a participant into agreement or make a substantive decision for any participant.

RESPONSIBILITY TO THIRD PARTIES

The mediator has a responsibility to promote the participants' consideration of the interests of children and other persons affected by the agreement. The mediator also has a duty to assist parents to examine, apart from their own desires, the separate and individual needs of such people. The participants shall be encouraged to seek outside professional consultation when appropriate or when they are otherwise unable to agree on the needs of any individual affected by the agreement.

PROFESSIONAL ADVICE

INDEPENDENT ADVICE AND INFORMATION

The mediator shall encourage and assist the participants to obtain independent expert information and advice when such information is needed to reach an informed agreement or to protect the rights of a participant.

PROVIDING INFORMATION

A mediator shall give information only in those areas where qualified by training or experience.

INDEPENDENT LEGAL COUNSEL

When the mediation may affect legal rights or obligations, the mediator shall advise the participants to seek independent legal counsel prior to resolving the issues and in conjunction with formalizing an agreement.

PARTIES' ABILITY TO NEGOTIATE

The mediator shall ensure that each participant has had an opportunity to understand the implications and ramifications of available options. In the event a participant needs either additional information or assistance in order for the negotiations to proceed in a fair and orderly manner or for an agreement to be reached, the mediator shall refer the individual to appropriate resources.

PROCEDURAL FACTORS

The mediator has a duty to ensure balanced negotiations and should not permit manipulative or intimidating negotiation techniques.

PSYCHOLOGICAL FACTORS

The mediator shall explore whether the participants are capable of participating in informed negotiations. The mediator may postpone mediation and refer the parties to appropriate resources if necessary.

CONCLUDING MEDIATION

WITH AGREEMENT

Full Agreement

The mediator shall discuss with the participants the process for formalization and implementation of the agreement.

Partial Agreement

When the participants reach a partial agreement, the mediator shall discuss with them procedures available to resolve the remaining issues.

WITHOUT AGREEMENT

Termination by Participants

The mediator shall inform the participants of their right to withdraw from mediation at any time and for any reason.

Termination by Mediator

If the mediator believes that participants are unable or unwilling to participate meaningfully in the process or that a reasonable agreement is unlikely, the mediator may suspend or terminate mediation and should encourage the parties to seek appropriate professional help.

Impasse

If the participants reach a final impasse, the mediator should not prolong unproductive discussions that would result in emotional and monetary costs to the participants.

Protocol

USE OF ACADEMY NAME OR MEMBERSHIP DESIGNATION

The following procedures and rules are adopted by the Board of Directors of the Academy of Family Mediators, and shall govern the use by all members of the Academy name and membership status; including by way of example but without limitation, on letterhead or business card, telephone directory listings and advertising, promotional literature, and professional journals or other periodicals.

PROHIBITED CONDUCT

No member may indicate any communication that she has been certified by the Academy, or that the Academy endorses her credentials, skills, or experience; except as specifically provided in this Protocol. For example, a member shall not list the Academy's initials or membership initials after her name (A.F.M.S.M.—meaning a Senior Member of the Academy); nor state that she is approved by the Academy (implying a licensing or accreditation), nor by any other means attempt to suggest that the Academy has qualified the person as a practicing mediator. A member may use the terms "approved," "certified," "accredited," "authorized," "licensed," or similar words only in the manner and for the purposes specifically described in this Protocol. A member shall not describe himself in any promotional literature either as having attained some professional status, or as having received a professional accolade, by virtue of his membership in the Academy.

PERMITTED USES

The following are permitted uses of a member's affiliation with, or status within, the Academy:

(1) Approved trainers may indicate that their training programs have been approved for qualification for membership. A member shall not, however, indicate that either they or their training programs have been licensed or endorsed by the Academy; except for purposes of meeting the Academy's membership criteria.

(2) Senior Members and Associate Members may list their Academy membership status in professional publications, promotional pieces, and in other materials intended to be read by other professionals.

(3) Approved Consultants may identify themselves as certified or approved by the Academy; provided such identification is for the purpose of providing required case consultation.

(4) In promotional pieces, members may include the statement of membership status without embellishment. Notwithstanding the foregoing, members may identify their membership and/or consultant status in any publication accompanied by a complete explanation of the meaning of such designations.

* * *

Table of Cases

Index

About the Author

WARREN FREEDMAN has written more than 45 legal treatises, more than 100 law review articles, served as State Trial Referee in Connecticut and a Hearing Examiner in New York, and continues to lecture at various educational and legal forums. He served as an Attorney Examiner with the Federal Trade Commission, a member of the faculty of Rutgers University School of Law, practiced law in his own New Rochelle, New York law firm, and for many years was Assistant Secretary and Legal Counsel for Bristol-Myers Squibb Co.

www.ingramcontent.com/pod-product-compliance
Lightning Source LLC
LaVergne TN
LVHW011800200926
848484LV00003B/741
* 9 7 8 0 8 9 9 3 0 9 0 9 5 *